Praise for
The Road Between Hearts

"A good memoir must meet one key test: the reader must care about the protagonist. Leslie Powell Ahmadi passes that test with flying colors; she is so honest, so fearless, so funny—and her story is by turns gripping, inspiring, and full of cross-cultural truths. You keep reading, not only because you are rooting for Leslie at every turn, but also because there is always the next challenge looming just around the corner. 'The Road Between Hearts' is a road well taken."

—Craig Storti, author of twelve books in the intercultural field including "The Art of Crossing Cultures" and "Why Travel Matters"

"'The Road Between Hearts' is an honest and heartwarming account of Leslie Powell Ahmadi's four-year sojourn in post-revolutionary Iran.

"On the brink of embarking on the journey with her Iranian husband, Leslie wrestles with her conflicting emotions, and you find yourself taking sides. Yet as she takes you into the homes of her husband's families, you have a sensory experience of the hospitality, hugs, laughter, and cuisine. By the end of the book, Leslie's Iranian family had become my family.

"The book reads like poetry—effortless poetry—as Leslie artfully weaves suspense and humor into her story, keeping you hooked and smiling. And whereas this book dispels misconceptions about life of women in Iran, it also gently introduces you to an understanding of Islam.

"In the end, this memoir is a story of resilience, unwavering support, and the beauty of familial bonds. This book is for anyone who wants to experience Iran from the inside."
—Sabeeha Rehman, author of the award-winning book "Threading My Prayer Rug: One Woman's Journey from Pakistani Muslim to American Muslim

"'The Road Between Hearts' is a memoir, an adventure, a detailed travel journal, but most of all, a love story. Through her lyrical prose and the gentle, steady voice permeating her narrative, we discover another Iran.

"With grace and understanding, Dr. Ahmadi navigates what seems to be an insurmountable array of cultural differences, from language to religion, amid the nuances of intimate and familial relationships. And as a Black American, she also brings a unique history and perspective to her experiences in Iran.

"The Nigerian writer, Chimamanda Ngozi Adichie, warns of the 'danger of a single story' limiting our understanding of a subject. If we only know one story about Iran, Dr. Leslie Powell Ahmadi has graciously added another story, filled with compassion, understanding, humor, and love."
—Joyce Hansen, author of historical fiction and non-fiction and recipient of several Coretta Scott King Honor Book Awards

"Leslie Powell Ahmadi's memoir is a captivating, beautifully written love story of a different kind—one that pulls you in from the very first page and feels less like reading and more like living it yourself. The exquisite language and emotional depth make every moment linger. Impossible to put down!"
—Camilla Quintana, founder and author of "The Empowered Expat Woman"

"While most Iranian American memoirs capture the pain of inserting into sharp-elbowed American life, this poignant memoir flows in the other direction. Follow Ahmadi's journey of discovery, as she leaves Ohio to enter her new Iranian family's culture with its cast of theatrical characters, whether in the tiny *village of Duzaj or bustling Isfahan. Heart to heart, they populate the scenes as she grapples with building bridges, learning from her wise 'Baba' and 'Maman,' while also facing the inner turmoil of separation that bi-cultural marriages confront on one side of the Atlantic or the other.*

"In spite of the Islamic Republic's rigidity, she taps into the timeless soul of the Iranian people, deeply moved by their humanity. And, in the end, we too come to savor her daughter's nostalgia for 'a world of rosewater and pistachio ice cream, the sweet orange ripeness of a full moon, bridges descending into the night-lit water, and saying goodnight to the home of my first memories.' Ahmadi has offered a rare treat for our cynical age."
—Terence Ward, author of "Searching for Hassan"

The Road Between Hearts

A Memoir of a Black American Woman Discovering Iran

Leslie Powell Ahmadi

ISBN: 978-1-960876-98-0 - Paperback
ISBN: 978-1-960876-97-3 - Hardcover
eISBN: 978-1-967703-20-3 - eBook

Library of Congress Control Number: 2025942878

Printed in the United States of America   0 3 1 8 2 8

∞This paper meets the requirements of ANSI/NISO Z39.48-1992 (Permanence of Paper)

Muse Literary Publishing
Send feedback to hello@museliterary.com
Special discounts for bulk sales are available, please contact operations@museliterary.com

To Mahmoud —
Without whose irresistible combination of wisdom, wit,
humility, and tenderness, this true story would never
have happened.

And to my beloved late mother,
Margaret Dunn Powell —
Had she been alive when Mahmoud appeared, she
would have recognized his substance
even sooner than I.

Contents

Foreword

I first had the privilege of meeting Leslie Powell Ahmadi nearly a decade ago, after delivering a keynote at a conference in Akron, Ohio. As an Iranian American Muslim woman who writes about religion, culture, and mental health for a living, I am always grateful for the opportunity to travel and meet my readers. But that morning, I was tired and in dire need of a physical and psychological boost. Leslie provided both, graciously greeting me after my speech with a cold glass of water and a warm-hearted conversation I remember from nearly a decade ago.

With the beautiful book that follows, Leslie does for her readers what she did for me on that gloomy November day in 2016. She soothes a human need just as vital as thirst: connection.

A masterful memoir of love, family, and discovery, *The Road Between Hearts* delighted and comforted me on every page. As one of its earliest readers, I found this book healing and transformative. I also found that it filled a massive gap in the literature and reflected an important step in the evolution and expansion of representations from within and across the American experience.

As such, I'm elated to be writing this foreword. Because here I can do what Leslie is too humble and wise to do in the pages that follow: I can tell you how important this book is. Not just to me or its other lucky readers, but to the country that has made the stories and people within it possible.

The book you hold in your hands is such a great read that I'm jealous of those of you encountering it for the first time. Because it's so much more than its lovely title or subtitle could relay. More than an intriguing and inimitable "memoir of a Black American woman discovering Iran." More than even a "road between hearts" and all the wonders that phrase gains and loses in translation from the original Persian.

This stunning debut memoir is a deft and delicious mixture of modern literary alchemy, hospitality, and diplomacy that reveals what it means to be and become American. It celebrates the power of connection across differences. It champions sanity and humanity at a time in desperate need of both. And it invites us to expand our mental and emotional palates with delectable delights that nourish the soul on every page.

—Melody Moezzi, award-winning author of *The Rumi Prescription: How an Ancient Mystic Poet Changed My Modern Manic Life, Haldol and Hyacinths: A Bipolar Life,* and *War on Error: Real Stories of American Muslims*

*"The real voyage of discovery lies not in seeking
new landscapes,
But in having new eyes"*
—Marcel Proust

Chapter One

Shadows of Doubt

I never told Mahmoud about the dreams: those ghastly, shadowy figures that infiltrated my sleep for weeks before we took that first flight from Columbus, Ohio to what eventually would be our new life together in his homeland, Iran.

Why couldn't I bring myself to tell him—my husband of two years—or anyone else about the dreams? I barely wanted to admit to their existence myself. Besides, I didn't feel the need to consult with anyone. I had a good enough sense of what the billowing figures, veiled head to toe in somber tones and drifting back and forth over a tiled surface, revealed about the state of my psyche regarding the move. In that silent world I would tiptoe across each tile whenever I dared, trying desperately to avoid a brush with the drifting phantoms and being careful not to tread on any of the lines. I would usually wake up at that point, heart balled up in my chest, terrified to return to the same eerie dream in black and white.

That was how I spent several nights in the weeks leading up to our departure. During my waking hours it was a different story. Rather than face my own nagging questions, I spent time working to reassure friends, family members, and anyone else who asked if my plan to move to Iran with my husband wasn't a misguided decision, a terrible mistake. After all, I'd tell myself and others, wasn't I the same person who had embraced language and culture as her chosen field of study? From the time I was three years old, I'd been fascinated by sounds and sights that contrasted with America's and spent untold hours speaking myriad made-up foreign tongues. And thanks to the recordings of my earliest hero Harry Belafonte—Black Jamaican American singer, songwriter, and civil rights activist—I'd belt out tunes I'd heard from other lands. Mom had played them alongside the jazz, the blues, the opera, the spirituals, the gospel songs, and the classical music that continually filled our home.

At other times I'd stomp and pummel the floor with my feet, imagining myself the world's most renowned flamenco dancer. As young as I was, I still felt her love for life's pulse and drama, her hair unfastened, and her bare arms outstretched toward the sky. This little brown-skinned girl of the fifties—with two crinkly fat braids, a child's soaring imagination, and Black American parents who raised her to believe in herself and whatever she wanted to be—wanted to see the world.

Hadn't I lived out my commitment to that dream—pursuing two university degrees in Spanish and another in teaching foreign language and culture? Hadn't I demonstrated my ability to study, teach, even live successfully in other countries—Italy, Spain, Mexico? Was there any reason Iran couldn't be next?

More than any friend, enemy, or family member, it was the flamenco dancer's voice in me who talked back most compellingly, the one whose words of warning grated and burned and haunted me in my dreams. *Yes,* it retorted, *you've wanted to see the world, but the world you long for is dressed in colors and rapt in song. It's tinged with drama, and leaps and twirls freely in expression. As the child who once loved to run barefoot in the rain and taste the raindrops, you wish to run into new worlds, open your mouth, and drink freely without fear. You love to feel beautiful and not have anyone tell you that you're not supposed to love that feeling.*

Fortunately, or unfortunately, by day I was so busy addressing the angst of others that I managed to hold my own inner voice at bay, save on those eerie, dream-filled nights. I suppose it was just too threatening for me to admit that a PhD graduate, who'd already spent years studying language and teaching about crossing cultures, could attempt the exercise herself and utterly fail in the process.

This ongoing banter with myself and others had begun since Mahmoud proposed to me in June of 1984. There were also exchanges with those dear family members and friends who understood all the struggle and soul-searching I was already putting myself through—and decided not to make things harder for me. I felt tenderly toward them for the valiant effort they made to quell their own inner voices of doom. Even so, each person succeeded in varying degrees.

For Aunt Annise, my father's glamorous sister from New York City, Mahmoud had long ago passed the test as far as being a suitable suitor for her niece. From the first days of their encounter in December of '84, he would do things like quietly slice up fruit for me or drape my shoulders with his sweater on a chilly evening. And when Mahmoud extended her similar courtesies, she was duly impressed. If only, perhaps she thought, he could simply remain my perpetual suitor, without the relationship evolving as relationships tend to do. If only he hadn't committed to taking his life and education—and anyone married to him—back to Iran. Being the mid-eighties, it was probably the worst of times to be "starting fresh" as an American in Iran, with a debilitating, ongoing war between Iran and Iraq, the peak of the Ayatollah Khomeini's religious rule in the country following the 1979 Iranian revolution and American hostage crisis, and severely strained relations at best with the United States.

As if the political drama weren't compelling enough, there was also a best-selling book circulating at the time: *Not Without My Daughter*, the autobiographical account of an American woman, Betty Mahmoody, taken hostage with her daughter to Iran by her Iranian husband. In the book, the author reported that Dr. Mahmoody, an established Iranian physician practicing in the States, had taken her and their child on a purported two-week vacation to Iran for a visit with family—only to announce later that he'd brought them there to stay. After enduring the many substandard conditions and hostile encounters she described, Mrs. Mahmoody was finally successful in escaping with her daughter, just barely, through Turkey. The book drew national attention, seeming to touch a raw nerve in the popular American consciousness. It was even made into a major motion picture starring Sally Field, a popular artist and sweetheart of the era.

Not one week after Mahmoud and I had said goodbye to Aunt Annise at the end of a wonderful visit, I received a brown package from her in the mail. It was a copy of Betty Mahmoody's book. Given the personal affection my aunt had so quickly developed for Mahmoud, she might have felt as baffled and conflicted by her own behavior in sending it as I was in receiving it. Could it be that she wondered whether once in Iran, Mahmoud would trade in his lovable, reasonable nature for a dangerous and maniacal one, just like what Mrs. Mahmoody reported had happened with her husband? As a woman of color who knew how it felt to be judged based on preconceptions, I battled back and forth in my mind as to whether to read it—and finally gave in. And as much as I questioned some of the details surrounding the story, I still wondered how much my reading *Not Without My Daughter* contributed to the ghastly dreams that had seeped into my psyche.

Both my sisters, Pat and Sylvia, warmed quickly to Mahmoud when we traveled to Boston to see them. His down-to-earth and winsome ways quickly made for comfortable and lively exchanges between them. They liked his energy, his good-natured laughter, the whimsical way he belted out *Singin' in the Rain*, Persian style, his ease with stepping in to help with tasks—any task, hard or simple. After just one weekend, Pat described him as the brother none of us had ever had. And when the time came, I was delighted when Pat and Sylvia both gave their blessing to our engagement.

At some point, however—her eyes apologizing for what she was about to say—Sylvia opened her mouth and let it out:

"Leslie, I definitely think you should marry Mahmoud, but I think he should go over *there*, and you should stay over *here*!"

I paused, took a breath, and mentally counted to three. "Really? And what would the point of a marriage like that be?"

Poor Sylvia! In my heart of hearts, I couldn't blame her for her suggestion. After all, *I* was the one having the spooky dreams about my future life in Iran, not she. Could it be that my inner self agreed with my sister's sentiments more than I cared to admit? Could it be, in fact, that I had been playing games with myself all along by postponing the hard questions from the very beginning?

Chapter Two

First Encounters

I first met Mahmoud in January of 1984, when I was 29. Mahmoud was three years older at 32. I had never planned on cultivating a romance, let alone commitment, with this man—the first (well, second) Iranian I had ever met. At the same time, I did not resist the opportunity for friendship, which evolved easily on its own.

Our first encounter was in our graduate student dormitory elevator, two days after I had moved from North Carolina to Columbus, Ohio, to begin my doctoral studies in foreign language and culture education at The Ohio State University. He smiled at me, and as a matter of course, I smiled back. I found him attractive, with bright dark eyes and a winning smile. He had a ruddy complexion with a healthy glow, and I noticed I was just a little taller than he was.

We both got off on the same floor, where we eventually discovered we were neighbors, just a few doors away from each other. Our frequent chance encounters led to casual planned ones—first to a campus movie, then to the campus McDonald's, then to a simple bachelor's meal in his dormitory room. For that first meal, he shared the full store of his fridge: plain yogurt, pita bread, walnuts, processed American cheese, and green onions. I joined him down on the carpeted floor, where I later discovered he often sat when he ate at the dorm, and we talked and talked. It all tasted so fresh and strangely delicious, both the foods we ate and the tales he told. A wonderful storyteller, he painted a side of Iran I'd not been exposed to—sweet and romantic tales of growing up with his family in the village or in Tehran. Tales that took place among mountains or pomegranate orchards. Tales of the partridges, foxes, and mountain goats he hunted on foot or horseback with his father and brothers. Tales of the livestock he inoculated as a young veterinary technician. The most notable thing about his stories was how he lit up whenever he mentioned his parents, grandparents, sisters, or brothers. He'd be returning to them, he told me, once he completed both his master's and doctoral degrees in agronomy (crop science) in the five years or so ahead.

To top off his stories, he peeled us an apple for dessert. I remember watching his masculine, sinuous hands in quiet admiration as he sat on his haunches and peeled with a ritual, artistic grace. There was something so earthy and wholesome about him, and it amazed me that he commanded such presence with such a simple act as carving an apple.

At the time, and for three full years after that, I preferred to think of us as "the best of friends," which would make things so much simpler. It wouldn't require anything beyond the present, which felt safe and perfect, and wouldn't have to rock anyone's belief system, vision, or imagined future—not mine, not Mahmoud's, not our families'. In the meantime, I told myself, I'd be grateful for that wonderful companion, that beautiful listener, that fascinating teller of tales from a world I didn't know, the humble sharer of fresh and nourishing foods, the magical, meticulous carver of fruits.

But then, there was the thrill of the first touch of his hand.

Still, telling myself everything from, "He's returning to another world, faith, culture," to, "He's two inches shorter than I am," I could not admit to myself that within a very short space of time, my heart had chosen Mahmoud. Had my mother still been alive (she died in 1977, the same year Mahmoud arrived in the States), I believe she would have recognized it sooner than I did, admonishing me to "wake up" and get on with what my heart was telling me. I'd never seen Mom as a sentimental woman but as a practical, sensible one—one of very few individuals who could effectively use logic to argue matters of the heart and be right about it. True, Mahmoud did not match the image I'd carried so long in my head of the man I would someday marry—not in nationality, not in skin color, not in faith. Still, I could imagine Mom saying something like, "Use your head. He's been constant, loyal, respectful of your person and morals;

he's intelligent, non-egotistical, and he doesn't play games. How easily can you find someone from your own country like that? You claim you've always wanted to see the world. Well, now that you have your chance, what's holding you back?" What's more, I have little doubt that Mahmoud, whose ways of thinking and speaking had frequently reminded me of my mother's, would have openly agreed with her.

Yes, he had asked me to marry him six months after our friendship began, but he never pushed me to make the commitment. In that same sensible, logical style as my mother's, he responded to my questions and hesitations without drama or sentimentality.

"Take your time to decide," he told me one day in his dorm room. "Whenever I marry, I want it to be for keeps. I'm pretty sure I can be a great husband to you, but before making your life with me in Iran, I want you to be sure for yourself. If you decide you can't, that's okay. I'll always be your friend."

I loved his straightforward talk and his lack of pretense, and I trusted his statement of unconditional friendship. Even so, the simple promise "I'll always be your friend" haunted me more than it offered comfort. These were the words we'd say to each other if we ever went our separate ways. They were the words that would mark the time when we could no longer cuddle, no longer kiss. Ironically, this phrase suggesting duration, "We'll always be friends," would mark the beginning of the end, the end of a relationship I loved as it was. I wasn't ready to see the end of it. But I also wasn't ready to commit to a life in Iran, sight unseen.

"I just don't know if I can really do this. Or even if I should," I murmured, eyes to the ground.

As we sat across from each other, the room fell silent, and my heart felt swollen. There was nothing more either of us could say. Then Mahmoud, the one whose proposal had been left undecided on, came over to console *me*. Placing his warm hand on mine, he spoke to me gently, "I don't want you to feel any pressure over this. From June to August, I'll be away working with my cousin in New Jersey. You'll have the whole summer to take a break from thinking about this."

Going away for two months? Away to New Jersey? The floodgates broke open and I bawled in his arms as I never had. Having already imagined a future moment when the two of us would say goodbye, I could not bear the thought of any separation at all, even a temporary one. What I remember most is how my streaming tears tickled as I pressed my face against his. What Mahmoud remembered, whenever we reminisced, was "how hot your lips felt when I kissed you."

Thanks to the public telephone on the eighth-floor hall of Jones Graduate Tower, I was able to stay in touch regularly with Mahmoud while he was in New Jersey over the summer. About halfway through, I even managed to spend a wonderful week there, visiting him at the home of two best friends he had grown up with in Iran: Mahmood Saeedi and his adorable wife "Fati" (short for "Fatemeh"). Together we devoured Fati's amazing Iranian cooking, traipsed through the Big Apple's splendors, and belly laughed our way through the week.

But even after I was back in Columbus from New Jersey, Mahmoud's absence turned out not to be the break from my heart's deliberations that it was meant to be. How I missed his infectious smile, the light bounce and swagger to his step, and the adorable way he squeezed his eyes—Mahmoud's signature way of winking. But it didn't bring me any closer to a resolution—not even after his eight weeks away in New Jersey.

Strange as it may sound, it wasn't the ongoing war between Iran and Iraq that held me back from committing, nor was it exactly the aftermath of the Iranian revolution. It wasn't fear of a brand-new language—why, I would welcome the chance to learn another one (this time Persian, or *Farsi*, as the Iranians call it). It wasn't concern over facing a new diet. In Mahmood and Fati's home in New Jersey, I'd already feasted on the succulent stews, the sizzling kababs, and the fragrant rice dishes of Iran; if anything, that was a draw. The long distance from home didn't trouble me either. After all, it came with the territory of seeing new worlds, and I trusted that somehow we'd figure out a way to make those visits back to the States. Nor did I fear I would ever be kept in Iran against my will. Despite others' concern for my naivete, in my heart of hearts, I believed Mahmoud the day he told me, "If for some reason you are unhappy there, we will come back."

Even so, there were plenty of issues for me to work through on whether or not I should marry Mahmoud. Among the questions that pressed my heart most were those related to faith: Would I, a wife whose Christian faith mattered to her, be kindly received in the Islamic Republic? For that matter, would I be able to demonstrate appropriate respect for the faith and religious practices of the country's majority of Muslim residents? Yet, in so doing, would I also do right by what I understood to be my calling as a Christian?

While these questions didn't keep me from spending time with Mahmoud daily, they replayed in the back of my mind for months after his proposal.

Then, one snowy day, as if out of the blue, a former Spanish professor from Gordon College, my alma mater on Massachusetts' North Shore, reached out to me in a phone call, encouraging me to apply there for an assistant professor position in Spanish.

I had at least another year to go before completing my doctoral research at Ohio State, so I wasn't looking for a position at the time. What's more, the invitation wasn't coming to me from any college, but from a *Christian* college. That's when I began to wonder: *Is God trying to tell me something? Is He gently steering me in another direction?*

While I finally voiced my thoughts to Mahmoud about possibly applying to Gordon College, he shifted his gaze from me to the carpet. Barely moving, he finally spoke:

"I'm not crazy about you going away so far. But I told you to do what you need before deciding about us. If that means you take a job at Gordon … then I suppose that's what you do."

Both of us were silent for several moments. "Are you sure you're okay with this, Baby?" I finally said.

"Country boy will survive!" he answered with what was almost a smile, squeezing both eyes in that singular way.

When I applied to Gordon for the Spanish position and then got "an offer I couldn't refuse," we both knew by then that I'd accept it. I did—which, in turn, set us in motion toward a physical separation between us, at least for one academic year. So, at the end of summer at Ohio State, I would leave for Gordon in Massachusetts—and Mahmoud offered to drive me the long distance there. After helping me settle in, he'd return to Columbus alone, staying on course to complete his master's and doctoral degrees in agronomy, three to four years ahead.

We didn't decide on a set time to check back with each other. Neither of us knew how long an appropriate "trial period" should be. Instead, we agreed I would get in touch with him only when I had decided one way or the other—and that, conversely, he would be back in touch only if he no longer wanted us to get married.

No longer … get married?

Long after the conversation, I lingered with my thoughts about what that could mean.

Chapter Three

The Test

After I moved to Massachusetts to start my job as a Spanish professor, Pastor Bob Christiansen—senior minister at Boston's historic Old South Church and deeply trusted by my sister Sylvia—did more listening than talking with me for nearly ten months as I sought his pastoral counseling. It was a pleasant but also soul-searching period when I no longer talked *with* Mahmoud—but did all kinds of talking *about* him. And Pastor Bob was the lucky one who got the monthly earfuls.

At our initial visit, I told him how the whole separation agreement was *my* idea … and on my terms. "That means no phone conversations, no letters, no occasional visits—no communication … *nothing*," I told him resolutely.

Pastor Bob raised his eyebrows like two furry question marks, but he said nothing.

"To my mind," I went on earnestly, "anything else would be breaking the rules and defeating the purpose: to consider the possibility of a life and calling apart from Mahmoud. To give things a fair shake, I need a neutral space and a clear head, which will not be the case if I keep any ties with Mahmoud."

"Okay …" His voice went up slightly.

"And the separation *also* means we're both free to explore *other* relationships—me here in Massachusetts and Mahmoud in Columbus." A sigh slipped from my lips before I could catch it.

"At the time it made sense to me, Pastor Bob, but now my heart isn't in it. And even though *I* was the one who set the terms, I still wasn't ecstatic when Mahmoud agreed—especially to the part about his being free to date other people, too. But okay—fair is fair," I added, reminding myself more than anything else.

"And have you been able to stick to the terms?" Pastor Bob asked.

"I have so far. But I can't say I've been having fun," I said. "A couple of weeks ago, I accepted an invitation to dinner and a movie. Was it a date? You could say it was. He was always a gentleman—and I did find him attractive. But the movie wasn't the kind I was used to: a dark comedy about a haunted house. One of the main characters was kind of creepy—with bright green hair and blackened eyes."

Pastor Bob laughed, "Oh … you must mean *Beetlejuice*! Okay … And?"

"I'm sure the film would have been okay, except that I was already a little freaked out. My date, well, he used to be one of my instructors when I was an undergrad—from, like eight years ago. The combination of factors made the night a little too much for me."

"And dating your former instructor is your only option?"

"No," I admitted, "but he might as well be. There have been other guys and other well-meaning matchmakers, but I don't know—maybe I'm not ready for any of them."

Pastor Bob's blue eyes flickered softly as he listened in those moments. They always reflected compassion as I went back and forth, visit after visit, with theological and practical questions for which I could find no pat answers. There would be many more conversations as the months rolled by.

One day, Pastor Bob surprised me at the end of my deliberations with an uncharacteristically pointed question—one that really felt more like a pronouncement.

"Leslie, don't you think marrying Mahmoud is simply your destiny?"

Man—what on earth was Pastor Bob saying? I certainly didn't expect him, a Christian minister of all people, to answer like that. And what did he mean by "destiny"? Was that the same as "the will of God?" Or was he suggesting that the answer I was seeking might not be found as simply as weighing one set of scripture verses against another? I was so caught off guard, I couldn't even formulate my questions. Nor do I remember how I responded to his. But I do remember that visit marked the end of our special months together. I think that to Pastor Bob's mind, there was nothing more to discuss.

We hugged, I went my way, and his final words went with me—both as a lingering question and a ray of hope. I cried when I heard of his passing from cancer thirteen months later.

***

As I kept considering marrying Mahmoud back in Columbus, there were plenty of other issues for me to unpack apart from just the theological ones. For one thing, I was Black, and Mahmoud wasn't. Was that a big deal to me? In some ways, yes; in some ways, no. I had long carried the ideal of marrying a Black man—not only for my tendency to be attracted to Black men, but for our shared racial identity as the basis for solidarity. And yet life had already taught me that solidarity can never be assumed based on race, nationality, or even faith tradition. Even so, I pondered, if I was to be fortunate enough to find genuine solidarity based on a shared experience, like growing up Black in America and the duality of belonging and unbelonging that comes with it—well, that might indeed be something to hold out for; that could be a treasure.

So, before there was Mahmoud, there were other men I had been attracted to, men who had mattered to me, most of them Black men. Parting ways with one of them was especially hard; it took nearly two years for me to get over him. But the gift in that broken relationship was a newly emerged sensibility—one that freed me to recognize common ground in a partner who might or might not share the same race with me.

Years down the road and quite unexpectedly, Mahmoud appeared—a potential candidate for partnership. With our vastly different backgrounds, it didn't make sense on the face of things. But whatever it was that made us fast friends and knit us together was there nonetheless, lying deep beneath the surface without naming itself. Even so, the strength of our solidarity would be tested if we left Columbus and plunged headlong into Mahmoud's world.

Different faith identities. Different race identities. The composite differences between our countries, both visible and hidden. All these issues were big enough for me to own as "legitimate." What I couldn't bring to anyone's attention, my own included, was something that seemed so miniscule, so petty by comparison. But for me, this little issue was huge. Not that I didn't recognize that many, if not most, American women would also find the matter of *hijab*—the head and body covering required in public of all women in Iran—challenging at the very least. But realistically or unrealistically, I'd set a different standard for myself. In addition to being a woman of color, I was the professor who had always urged my language and culture students to replace prejudice or fear of the "different" or unknown with an open mind—and I felt I had no choice but to do the same. And even if I did, I'd still have the "flamenco dancer" in me to contend with, the same one I'd grown up and lived with all my life. I might never literally dance the flamenco, performing for people on a physical stage. But I still felt the need to freely express the feminine spark that fueled my joy. Without that freedom, how could I hope to make the flamenco dancer understand, let alone change? What would happen to "me" if she did? And even if I did manage to ignore the fact that I looked and felt different with my head, arms, chest, and legs perpetually covered in public, she would no doubt find a way to remind me.

And so ironically, it wasn't the "big" issues, but my "small" and private one about hijab that loomed large, and because I had trouble owning it, I simply kept pushing it to the back of my mind.

Since that was my Question Number One, it was even easier to ignore my Question Number Two—namely, "What could I expect of a life in Iran?" It made no logical sense for me to tune out that major question, of course, but it made all kinds of emotional sense to avoid the risk of hearing answers too hard to handle. Still, even if I *had* been strong enough to pursue the question, how much could I really expect Mahmoud to know? He had spent the last several years living *outside* of Iran and had not witnessed his country become an Islamic republic. I might have considered going with him on a look/see trip to see for myself, but there was no provision within the republic's code to allow me to travel there with Mahmoud while we were still single. On top of that, at the time, there was no Google, no Yahoo, and no internet resources at my fingertips to provide any answers. And as far as the eye could see during my time in Massachusetts, there were no Iranians in my world to ask. So, apart from my monthly sessions with Pastor Bob, I worked hard to keep any conscious thoughts about Mahmoud, or a possible future with him, at bay.

That is, until one crisp Saturday morning when I rolled out of bed—only to be startled by four or five scampering gray mice, who apparently lived with me in my beautiful oceanside studio sublet! My wily landlord, a fellow professor, had apparently "forgotten" to mention their presence when he signed me on.

The next thing I remember was hearing myself over the telephone, screaming the same words again and again, "They're here in the house! They're in the house with me! What do I do? *Mahmoud, please help me!*"

It was the first time Mahmoud had heard my voice in over a year—and the first time I had also heard his. I could have called my sisters, my father, my aunt, my "bestie," my friendly neighbor around the corner … my wily landlord. But I didn't call any of them; I called Mahmoud—and oh, how I drank in the sound of his voice! It brought me gently down from my terror, providing a refuge from me and my panic. But it had been worth the terror just to hear him again—his at once bright and soothing tones, his easy pace and familiar accent, his down-to-earth choice of words with an edge of humor. Of course, "Call your landlord" or "Buy some traps" were included in his commonsense advice, which I probably would have concluded myself. But when he added, "Don't you know? Mice are 40% protein!" I laughed out loud. I hadn't expected that playful poke in the ribs; I'd been way too long without it.

After that all too brief seven-minute conversation, the question occurred to me: *If I dialed him without really being conscious of it, did it still count as "breaking the rules"? But then,* I thought, *now that the silence barrier had been broken, did the answer really matter?*

I sat on the bed, hugging my pillow as if it were Mahmoud … I don't know for how long. I had no thoughts of mice—they'd been obliterated by the mental replay of Mahmoud's voice. I opened the dresser drawer at my bedside and reached deep inside for a special pile of photos that had long been awaiting my attention. Photos of Mahmoud in careless poses and moments of laughter. Photos of him with those masculine ripples along each cheek that turned into dimples whenever he smiled. Photos of both of us back in Columbus … at the park of roses, at the university library, out in a cornfield, hanging with friends. I spent the next hour pouring over those pictures. And when there were no more pictures to look at, I remembered to call my landlord about the mice.

In the week or so that followed, I came to realize something. The *real* question that lay in my heart wasn't so much "What would life be like in Iran?" as "What would life be like *without* Mahmoud?" I thought back on that final, lingering question of Pastor Bob—*marrying Mahmoud, my destiny?* And I remembered imagining Mom again asking me pointedly, "What are you waiting for?"

It happened not two weeks after that—at least on my end. Nearly two years since Mahmoud's proposal, my time of thinking, waiting, soul searching, and trying life on in Massachusetts without Mahmoud was finally over—and I made the life-changing decision to marry my soulmate back in Columbus.

So, I told Mahmoud. I called him. I picked up the phone and dialed.

"If you will still have me," I told him on the other end, "I'll turn in my resignation to Gordon, finish out spring term teaching here, and return to Ohio State in the summer to finish my dissertation."

"Okay, that's good!" were the first and only words I heard—a reply that made sense if you knew Mahmoud. His simple response was like one to a favorite story whose ending the listener already knew… and had trusted all along.

I would miss my students, my church, and being close to my sisters in Massachusetts. But come the end of the college semester, it would finally be time for me to go "home" to Columbus.

One week later, in a phone conversation, Mahmoud asked me about the mice.

"Yes, my landlord finally got rid of them," I said.

"That's good," said Mahmoud.

Then, after a pause, he added quietly, "Poor guys."

Chapter Four

The Meeting

So, our decision to marry had finally been made. My secret, unresolved "little issue" about hijab would have to wait another three or four years until after we made the move to Iran.

What couldn't wait was the one major step that remained before setting a wedding date: introducing Mahmoud to my characteristically overprotective father in Connecticut as a first step to asking his approval of our marriage. Guessing I knew how he'd respond to the future I was considering, I had put off telling him the story of our serious courtship for as long as I thought I could. My sister Pat knew, my sister Sylvia knew, and my aunt Annise also knew. But the time to talk with Dad and introduce him to Mahmoud had finally come.

In Mahmoud's mind, there was never any question that we would do anything else. In his culture's tradition, the family was always involved in such matters, and it would be unthinkable for him not to ask my father's approval of, if not permission for, our marriage. It didn't matter that he was thirty-six and I was thirty-three at the time. It didn't matter how uncomfortable it might make him feel. For him, it was the only honorable thing to do, and we owed my father that respect.

Even so, perhaps from my father's perspective, it made sense to resist such a potentially risky union for his daughter—a rationale that may have predisposed him not to want to like Mahmoud from the start. It certainly would help explain the drama of their first encounter, the day when Mahmoud and I arrived at his Connecticut doorstep after heading out from Massachusetts.

Aunt Annise had driven in from New York City at Dad's request and was also there to receive us. Was it possible she had already clued her brother in that we were already "serious"? Despite her earlier "gift" of the book in the mail, I could feel she genuinely liked Mahmoud, and I took comfort in knowing that she and my father had always been close.

After Dad shook hands with Mahmoud, exchanged a few polite and perfunctory comments with him, and retreated to the back room with his sister, we could only hope she might put in a few good words on Mahmoud's behalf and that the evening would progress more warmly than it had started.

It didn't.

Perhaps if I hadn't wanted quite so badly to make things work, my nerves would have been under better control and things would have gone more smoothly. The Iranian dinner that I had insisted on cooking all on my own would have turned out reasonably well, and the items in Dad's kitchen would have all remained in one piece. Instead, within the first hour of our arrival, the meat started scorching while the rice and split peas went mushy on the stove. And the glass of ice water Dad had asked me to fetch slipped through my tense fingers—ending up a thousand wet splinters all over the kitchen floor.

Dad, not thrilled to begin with, was not pleased by what he saw when he rushed to the scene and started venting immediately.

"You know, you can get a nasty cut stepping on one of those shards," he said, his voice growing tenser with every sound bite. "Not to mention how they will scratch up my floor!" Then, turning and looking straight at me, he went on in deep, reproving tones, "This will all have to be cleaned up thoroughly. Every bit of it. Immediately."

"Okay, Dad. Of course—sorry." Suddenly, I was a ten year old.

"Dr. Powell," another deep voice with a round, flowing accent drew all our faces in a new direction. "I will clean it up," it said.

It was Mahmoud speaking, politely but firmly. He would not let my father reprimand his daughter in his own home.

Dad, decidedly the king of his castle and not accustomed to being stood up to by anyone (let alone by his daughter's newly introduced Iranian boyfriend), paused before he redirected his remarks to me—again pointing out the gravity of the shattered mess on the tiles. To my horror, however, Mahmoud stood his ground.

"Dr. Powell," he repeated calmly from several inches below my father's eye level, "I said I would clean it up."

There was a pregnant silence in the room as Mahmoud made good on his word—all while father, daughter, and aunt stood frozen and watching—watching him on hands and knees as he wiped up tiny daggers of glass and ice until Dad retreated in silence to the back room again.

It seemed to me that things couldn't have been worse. And yet, I've learned as a mother myself that parents often have a way of surprising their children at all stages of life. Both Dad and Aunt Annise received the unmistakably mushy and singed meal I'd prepared with graciousness and gratitude. What's more, the conversation was decent enough, and I concluded that the equilibrium must have mysteriously been established among us while I wasn't looking.

After the meal, I offered a round of coffee or tea, and Dad suggested I bring the beverages into his room so that he and Mahmoud could continue in conversation. Not certain I had heard him right; I brought in the hot drinks while searching for an empty chair.

"May I join you?" I asked, smiling.

"No," Dad said.

Aunt Annise rose slowly from her chair.

"Thanks again for the dinner, Sweetheart," she said to me warmly, then turned back toward her brother and Mahmoud. "I'll leave you two gentlemen to get better acquainted."

And so, after catching a wink from Aunt Annise, I followed her to her bedroom and onto her bedside—all while Dad and my nearly betrothed sat alone in the back room and spoke together for one, two, three … four hours into the night. Their conversation outlasted Aunt Annise's and my ability to wait it out. It would be morning before we'd see either man again.

"What did you talk about for so long last night? Did you even sleep?" I asked Mahmoud in a private moment the following day.

My next surprise was learning that whatever they talked about had nothing to do with me. They did manage to touch on a range of other topics: from politics to civil rights, to economic theory, to philosophy.

My father, a brilliant cardiologist and a true intellectual if I ever knew one, had always taken delight in exploring such subjects, both on his own and with others. On this markedly unique occasion, however, I couldn't help but wonder whether the intent behind the discussion was not so much for intellectual stimulation as for putting his somewhat controversial guest to the test—and in his place—with a little battle of the wits. It appeared, however, that whatever knowledge my father had dished out to Mahmoud, Mahmoud was able to digest, savor with appreciation, and dish back in return. Evidently, by the end of the night, both men had thoroughly enjoyed their marathon discussion and what each of them had learned from the other.

Although I was duly proud of my father's intellectual prowess, I was completely blown away by Mahmoud's ability to keep up with him. All he said, in humble explanation, was that he'd been taught the value of educating oneself in a wide range of topics. Then, summing up his thoughts in six words, he added, "I like Doctor Powell very much."

As for my father, Aunt Annise later told me he'd confessed to being "pleasantly surprised" by the knowledge and substance of a man almost thirty years his junior.

I cannot say what made the most inroads in their relationship: the four-hour discussion in the back room that night, the respectful way Mahmoud had managed to stand up to Dad from down on the kitchen floor, or the special trip Mahmoud made back to Connecticut one month later to ask Dad's blessing on the marriage. With my father accustomed to being regarded highly in both his profession and his household, it didn't hurt that Mahmoud acknowledged Dad as one with a say in the matter.

Dad himself had grown up in a household where the husband's and father's word ruled supreme. And I imagine that as a Black physician since the early fifties, Dad must either have had or developed some bravado to retain his standing in the society he practiced in. I'm guessing he was also glad to have recognized some of that bravado in Mahmoud.

What I can say is that my father's delayed but ultimately favorable response to Mahmoud's gutsy stance in the kitchen on his daughter's behalf surprised me.

"Before I met him, I'm not sure what I was expecting," he said almost contemplatively in a rare moment when he and I were alone together, "but I can tell you I think he's a wonderful person and a wonderful man."

"Oh, Dad…! My eyes grew damp as I scoured my brain to find the right words to respond.

"—But if you decide to marry and go to Iran with him," he added rather abruptly, "I cannot condone it and may have to disown you."

Any words I'd collected to express my feelings blew right out of my mind that very instant.

Perhaps it shouldn't have been hard for me to say, at least, "WHY, Dad?"—not at age thirty-three. But I had learned over a lifetime not to question him, and I wasn't about to start practicing then. Anyway, we were both relieved when Dad turned around and headed slowly down the hall.

As my eyes followed him moving toward his bedroom, I felt … empty. On the one hand, with Dad being Dad, his laying down the law like that really wasn't unexpected. On the other hand, even his suggesting the possibility of disowning me was just too much to take in. It would take a day, perhaps even more, for what had just happened to penetrate my heart. That's what made it possible two hours later to kiss him and Aunt Annise goodbye without too much drama.

I didn't tell Mahmoud about my conversation with Dad until we were thirty minutes into the drive back to Columbus. After listening to me quietly, he paused for a moment, then said, "He's your father; he has a right to worry about his daughter." He paused for another moment and added gently, "Things work out, Baby. Didn't you say we 'Trust in God'?" Just wait for the right time."

Two days later when we were back in Columbus, my heart knew what to do. I pulled out a pen and paper from the desk in my dorm room (good old Jones Graduate Tower again!), breathed a prayer, and wrote Dad a letter—one whose opening lines were unlike anything I'd ever written to him before:

> *"Dearest Dad:*
>
> *You know I love you, and I've always done everything you've asked of me. But when it comes to choosing a life partner in marriage, I feel I'm the only one who can make that choice. And because you matter so much to me, I hope you'll understand and can somehow be happy with my decision to marry Mahmoud.*
>
> *Love, Leslie."*

Dad never answered my letter—at least not directly. But shortly after I sent it to Dad, Mahmoud received a letter that Dad had sent to *him*. It contained a check of "gas money" for Mahmoud's recent trip to retrieve and assist his daughter—plus a short explanation to that effect. An explanation that started with the greeting "My Son"—even before the day Mahmoud asked for his daughter's hand!

"Not only that," said Aunt Annise. "He could tell you were in love with Mahmoud from the very beginning—from the moment he saw you together and how you looked at him. And when he told you, nonetheless, that he didn't want you to marry Mahmoud, Chuck noticed a 'quiet resolve' in your eyes for your future husband. And so, I asked him if that made him angry.

"'On the contrary,' your father told me, 'it just got me thinking about my daughter. She looked like a woman in love, aware of the stakes, and knowing exactly what she was doing.'"

I paused silently at my phone for a moment or two, loving Aunt Annise for telling me this. It was another moment I realized that if Dad was learning new things about me, I was learning another side of Dad, too.

One year later, the summer following my graduation from Ohio State, he would come to Columbus to give me away at our wedding.

***

As far as I know, Mahmoud's and my difference in race was never an issue for my dad, my sisters, my aunt, or other family members, for that matter. I never brought it up as a point of discussion, and they never asked. Mahmoud and I never had that conversation either. I guess none of us felt like we had to. Dad, an early proponent of Dr. Martin Luther King, Junior's declaration that people should "not [be] judged by the color of their skin, but by the content of their character," didn't seem to give Mahmoud's race a second thought. Besides, throughout our friendship or during visits with family, Mahmoud's knowledge and interest in America's racial struggle became apparent, emerging naturally in conversation.

"Back home, I used to wonder what Frantz Fanon meant when he said Black people must struggle against 'being injected' with a feeling of inferiority," he once told me, then paused for a moment. In that moment I paused in my thinking too. Fanon, a writer Mom used to read, was a Black Caribbean psychiatrist known for his writings on colonization and race issues. *So, Mahmoud had read Fanon before he came here? Before he even **knew** he was coming?*

Mahmoud continued. "But now, after the Iranian revolution and hostage crisis in '79, maybe I know a little bit how it feels when people look down on me because of my group. But still, I don't know what it's like *to feel that way in my own country*." He paused for another moment and shook his head.

Whenever Mahmoud spoke on related matters, he spoke as if

Black people were in some ways *his people*—fellow strugglers in America—making our issues something he cared about. He never said it outright, but you could see it in the books he was reading; you could hear it in his voice. Not that every Iranian so identified, but Mahmoud did. In any case, whether or not he was talking about race, the mutual respect and unspoken connection between him and my family were already planted.

I, on the other hand, could claim no such status with Mahmoud's parents—or any of his family. With the language barrier, we had not exchanged so much as a "Hello" with each other.

What would they think of their American "bride" (daughter-in-law) when they'd finally meet me after the fact?

Chapter Five

Leap of Faith

On the day of our wedding, we followed both American and Persian traditions in a lush Ohio garden before God on June 25, 1988. A Presbyterian minister, a Muslim imam, two additional clergy members, thirteen members of my immediate or extended family (the latter mostly from Cleveland), sixteen Iranians, out of town and local, and a whole host of local and international friends from ten different countries attended. In their presence, we recited our vows and sincere intention to live out a marriage that *would* be "for keeps."

How I wished Pastor Bob could have been there! In a way he was, just like Mom was.

Sadly, none of Mahmoud's immediate family could be present, although they were also with us from thousands of miles away, extending their earnest moral support. At least, I hoped they were. Putting myself in their position, I wasn't so sure how earnest I could have been. But standing in for Mahmoud's family in their painful absence were Mahmood and Fati Saeedi—Mahmoud's closest friends and distant relatives from Iran whom I had met in New Jersey, where they had resettled. Among other things, Fati would walk as a bridesmaid.

The celebration took place in the backyard of an older couple, Canadian and American, named Andy and Gwen Trudeau. Former landscaping clients of Mahmoud turned weekly yard sale buddies, Andy and Gwen became Mahmoud's surrogate parents in the absence of his own parents, who were worlds away. The fact that the Catholic couple had nine children of their own, similar in age to Mahmoud and his eight siblings, reminded Mahmoud even more of his family back home. And lovers of travel, the Trudeaus had even been to Iran—not just once, but *twice*, on sightseeing trips.

With all the serendipitous planning by so many parties that led to the merging of cultures and traditions on our wedding day, our coming together felt not only miraculous, but surprisingly easy. Like stirring a unique blend of ingredients into a thick, rich, and delicious soup. A soup that, wonder of wonders, proved not to have too many cooks after all. The downside, admittedly, was that without a central coordinator, the proverbial "right hand" frequently didn't know what the "left hand" was doing during the planning process—leaving a few things that fell between the cracks. Like the fact that a wedding rehearsal the night before had never been formally planned—meaning that at the wedding event itself, I would be "learning as I go." ("Don't worry!" said this one and that one to me, "We'll be here to guide you along!") And while this did not make for an ideal situation, it certainly increased the potential for fun!

Even so, every now and then my heart felt the twinge of someone taking "a huge gamble," as some would say; "a leap of faith," as others would say, including me. Faith that God had made a way for us. That He had blessed our bond and would continue to do so. That we were each the answer to the other's prayers for a spouse after all those long years of praying. Today was the day to acknowledge that leap of faith. Not just *my* leap of faith, but Mahmoud's too: to be marrying this American Christian woman who had never set foot in his home country.

As I stood in my white bridal gown, clinging to Dad's arm just before the processional, I heard in the background the soulful singing of a Spanish guitar played live at the hands of Byeong, our former dormmate from Korea. Was it possible that my father, standing quietly beside me and breathing tightly to contain his emotions, had once resisted the thought of Mahmoud as my life partner?

The musical recording of the processional began, and the bridesmaids in front of us gently began to step to the beat. I watched Pat, my beautiful sister and maid of honor, move with such grace to every step. I thought back on a time she had gently ribbed me about this song: its delicate, tinkling, faraway melody by the Greek composer Manos Hadzidakus. After hearing me play it again and again on the cassette recorder that day, she playfully mimicked its music box quality in a way that implied she clearly questioned my choice. I had laughed outright then, as I almost did this second time around—but I was glad I had stuck with the song. Why a Greek melody as the processional? I *liked* it! Plus, with no connection to either his heritage or mine, the music felt more encompassing and universal, like an enchanted space that was neither American nor Iranian–symbolically welcoming everyone present, regardless of race, culture, or creed. As I walked down the aisle with my father, I felt encircled by the love of all kinds of people from around the world.

Dad and I approached the front where Mahmoud, dressed in a formal black suit, stood beside his two groomsmen, similarly dressed: Mahmood, Fati's husband, and Martin, our fun-loving dormmate and so much more. As we were drawing closer, I could sense a subtle shift taking place in my dad. A relaxation, a letting go, an energy released. With a side glance, I stole a peek. He was grinning with wet and glistening eyes, and I felt the tears starting to brim in my own.

In fact, nearly *everyone* I was able to see in the garden was either smiling or tearing up with joy and anticipation. But Mahmoud wasn't one of them.

Was he sad? Was he pensive? Was he moved? Wait—was he *hot*? At six o'clock in the evening, it peaked at 101 degrees. The hottest temperature ever recorded in Columbus's history to that date.

My eyes met Mahmoud's for the first time that day. He smiled, but there was no light in his eyes. And the double-barreled blink of his I'd been hoping for … it wasn't there.

The imam from the local Islamic Center, a distinguished looking, brown-skinned man from Pakistan, welcomed the guests and introduced Mahmoud and me as a couple. With his hands he directed us to the Persian table, known in Persian as the *sofreh aghd*. And there we sat beside each other: this gentleman from Saveh, Iran, and his Black American bride.

I had never experienced a Persian-style wedding before, and the newness of each experience felt both strange and delightful. Strange to sit with Mahmoud on two satin pillows and be treated like "King and Queen for a Day." Delightful to have a white linen tablecloth laid at our feet and be invited to ponder the deeper symbolic meaning of each item displayed. Flowers for splendor. Candles for purity and enlightenment. A mirror for insight into oneself. Silver eggs for fertility. Crystal candies for joy and sweetness. A copy of the holy Qur'an to invoke God's presence. And a plaque all in brass, whose words scripted in Persian meant *May your bond be blessed.*

It was the first time I had laid my eyes on any of those beautiful items reserved for our wedding. I never even found out who had lent them. Apparently, no one cared about getting the credit.

Each of the rituals that followed were either familiar or pretty straightforward, happening mostly as I had anticipated—except, of course, for the ones I couldn't anticipate! I couldn't imagine what "the weaving of the tapestry of betrothal" would look like, for example, and I couldn't imagine what the "sugar blessing" would look like, either. But fortunately for us, Mrs. Khabiri, a matriarch of the local Persian community, was there to guide us through both, just as she had promised. It turned out that the two rituals happened almost simultaneously:

First, while Mahmoud and I were still seated at the Persian Table, four attending Iranian women held delicate embroidered netting over our heads, like a kind of human canopy. As I turned to look at the attending women's faces, I opened my mouth wide when I saw that one of them belonged to Fati! *When had **that** happened—and when had she found time to be a part of this ritual too?*

Then Gwen, the hostess, and my sister, the maid of honor, rubbed cones of sugar together over the netting (as Mrs. Khabiri had directed), so that the falling sugar crystals would pass through it and onto our heads—to bless our marriage with sweetness. And, as if our bond hadn't been sweetened enough, we were directed to top it all off by eating honey off each other's baby fingers. I found out later that as the bride, I could have given my future husband a playful nip before polishing off the honey—a way to show a little bravado. An opportunity missed!

But the "unity candle," with both new and familiar elements, was the ritual I remembered most:

A pretty Black woman in a splendid striped robe approached a table behind Mahmoud from the left, while a handsome Iranian man with dark hair and eyes approached the same table from the right. The woman was my younger sister Sylvia, and the man was none other than "Fati's Mahmood," the best man. Each holding a flaming candle, together they lit a third "unity candle"—but a unity candle of a different sort. It wasn't just representing two individuals or families united; it wasn't just representing two faiths or cultures. What flickered and burned in that unity candle represented all the individuals, identities, and communities present—all contained in that single flame. It acknowledged us as a community all our own ... a singular community brought together by love.

Sadly for Mahmoud, a part of him was grieving. He was keenly feeling the empty spaces of missing family members on this pivotal day—of everyone who would have wanted to merge their flames with the burning flame of the unity candle. To be present for their son, their grandson, their brother, their uncle, their nephew. To laugh, to cry, to witness his joy, to welcome his bride into the family. They wanted it badly, and he wanted it badly, but it didn't matter; with access to funds and visas to America so hard to get at that time, it just could not be. I could still see the shadow in his eyes; *was there a shadow hanging over his family in Iran, too?* I put myself in his place for a fleeting moment—and I understood that my turn would come. It was part of the price that came with the package of living and loving between two worlds.

Things might also have fared differently for *me* at the ceremony had someone from his family been there to coach me, to warn me.

They likely would have admonished me *not* to respond immediately when the imam asked if I'd take Mahmoud as my husband. As things were, however, the imam didn't ask me just one time, but *three*. Each time he did, I answered with a clear and resounding "*Yes.*" And each time I said "*Yes,*" I heard an annoying titter ripple among the guests.

Any Iranian bride—or Iranian guest, for that matter—would have known that the only proper response to a "Will you take this man?" question is silence, so as not to appear overly eager. Her initial silence also would have signaled that she had a right to refusal, that she wouldn't be forced. But, well, I *wasn't* an Iranian bride. All to say that I flunked the "play it coy" tradition at my partly Iranian style wedding that day. The good thing, I suppose, was that the imam still married us. "And anyway," I promised everybody (who laughed along with me), "I'll get it right the next time around."

After they pronounced us married and gave us the nod, Mahmoud leaned over and kissed me softly. (A few people hooted. *Who were they? Were they American? Were they Iranian?* I couldn't tell.) In any case, his eyes were bright and clear again, and while he still looked hot, he also looked *so* much better.

Finally, it was time for me to end our wedding with my love offering! So, I presented it to Mahmoud in the form of a song—not in English, not in Persian, not in Spanish, but in American sign language with my arms and hands—all without speaking a single word. I signed to the words in a recording of *Longer*, by Dan Fogelberg: tender, cheesy, romantic. *Me,* honestly.

***

I hugged a lot of people after the ceremony. My hair was mussed, my makeup melted, and I'd lost track of how much time had passed. The evening air on the patio was still hovering at close to 100 degrees—and although I still had my gown on, I felt like just another overheated person immersed in a crowd. *But where was Mahmoud?* Looking around me, I made out the form of my new husband, a few yards away. Like me and pretty much everyone else, he was busy with mingling, laughing, speaking English or Persian, wiping the sweat off, hugging or being hugged.

Suddenly, it struck me that, from a Persian perspective, everything was going just as it should have been.

***

We danced! Most of us weren't familiar with Persian style dancing or what to expect—but to my delight, that didn't matter. Within the first minute of absorbing the jubilant tones of Iranian love songs, everyone's musical instincts took hold. Pairs of arms began shooting up all over the patio. And men, women, and children started mingling as we pivoted and swayed to the rhythm, moving our hands like birds in the sky. In the grip of a fierce heat wave, no one was deterred by the temperature or mugginess. And if anyone dancing was short on grace or rhythm, nobody cared.

As I glanced around, my eyes fell on my sister Sylvia. She was laughing and dancing with a cluster of people, her arms also stretched high in the air. Just a few feet away, a handful of my cousins from Cleveland were doing exactly the same. I laughed along with them.

And at one point, go figure: as the bride and groom, Mahmoud and I *even danced with each other!*

The symbolic flame of the unity candle was burning and flickering as brightly as ever.

***

We ate—no, we feasted! We feasted on kabab, saffron-laced rice, and a dish called *khoreshte bademjan** (Foods sounded even more delicious to me when called by their Persian name!) A heavenly favorite, it was a succulent stew made with lamb, fried eggplant, and a tangy tomato sauce—all crowned with a crispy garnish of shoestring potatoes. Not coincidentally, it also happened to be the first dish that Mahmoud had ever made for me, along with that fragrant Iranian rice.

But how many eggplants, potatoes, and onions would have had to be washed, peeled, sliced, and fried in record heat to make a stew to feed *over 60 people*? Even more to the point—who on earth would have been willing to do it? With the help of just two other people, it was magical *Fati* again, who had cleverly planned it, cooked it, and made it all happen. And it was the very same day she walked with me as a bridesmaid and stood by Mahmoud and me for the sugar blessing. No wonder she had come late to the bridal parlor earlier that day!

[*khoreshte bademjan* = horeshtay bottomjohn]

***

The evening was over; we said our goodbyes. Our old friend Behzad dropped Mahmoud and me off at the downtown Hilton, at an elegant bridal suite he had booked for us as a wedding gift. It offered a refreshing refuge from the blistering, sweltering heat of the day. And inside the suite, the cool swirls of air conditioning goose bumped our skin. But the warmth and wonder birthed from our wedding were still in the air—even with so many questions unanswered, so much unknown about what lay ahead.

***

In the two-year period that followed our wedding, the experience symbolized by the honey we had fed each other was realized daily in my life with Mahmoud. We settled into our cozy Columbus home, Mahmoud completed his doctorate, we both found work at Ohio State (I in teaching Spanish, and he in postdoctoral research), and we enjoyed visits with friends and my family. At the same time, we began to set our sights and establish our path, piece by piece, for Iran.

Chapter Six
The Gift

My first encounter with Baba and Mamán was not face-to-face. Nor was it in Iran. It was in the summer of 1989, one year after our marriage in the States and one year before the mysterious dreams began.

The encounter took the form of a tiny slice of something—smooth, cool, and razor-thin—an object that Mahmoud gently pushed into my palm, ceremoniously curled my fingers over, then stepped back with satisfaction.

"A gift from my father and mother," he said proudly.

Just back from his long-awaited trip to Iran, Mahmoud had the beautiful face of someone who had made peace with himself. He had finally managed to close the gulf of that agonizing twelve-year separation from his family, at least enough for a two-week visit. It was also clear that for my husband of one year, the tiny gift from his parents lying nestled in his wife's palm was as much a treasure and affirmation for him as it was for me.

Whatever lay inside had already relinquished its coolness to take on the warmth of my palms. I uncurled my fingers to what lay flat and shining underneath: a delicate, rectangular-cut pendant of fine gold. To my surprise, on the face of it was something inscribed in English: a three-letter word. Not *any* three-letter word, mind you, but the word "GOD" etched boldly on its delicate surface.

What to think. Gazing at the gift, I hesitated, hardly knowing how to respond. Rightly or wrongly, I assumed I understood the implied message behind a gift of gold: the ascribing of great value—a value of the highest worth—to the recipient. Small wonder that in Iran a gift of this precious metal was traditional for parents to bestow on their son's chosen bride. Still ... had the center on the gold face simply been a *heart* or some other symbol of love, it might have been a less complicated moment. I might have let myself be convinced that the gold also conveyed that good faith declaration of acceptance from his parents I'd been hoping for. But with that gigantic three-letter word relentlessly gleaming, the same word that throughout history men have allowed to elicit both the best and worst from their hearts, to unite or divide people of faith, to build community between nations or destroy it with the most paradoxical brand of violence imaginable ... I held back, asking myself, *How can I be sure?* Never having met his parents, how could I be sure of the intention behind the word? Was it truly meant as an affirmation for the bride, or was it a kind of ultimatum, an implied demand for something?

Suddenly, I felt the presence of my husband's trusting gaze, his love for both his parents and his wife, and his childlike moment of waiting for what I would do or say next. I knew I didn't dare take the hours, weeks, or years I felt I needed to sort through questions to which I had no answers or promises. With Mahmoud waiting and no time or space to allow for doubt or hesitation, I had only moments to respond. A deluge of thoughts, memories, images, and past conversations spiraled through my head.

...Like the way Mahmoud listened to me one day as I sat across from him in his dormitory room and carefully explained my simple message of faith that centered on the figure and person of Christ. I had not taken the step lightly, especially since I believed in respecting people in whatever faith or ideology they embraced or were in some way aligned, as Mahmoud was with Islam. But three weeks into a friendship I'd told myself could never be anything more than that, I had found myself falling in love and wanting to share the things that coursed deepest within me.

What I noted most was the lack of tension in his face, his attentive, non-argumentative eyes, and how unconcerned he seemed with countering my statements with the views he had no doubt been taught as a Muslim.

And on this particular afternoon, both my introduction to the

Islamic faith and my deeper discovery of the man Mahmoud came in the form of his gentle response to my words of devotion for Christ:

"Jesus?" he said. "Oh, yes—well, we like him too! It's just that maybe we don't like him *quite* as much as you guys do."

Taking "we" to mean the community of Muslim believers and "you guys" to mean the community of Christian believers, I was taken aback, and yet totally disarmed, by his simple response. The tone of his voice was kind and affirming, and his straightforward words were trustworthy. What more to do with a statement like that than simply receive it—as graciously and uncontentiously as Mahmoud had received mine?

***

The memories kept coming as I stared at the fragile chain attached to the pendant. I saw the image of Mahmoud, my new friend and dormmate at the time, chattering gleefully, noisily in Persian with his parents on the eighth-floor telephone, as if neither he nor they had a care in the world. I had always been intrigued by this man's fun-loving, easygoing spirit, his ability to laugh at life with gusto and a "live and let live" humility, even in the face of pain, misfortune, or disappointment. It was a quality that seemed to run deep, apparently as much a reflection of his strength and philosophy toward life as it was of his personality. But I never saw that trait more colorfully evident in him than I had in that dorm hallway, set to the tune of his unfettered laughter and noisy free exchanges with his parents on the phone. Did I dare hope that this beautiful trait I so admired in Mahmoud—his uncomplicated acceptance toward life and people—had been passed on to him by his parents and accurately echoed their spirit as well?

***

The question jogged me out of my thoughts and returned me

to the moment, reminding me that Mahmoud was still waiting for my response to the gift from his parents.

"Oh, it's so beautiful," I said, meaning it and looking closely at it for the first time.

I had missed a detail. As I elevated the pendant to eye level, the light hit it in a different way—and I noticed the faint but unmistakable image of a cross, which had also been engraved onto the surface.

Startling me like an unexpected apparition, it took my breath away.

I had not yet come to realize how, in the faith of Islam, Jews and Christians are considered "people of the book": fellow members of a common spiritual and historical heritage, starting with the prophet Abraham and continuing over generations. As Mahmoud had suggested, the person of Jesus Christ is therefore highly regarded by Muslims, not as the son of God but nonetheless as a central prophet of God commanding their highest recognition, respect, and affection. Even so, it is also true that the teachings of the prophet Mohammad are recognized by Muslims as the source of God's most recent and accurate revelations, much like how the teachings of Christ are generally recognized by Christians as the ultimate authority. That being so, I often asked myself just how many people devout in their own faith would as freely and tangibly affirm the faith of another in the same way my mother and father-in-law had chosen to affirm mine—even before laying eyes on me or exchanging a word.

Mahmoud said nothing as I reflected, but I think he was pleased by my stunned silence, my glistening eyes. It wasn't long after that he finally admitted to the initial reluctance his parents had expressed years earlier when they first heard the news of my entering their son's life—but that over time, when they saw how frequently he spoke of me and that he was in earnest, they offered their support. At one point, he told me they had even urged him to "stay close to Miss Leslie; it seems she will keep you close to God out there."

Mahmoud's father and mother, parents of nine living children and working daily to maintain their small farm in the arid village of Duzaj, were not a family of means. Even so, Mahmoud's father had continuously helped finance his son's education in the States to the extent he could, on borrowed money alone. Knowing that, I valued the gift of gold on the fragile chain that much more.

Imagine my surprise, then, when Mahmoud pulled out something else: a tiny gift box with a colorful paper lid whose folds, in typical Iranian style, had been cleverly cut and fashioned into a bow. "*Also* from your parents?" I asked. Playfully, he squeezed his eyes in his bright, double-barreled blink and handed me the box.

Curious, I lifted the lid. Inside was a *second* gold pendant, also rectangular cut. This time, etched upon the surface were the dainty figures of a man and a woman. Their heads were joined as one, as if they were sharing the same face, the same vision. Straight from the hands of my parents-in-law, I had gotten my wish after all: a gift that represented that simple, unmistakable symbol of love.

These were moments that touched me and gave me pause — but moments that were all too fleeting. The nature of fretting is such that it sometimes confounds the cues life sends you — even the ones glimmering and set in gold.

Two months before we were scheduled to make the flight, the haunting dreams that would flag my attention began.

Chapter Seven
In Transit

Three days before we were to leave for my first visit, my chance to traverse a whole new universe in two weeks, I hadn't packed a single item.

A seeker and dreamer of cultural adventures since childhood, I'd been in "new universes" before: a week in Rome with my ninth-grade Latin class, three months in Madrid my sophomore year in college, eighteen months as a fledgling teacher of English in Saltillo, Mexico, a year after I had graduated. But this trip was different.

All I could remember was what Dr. Wilson, a favorite college professor from my undergraduate days, had stated so poignantly in Old Testament class in an early morning lecture. "When you marry someone," he said, "you're not just marrying the *person*. You're marrying the family and culture that come with the package." This was the trip that would reveal what I had committed myself to, sight unseen. For me, packing would force me to face all the invisible baggage I'd be lugging along for the ride. Maybe that's why I postponed the inevitable task till the very last minute.

What finally drove me to jump to the ticking clock was the gnawing anxiety around what exactly I had, or rather *didn't* have, in terms of suitable clothing for the trip. As I stood in my bare feet perspiring in our humid, eighty-degree plus apartment in July of 1990, the whole drama around planning and packing a wardrobe for Iran became all the more torturous as I vaguely imagined myself wrapped up in some kind of layered, fettered existence. By American standards, many might have considered me a modest dresser to begin with, so it wasn't a question of my having to leave any short shorts, halter tops, or even sleeveless shirts behind. The real issue was the notion that at thirty-six years old, I had to worry about adhering to someone else's standard of how to dress.

The irony was that Mahmoud ended up telling me, as an odd reassurance, that if anything, the clothes I had to choose from might just be too *plain*, lacking in some basic fashion finesse. I had been terrified that once we arrived at the other side, I would sooner or later end up violating some dress code I knew nothing about. Even Mahmoud had been in the States too long, I thought. I couldn't rely on his judgment or well-intended guidance. The idea crossed my mind more than once that perhaps I would need to watch out for him too. Would he even know when either of us was violating a rule?

The most immediate question was what I was to wear as an outer garment. Temperatures, some had told me, could reach 100 degrees Fahrenheit or more in summer. I had no *chador* (the one-piece, generally black outer wrap for women that literally means "tent" in Persian), nor could I bring myself to ask about one. Although I still couldn't admit it to myself, the chador represented everything I thought I was giving up about being an American, and, perhaps worse still, about being a woman: freedom of choice, assertiveness, and "feminine expression" in my own signature ways. Wearing the chador would be like wearing a silent stranger. So, unaware that women had options for outer garments besides the chador (like a long overcoat that Iranians called a *manteau*, a term borrowed from the French), I quivered at the thought of having to wear it and tried my best to shut it out of my mind.

Strangely enough, Mahmoud hadn't mentioned the chador either; in fact, he hadn't mentioned *anything* about an outer garment, period. I had heard from other Iranians that Iran Air had strict rules about being dressed on the flight according to Islamic code, whatever that meant. Three days before the flight, I concluded that conforming to the code would feel much better than agonizing over the prospect of not conforming.

Not sure I was sweating from heat or anxiety; I finally called Mahmoud over and demanded an answer.

"Come on, Baby; I really don't get it! We're traveling to Iran, the Islamic Republic, aren't we? For all I know, we might as well be packing for the Bahamas! Please, just tell me straight: WHAT SHOULD I BE WEARING? On the plane? At the airport? In the streets? With your family? You don't look concerned, and that makes me nervous!"

Mahmoud paused, walked casually to my closet, and flipped through my meager inventory of warm-weather clothes: A few midcalf or maxi skirts and dresses. Some tops, tunics, and blouses with sleeves. No shorts, some slacks, some knee-length culottes. Two pairs of blue jeans, not yet broken in.

Effortlessly, he handed me his choice. "Wear this," he said.

It was a simple but well-made and sturdy cotton dress. Although lightweight, it was cut from a crisp tan fabric and tailored in the classic design of a mid-calf length trench coat, with a fashionable wing-tipped collar and a buckled belt at the waist.

"Wait—*this*? But this is a *dress*! I meant, what should I wear *over* my clothing—on the plane and in the streets of Tehran? And anyway, isn't this style *way* too form-fitting?"

Mahmoud repeated pleasantly, confidently, and without explaining. "Yes, this one is good."

I looked at the dress again. Well, it *did* look something like a woman's trench coat, but would it really pass as one? Still in mint condition, it had stayed in my possession for some sixteen years. It was the one dress Mom had bought me that had lasted so long, making it a precious article of remembrance. It hardly seemed appropriate to use it merely as a counterfeit manteau, and by now a snug one at that. I moved on to the next question:

"But how will I cover my head and … chest?"

Mahmoud considered the dress for a few moments. "You're right," he acknowledged. "You'll need the right scarf," and with that, he opened my drawer of assorted accessories. To my surprise, he pulled out one of the "fanciest": a broad silk scarf in a fluorescent shade of orange and with chocolate brown splashes all over it. To this day I have no idea how or when I acquired it. "That should brighten you up," he said sincerely, confounding me all over again. Wasn't I supposed to *avoid* calling attention to myself?

Resisting an urge to put off modeling it, I slipped away to the bathroom and tried mom's dress on—then took a long, hard look at myself in the mirror. As I had suspected, it was snugger than the last time I'd worn it, accentuating a plumper hourglass figure since a couple of years earlier.

I groaned to myself. *This will never pass as an overcoat—let alone a modest one.*

But when I modeled it for Mahmoud, he smiled with approval.

Looking good!" he added with genuine admiration. Mahmoud had never minded my curves.

"Mahmoud, I think you are missing the point here!"

"Just wear it with the headscarf. You are fine!"

I returned to the bathroom and looked back in the mirror, taking a minute to study my face. I had always considered my features broader and more angular than my sisters': my forehead, my cheekbones, my jawline, my nose, my mouth. And with my dark brown eyes and thick bundle of hair, my features balanced each other out, I figured.

*But take my hair away and stuff it under a scarf—**then** what?* My thoughts both stressed me out and egged me on.

Still looking in the mirror, I tied the scarf on, squashing my volume of hair out of sight. Instantly I saw a different person looking back at me in the mirror, and I didn't like what I saw—I felt plastered down, like a cat dunked in water. The flamenco dancer inside me with the voluminous hair shrank back in horror. (*Who are you?* she said.)

A deeper voice from the other side of the bathroom door interrupted, "So, how's going, My Lovely Fellow?" Then Mahmoud poked his head through the half-open door, his sparkling dark eyes greeting my listless ones.

"It's amazing what no hair can do to a face," I said to him in a grumbly voice.

Mahmoud stepped in gently and took my face in his hands with another look of admiration. Without warning, he chucked me under the chin. I jerked back and a laugh slipped out.

"See?" he said, "That's the smile that lights up everything! No headscarf can cover that kind of pretty. Didn't I *say*, 'You are *fine*'?"

Something inside me bubbled all over. "I really love your smile, too!"

"The question is, 'Is it *working*?'" he asked mischievously, leaning in closely. He smelled clean and spicy, like pine and ginger.

It didn't change what I'd have to wear, or my opinion of how I looked in a scarf. But in those moments with Mahmoud, everything felt better.

***

Despite the backlog of packing details and last-minute preparations I faced, seventy-two hours later, I found myself ready for the flight in that tan cotton dress. In addition, the orange scarf with the brown splashes, which I would need for the flight from Europe to Tehran, was neatly folded and wedged inside my pocket. Even so, in its own way Mom's dress provided me with the comfort of her presence for the long, uncertain adventure ahead.

The first portion of the journey, which in twelve hours took us from Columbus to Detroit, then out of America into Glasgow, felt familiar enough. I had already traveled to Europe twice before. Before continuing to Tehran, we would spend a couple of days there with Mahmoud's Uncle Said, the baby brother of Mahmoud's father, and his Scottish wife Maureen. As fate would have it, Mahmoud was not the first of the Ahmadi family line to marry outside of his faith and culture. Two decades earlier, a severe earthquake had leveled a large collection of villages in Iran, resulting in an outpouring of international aid. That's when Maureen Andrews, the pretty but no-nonsense social worker from Scotland, met the charming and dashing Said Ahmadi, and the two of them soon became a couple. Two years later they married, and Maureen joined Said in Iran.

So, Uncle Said and Aunt Maureen had already blazed a trail

ahead of us, but *would it make things any easier for us?* It was promising that the couple had apparently been blissfully married for twenty-four years. What was less encouraging was learning that they had spent the last twenty of those twenty-four years living in Scotland, *outside* of Iran. Furthermore, during those twenty years, Aunt Maureen had visited Iran only once, which happened *before* the revolution. No doubt I'd gain insight into the reasons if only I'd *go to the source and ask.* Instead, Mahmoud and I chose to spend two days in light conversation with our hosts and their children, who stuffed us with savory meats and roasted vegetables and, between spells of torrential rainfalls, drove us through the misty fields of Scotland's breathtaking countryside.

In other words, I chose in the end *not* to ask Aunt Maureen the obvious questions: *Did you like Iran? If so, why did you come back? What was it like for you as a Western woman there? What advice can you offer me about my new home and new life?* For all I knew, perhaps she was even waiting for me to ask. It would have made sense if I had, of course, but frankly, I didn't want to risk hearing something I wasn't ready to face.

Still, as we took leave of Aunt Maureen and Uncle Said at the airport and they wished us the greatest success in whatever we were hoping for, I wondered when Maureen and I would finally have that talk, when I'd learn the details of her story, and how the path of my life as a Black American would be the same or different from hers as a White European.

Shortly before boarding the plane, I contemplated my face and bare head for a good long minute in the ladies' restroom mirror before ceremoniously tying the scarf on again. It was almost as if I were grieving the possibility that once tied on, it might never come off again.

We finally boarded the Iran Air carrier for the last leg of the trip. I glanced around furtively as we walked down the aisle and took our seats. All the female passengers, save the children in their bright new dresses and bows, were so neatly packaged and assembled—mostly in fashionable, dark-toned manteaus and chic scarves. Still, once the plane had reached cruising height, the same passengers around me slowly transitioned into varying stages of unraveling, quietly settling into a more comfortable state for the long ride. While all the flight attendants wore the standard *magnaeh*, the hooded headpiece that completed their simple, brown, nun-like uniforms, most of the adult female passengers wore scarves whose knots had somehow managed to become loose or undone altogether—leaving hairlines, locks, and sometimes even the suggestion of a luxurious coif in view. Even some of the manteaus had managed to get unfastened by several buttons. Surprised that no one, not even the flight attendants, seemed to take notice, I looked around again in fascination to study the local landscape.

To me, many of the women looked like cover girl material, with flawless complexions, marvelous dramatic eyes, and finely sculpted mouths and cheeks, the colorful canvas of an artist's steady hand. Complexion shades ranged from ivory to hazelnut, to olive, to a light or moderate brown—a few close to my own medium brown skin tone. (*Okay*, I thought, *maybe I won't stick out as so very different, at least not at first glance.*)

As I surveyed how fully cloaked the women were in their long, tailored manteaus, I thought back on the comments Mom used to make about how the suggestion of an ankle could be so much more alluring to the imagination than the whole leg bared. I considered how, similarly, one stray dangling strand of hair might also do more to command attention than a headful of wavy locks in plain view. In a way, by softly framing these women's beauty, both natural and painstakingly cultivated, these artfully draped headcovers somehow managed to showcase as effectively as they concealed.

I switched my attention to the male passengers. Looking rather drab and ordinary by comparison, they nonetheless stood out to me, blissfully unencumbered in their short-sleeved t-shirts, removable jackets, and streamlined slacks. Feeling harnessed in my orange scarf and the camouflage of my buttoned-up trench coat dress, I couldn't help but envy their bare heads and necks, their open collars, and sometimes their skin-tight pants. *Not fair, not fair, not fair.* And I wondered how they could be so oblivious to the plight of the women sitting beside them.

I suddenly thought, *But what about Mahmoud, seated right next to me? What is **he** thinking about the discrepancy?* Casting a side glance, I wanted to ask him—but what if he said something I wish he hadn't? We might end up not talking for the rest of the flight! So, I redirected my thoughts back to the other men on the plane.

Then it dawned on me. These men seemed no more concerned with the women upholding the letter of the dress code than did the women themselves. It was as if everyone on the plane, airplane staff included, had learned to go on with their lives either following or managing around rules that had been made at another time and place—rules that had been decided apart from their input or involvement. Perhaps for them, the rules were simply what they were.

Still in midair, we were within minutes of reaching Mehrabad Airport when the landscape inside the plane again began to change. Knots on scarves that had been loosened earlier on the flight suddenly turned taut again, and unbuttoned manteaus were tidily reassembled once more to conceal their wearers' frames properly. Once we had landed and the plane had reached a full stop, I adjusted my slipping scarf for the umpteenth time. Then I fell into line with the others to cross the threshold and exit the plane into the Islamic Republic of Iran. Although I was both aware and in need of Mahmoud standing close beside me, I felt scared and strangely alone, guessing that the world I was about to step into would be decidedly different from his.

Once out of the plane, everyone seemed to be making a mad dash from one checkpoint to the next, hoping to shorten the wait in each of the long lines that lay ahead. First would be passport check, then baggage claim, then review of customs declaration documents, then the customs inspection itself. Under dim fluorescent lights at one-thirty in the morning, we took our places in line, waiting to stop at the next station where a solemn-looking airport official in a gray-green uniform stood to review one document or another before flagging us through. For an airport as large as Mehrabad, it felt extraordinarily subdued and silent. At the same time, it felt strangely familiar, as if I'd been here before.

Suddenly I made the connection. The entire experience—the dim, unnatural light, the sense of being alone, the silent surroundings, and every self-conscious step I took as I stood in my tan cotton dress—had the same somber energy, the same eerie feel as the dream I had visited and revisited. *Had my dreams distorted my read of this place ... or were they an actual forecast of what was to come?*

As I waited in line, I sensed two bright eyes surveying me curiously. They appeared to belong to an Iranian woman, possibly in her late fifties, standing two to three feet ahead in the same line and smiling at me broadly. When my eyes finally dared to meet hers, she approached me immediately and began to speak, asking me questions in a blend of English and Persian.

"Are you from America?" she asked.

I smiled and nodded.

"It is your first time here?"

I nodded again.

"What do you think ... is US better or Iran?"

I paused. Had she been listening? I had just confirmed it was my first time entering the country.

"Um ... well, I—I think every country has its own beauty," I answered politely, then glanced off to the side, hoping she'd be satisfied with my answer and stop.

Little did I know that I'd be asked the same pointed question by Iranians over the years—whether it was a friend, family member, student, neighbor, or stranger like this lady. And although I could never be sure of the motive behind each asker (sheer curiosity? nationalistic pride? a friendly sense of rivalry?), my answer always remained basically the same, except perhaps with deeper conviction each time I responded.

In any case, I was still on guard with this sociable lady in line who was paying too much attention to me. From the way she'd been studying me, I wondered when she was going to work in some comment about my snug tan garment or the orange and brown scarf that kept slipping off. Instead, she turned to my husband with what appeared to be a few respectful words of acknowledgment in Persian. Then she turned back to me one last time.

"Welcome to Iran," she said warmly, in English, as if to a daughter. "You will do just fine here."

Although they were the words of a stranger, their impact surprised me. They settled like a salve on my soul and served to comfort me, if only for a few minutes as the line pushed us forward from one checkpoint to the next.

The final stop, several stations ahead, was the customs inspection line, where I could see officials carefully examining the baggage contents of many passengers ahead of us. I wondered if my nerves could withstand another session of being scrutinized and questioned, especially by a government official. When our turn came, I stepped forward with my husband and, flinching, passed the officer my handbag for inspection.

His response startled me. Although he accepted the bag from my hand, he promptly handed it back to me, waiting for me to retrieve it while turning to my husband with words I could not understand. Mahmoud interpreted them for me immediately.

"This bag belongs to the lady," the official said, tilting his head slightly toward me. "I have no business with it." Although it had happened too fast for me to process fully, it was clear that the officer had *every* authority to inspect my bag but simply had chosen not to. He then turned and looked at me deliberately, if only for barely a second or two.

"*Khanum* (Madame)," he said in Persian with a unique blend of formality and kindness I'll never forget, "Welcome to Iran."

Within fifteen minutes of setting foot in the country, I'd been welcomed *twice*, warmly and sincerely, by complete strangers. But with Mahmoud's family on the other side of the partition, what reception was awaiting me there? For that matter, what kind of response would they get from *me*?

Chapter Eight

"Madame, Welcome to Iran"

Having made it past customs by two in the morning, Mahmoud and I crossed into a wide-open area of the airport where the long glass partition stood a few dozen feet ahead. On the other side, we saw throngs of people, peering in, pressing on the pane, and laden with flowers, signs, and hopeful, bleary-eyed expressions. I knew that among those hundreds of peering eyes, two or three pairs must belong to members of Mahmoud's family, anxiously searching for us.

"There they are!" Mahmoud exclaimed, quickening his pace. Shyly, I followed along, spotting a few beaming faces vying for our attention.

How many people belonged to our party, waiting there to receive us? Not two, not three as I had imagined, but maybe *nineteen* or *twenty*—male and female, of assorted ages, sizes, and general appearances. As we reached the other side, seven or eight females draped in black gently flocked around us. The airport had been filled with similar figures and I'd noticed them all, of course; they reminded me of those threatening shadows in my dreams, traversing the floor tiles. And yet now I was standing face-to-face with some of those figures as members of my new family. *What to do next?*

I began focusing on faces, one by one. And Mahmoud proudly, almost ceremoniously, introduced each in turn, by name and relationship: "Badri, my sister … Jamshid, my brother … Mahmonir, Jamshid's wife … Mehdi, my nephew … Aunt Rahimeh, my father's sister …" I wondered how I'd possibly learn all these names and faces. I wished I'd made myself learn them before coming, but ambivalence had held me back like a strait jacket. No doubt I'd seen many of these relatives before in photographs that Mahmoud had shared from much earlier days, but I found it hard to connect a living face of the moment with a worn and static photograph of the past. At unexpected moments, though, I'd recognize traces of Mahmoud in someone's features: the dip of an eyelid, the slant of an ear, a crease at the jawline, the way an eye sparkled or how the laughter came out. It was both fascinating and unnerving ... just as it was to hear each new person mention *my* name with comfortable precision, as if everyone had already spoken it many times before. *"Khosh amadeed, Leslie Khanum* (Welcome, Miss Leslie)," I heard between kisses, hugs, outstretched hands, and gentle pats.

Mahmoud's parents, patriarchs of the family and the giants I'd already met without seeing, were there too—somewhat gentle and frail, laughing, with tears in their eyes. I later learned that Baba and Mamán rarely left the village for an urban, crowded place like this. Too much heat and smog for their health.

As for the figures draped in black, the ghostly aura around them had somehow evaporated after I'd made those first connections with that inventory of faces, and in its place there were *women* instead—with tired, lovely, kind expressions and cloaks on their heads and shoulders.

Finally, after all the anxiety and anticipation, we were meeting face to face. It was monumental, more than I could take in. How could one moment justly represent the culmination of so many years, of so much waiting and travailing? And yet truly I didn't have the language, the presence of mind, or the confidence to do much more than smile, express my shy gratitude with a glance and the standard greeting, *"Salam."*

Someone handed me a brilliant bunch of gladiolas, bursting in pinks and yellows. Next, I felt the small, warm hand of a child grasp mine and start tugging. Someone else relieved me of the bouquet so that another child could clutch and pull my other hand. Now, with two of Mahmoud's young nieces serving as friendly guides and chattering incessantly with words I didn't understand, I was led out of the dim, dreamlike chambers of Mehrabad Airport into Tehran's warm, bustling, and vibrant summer night.

Herded into one of the five or six cars in our party, Mahmoud and I rode the chaotic collision course of the dense Tehran traffic, where it felt like a bumper-car scene at an amusement park, with a near-miss at every turn. Pedestrians darted in and out of the steady flow of traffic. *How was this congestion possible at this time of night?*

Wondering why there were so few traffic lights and even fewer that anyone paid attention to, I tried to focus on the tall, knotted trees along the streets, the green and white street signs in both Persian and English, and the classic fountains at every other plaza. A bride and groom saluted us as they swerved by in a honking car with neon-pink headlights. *How could this lively, colorful conglomeration be Iran?* Other drivers flashed headlights with their own neon shades: green, purple, blinding white. Vendors with crates filled with bright yellow melons shaped like footballs stood at every other corner, and the delicious smell of kabab peppered the air.

When the sweeping, majestic curves of the *Azadi* Tower loomed into view, glimmering and dominating the sky with their compelling blend of modern and ancient lines, I couldn't take my eyes off them. For those hypnotic moments I was captive to my awe, and at three o'clock in the morning Tehran time, I grasped the realization that *I was in the great, historic, and unsearchable Middle East I'd heard about since I was a child.*

We arrived at a comfortable, modest, air-conditioned apartment with very little furniture, charming family photographs on the walls, and an ornate red carpet in nearly every room. It belonged to one of Mahmoud's younger brothers, Ahmad, and his soft-spoken wife Esmat, who would be our hosts for the next day or so. Welcoming us warmly, they showed Mahmoud and me an inviting bedroom with an adjoining bathroom and invited us to refresh ourselves as needed. The bathroom, although small, didn't look much different from what I was accustomed to, with one notable exception. In addition to a toilet on one side, there was another option for going: a rectangular ceramic basin on the floor with a large hole to squat over. And instead of toilet paper, a hose and pitcher nearby to wash with. Relieved to have a choice, I opted for the model I knew.

Before leaving the bathroom, I bravely glanced in the mirror to examine the likes of the new addition to the Ahmadi family. Yes, my makeup had all but dissolved hours earlier. And my date-colored, medium length hair—swept up in loose coils and secured at the top— had been plastered down for hours by the scarf, begging to remain covered and out of sight.

You are truly a vision, I quipped to myself as I splashed water on my face, readjusted the scarf, and exited the bathroom. Mahmoud took his turn to wash up and was out one minute later, face fresh and hair lightly combed. "Come on," he said, stroking my hand before grasping my fingers, "They're waiting to see us."

We entered the adjoining room. On the floor, we saw a circle of family members seated comfortably on the red carpet, sipping tea, and beckoning us with their hands to join them. As was the custom, many rose to their feet with surprising agility when they saw us, but Mahmoud gently waved them down to their seats again. I would later learn how much Iranian etiquette demands of one's thigh muscles, ankles, knees, and general balance every time a guest or senior person enters a room.

While I surveyed the floor, calculating how to join the circle and still be modest, a petite figure cloaked in black approached me. I would later learn that she was Badri, Mahmoud's sister, nearly the same age as me. Her name translated means "full moon," Mahmoud explained one day, and I remember thinking she'd been aptly named. She had a round, peaceful face that lit up merry and full of laugh lines when she smiled. She spoke to me slowly, kindly, and in a calming voice, deep-toned for someone so small.

"*Leslie Khanum,*" Badri said, looking way up at me. "Are you hungry? Shall I bring you some dinner?" Between her choice of words, her pace, and her gestures, it was somehow easy to follow her Persian.

"Nah, merci," I replied in my limited vocabulary, thanking her (with the word borrowed from French) but turning down her offer. I was already full from two rounds of food on the flight, and in any case more spent than hungry.

Studying my face in concern, she lightly fingered my orange scarf. "Leslie Khanum," she said again, softly and earnestly in Persian, "take off your headscarf. Be comfortable."

Remove my scarf? Was that even okay to do with men all around? It seemed that all the other women had *their* heads covered. I was surprised by the tender gesture from this kind-eyed lady in black. But how could I explain to her that, irony of ironies, with my hair so totally ravaged under that scarf, I'd feel much better keeping it *on?* "I *am* comfortable," I answered honestly, mirroring her words in Persian and no doubt panicking with my eyes.

Accepting my answer, Badri invited me to join the circle on the floor. On my somewhat graceless way down, I felt grateful to her for not insisting I take off the scarf. I finally managed to secure a seat next to my husband—my legs neatly, if not comfortably, tucked to the side and under my paltry mid-calf length skirt. What I'd have given to be wearing a pair of jeans.

Shortly after we were served tea and some melon that tasted a little too ripe, our first round of exchanges began. Every member of the family—male and female, from oldest to youngest—had joined the circle on the red and exquisitely patterned carpeted floor. Like a playful game of catch, each adult, in turn, would slowly "toss" me his or her name by pronouncing it. And I, by trying to repeat what I'd just heard, would "toss" it back. Praise for my efforts was generous, as was the laughter; corrections were minimal. Everyone seemed happy with that elementary, textbook-brand Persian I'd learned over ten weeks at Ohio State two years earlier.

Next, the conversation turned to the topic of *my* family—their names, ages, and states of health. Carefully, they practiced pronouncing the names of my father ("*Doktor Pahvel*"), of my two sisters Pat ("*Pah-tree-seeYAH*") and Sylvia ("*Seel-veeYAH*"), and of my brothers-in-law Jim and Don. They fussed with delight to learn I'd been blessed with a brand-new niece, Emily, born to Sylvia and Don just three months earlier. They asked all kinds of questions about her and devoted the rest of their practice time to mastering the pronunciation of her name (*"Em-ee-LEE"*). They made me promise to send regards to all my family members back home, to thank them for letting me come so far away, and to ask them to send lots of pictures. Finally, they gently expressed regrets over the untimely loss of Mom, whom they already knew had passed away years earlier. *"Khoda biamorze* (God rest her soul)," several in the room murmured quietly.

But it was a time for laughter and celebration, not for pain. So, after a bit of floundering and false starts, the family reestablished a lighter mood and began to toss me their next playful line of questioning, upped a few notches. "Now about Mahmoud," one of the women asked—with others of them joining in while the men stayed silent—"What kind of husband is he? Do you like him? Very, very, very much? Has he been a good husband? Has he been behaving himself?" This was the line of questioning where nuance meant everything, and at my level of Persian, nuance was a ball I'd be better off dodging. I answered nearly every question on the Mahmoud topic with a one-size-fits-all response: *"Khoob ... Kheilee Khoob* (Good ... very good)," and stuck to the script, even when I wasn't quite sure what was being asked. In every case, my polite but somewhat guarded responses proved to be entertaining, provoking peals of laughter from the most fun-loving members and energizing the group to keep hurling new questions.

Although I felt bashful and sometimes embarrassed during the exchange, I sensed affection behind their attention. So, for better or worse, in my halting, clumsy, limited Persian, I kept playing right back. Mahmoud, who intervened as an interpreter only when he absolutely had to, sat silently, proudly, as he watched things unfold.

There was one line of questioning that particularly threw me, though. It was when the conversation turned back to the names of the Ahmadi family, and for whatever reason, landed on a review of Mahmoud and his three brothers: Jamshid, Ahmad, and Ali. "So," a female member or two of the group initiated, as if out of the blue, "of the four brothers, which one would you say is the best husband?"

I hesitated, wondering if I'd heard the question correctly. *How should I know?* I thought wistfully and turned to Mahmoud for assistance. Shrugging with a sheepish grin, he only verified that the question they asked was in fact the one I had heard, and that the group was waiting for my response.

"But what if I say something wrong?" I asked him.

"Anything's possible!" he said impishly. But I saw confidence in his eyes.

The room was filled with eager expressions. Taking their mischievous question far too seriously, I fidgeted and stalled. If the question was meant to be funny, I thought to myself (rapidly losing perspective at 4:30 a.m. and after 30 hours of travel time), I didn't particularly find it so. How could they expect me to know the answer—and why would they even ask? Feeling a need to locate the brothers, I scanned the room and managed to identify Jamshid, Ahmad, and Ali, all grinning at me. *They* didn't seem to mind the question. As for their spouses, well, at this point of familiarity, I still wasn't sure who was who, whose face I should read, and whether the woman sitting beside each brother happened to be the spouse, a sister, or a cousin. In any case, absolutely no one was letting on—only laughing, watching, and waiting to see what answer I'd come up with next.

I thought of the woman at the airport who had asked me, "Which place do you like better, Iran or America?", and the answer I gave her. So, basing my answer on a similar strategy, I asked Mahmoud to tell them I was sure that each brother was the best match for his own wife.

"No, no, no!" they all said, laughing. "Wrong answer this time!

'Mahmoud' is the right answer! You are supposed to say *Mahmoud's* the best husband!"

Not wanting to insult the other brothers or any of their wives by implication, I shook my head bashfully and waved my hands, but all they did was laugh all the harder and stand by their assertions all the same. As exhausted as I was, I took note of their unanimous, well-coordinated response and their good-natured joking with me and each other. Even so, I wasn't sure I had quite gotten the joke, or even if there was something to *get*. Maybe the only thing I really needed to get—besides sleep, apparently—was the understanding that laughter for its own sake sometimes feels good, that no one was trying to "one up" anybody, and that everyone seemed happy for Mahmoud and his new bride.

Like clockwork, people began standing up moments later and thanking Ahmad and Esmat for the pleasant evening and their hospitality. Right after that, they turned to me gently, welcoming me one last time and wishing Mahmoud and me a good night's rest. *Had they noticed,* I wondered, *that my energy had started to wear thin?*

Esmat, the hostess, took me by the hand and led me to the bedroom door, which she opened a crack to let me through. "Here you are," she said under her breath. "You must sleep now."

My eyes opened wide, and my jaw dropped as I looked at my hostess. For the first time all evening, someone besides Mahmoud was speaking to me in *English*.

Responding shyly to my startled expression, Esmat explained that she was a high school language teacher and used English regularly with her students, but normally she didn't speak it outside of the classroom. She also admitted to feeling strange about using English in front of family members.

Feeling instant gratitude and tenderness toward her, I spontaneously kissed her on the cheek and we both laughed. Not only had I found someone besides Mahmoud who could interpret for me, but someone who truly understood. Here was another who also felt the lure and power of language, the desire to command it, and the discomfort of not feeling ready to take it on. A kindred spirit.

"Good night," she said. "*Shab-e-kheir*."

Turning back long enough to exchange a glance with Mahmoud, I pushed through the partially opened bedroom door to turn in for the night.

As I entered, I was startled by the presence of two young boys, not more than four or five years old. They looked sufficiently guilty, as if they'd been playing there for a while and knew they shouldn't have been. Standing between me and my bed, they faced me, waiting for my reaction and grinning broadly with their small, round, adorable faces. Exhausted beyond description, I did my best to ask them in Persian if maybe they'd be willing to play somewhere else and let me sleep?

With an upward tilt of the head and a click of the tongue, each broke into dimples before impishly saying, "*Naah* (No)." I would soon come to know them as Amin and Abolfazl, Badri's two darling youngest kids.

If I hadn't been so sleepy, I'd have been totally charmed by their innocent candor. Things being as they were, however, it was all I could do to walk past them, crawl up on the bed, and drag the soft covers over me. I was asleep before I could see them leave.

Chapter Nine

More Relatives and Rocky Road Trips

I don't know why the memories of those first few hours in Iran
stay so etched and anchored in my head, especially since much of
the rest of our two-week visit remains something of a blur—a
sketchy patchwork of hazy images jammed and melded together.
Perhaps we can blame it on jet lag, apprehension, or just feeling
overwhelmed. Perhaps it was a simple question of sensory over-
load: too many new images, messages, and interactions. Perhaps
it was the constant mental tug of war between Persian and English
draining my memory banks. Or maybe it was still the fear of discovering something I'd rather not notice or think about. Whatever it
was, it was as if after those first few hours of sleep in that cozy bed, I
never fully woke up or emerged from a dream. Like whatever I said
or did in my waking hours was operating on automatic pilot.

What I do remember are patterns, images, and a few events
whose imprints from ritual, repetition, pleasure, or impact made
them hard to forget. Elaborate, fabulous spreads of Persian food,
artfully prepared, exquisitely presented, seductive to the senses
and too rich for a Western-bred stomach used to more processed,
store-bought foods. Sitting at a tablecloth that lay stretched across
a carpet, my legs tucked, awkward, and perpetually crampy —
shifting this way, that way, then this way again. Sharing the company of twenty, thirty, forty people assembled in my honor and
eager to meet me, greet me, welcome me, kid with me … three or
four times a day. Struggling to my feet to acknowledge yet another caller, then making it down to the floor again while scooting
over to make room for just *one* more person. Gentle Esmat, a loyal
companion who often served as my interpreter, told me that *no
one* expected me to follow this Persian custom of acrobatics. I
didn't listen to her, to my aching joints, to my slightly bloated

stomach, to *anyone*. I only listened to my own expectations—and was met with appreciative or sympathetic looks at every honest effort I made to follow the local customs.

Travel was frequent, with a road trip for visits nearly every day. Traveling back and forth between Tehran, the city of Saveh, and the village of Duzaj, we were constantly piling into cars and jeeps with myriad family members. There would be many places, many homes to visit: one for each of Mahmoud's eight brothers and sisters, one for his parents, and a standing invitation at each of his parents' siblings' homes. Then there were all the cousins, cousins, cousins awaiting us.

Together with family, we'd face the traffic as we headed for a neighboring city, or town, or village almost daily, frequently in the intense summer heat. Uncomfortably clammy under my headscarf and wearing nothing but that cinched tan cotton dress meant to pass as a trench coat, I'd feel like a wimp when rubbing shoulders with my female travel companions, uncomplaining in their full array of bona fide manteaus and scarves. What was then the unpaved road to Duzaj, the village of Mahmoud's birth and where his parents still lived, made for an unforgettable, sweaty episode of plowing through dust clouds, teetering precariously over rough and ragged turf and bumping along endlessly.

That same road took us to my first and final visit to the home of Morraseh Khanum, Mahmoud's ninety-year-old paternal grandmother, who would pass away before my next visit. She spoke only the local Turkish Iranian dialect, and I didn't know a word of it. But she cradled my face with her hands and planted a strong, wet kiss on my cheek the first time she laid eyes on me.

"*Ghizim, Ghizim* ('My Daughter,')" she repeated two or three times.

It was a moment of mixed emotions for me. Knowing she was Baba's mother, the matriarch of generations, made me understand the import of her warm, unbridled acceptance. At the same time, it ushered me back to early childhood memories—bashful moments at those huge family gatherings on my mother's side in Cleveland,

Ohio, when I'd be smothered with kisses by one new face after another, all claiming to be an aunt.

In its own way, the remote village of Duzaj proved to be the ultimate port of call for the Ahmadi family—where everyone from the four winds gathered weekends and summers under the thatched wooden roof of Mahmoud's parents. Unlike the other stopping points planned for brief or overnight visits, we would spend several days and nights at a time in their cooler, modest, unfurnished space. For some of that time, Mahmoud would need to be away, making preliminary inquiries and preparing for our eventual relocation in two years. So, many of the family members, especially the sisters, brothers, and their spouses, took it seriously upon themselves to see I was never lonely or unattended. In the end, we'd do much the same at the parent's house as we'd done at the other households, only for longer stretches: sipping tea, eating fruit or salted cucumbers, discussing anything from recipes to politics, stealing a nap, dancing to music Persian style, or playing an occasional round of poker or blackjack—complete with petty cash. Poker was one of my favorite options: my dad had taught me a tip or two, and I didn't need to speak much Persian to use them to advantage!

Badri's husband Rasool *Aqa* ("Mr. Rasool"), a gruff personality in his fifties with a tender heart, took a somewhat fiendish delight in entertaining the houseguests by taking me through a daily drill of matching faces with names. The routine began with his pointing a long, thick finger to one of the guests and articulating slowly, emphatically, and loudly for me in Persian, "And this one, who's this? And that one, who's that?" It wouldn't have been so bad had I been even halfway good at it, or if Rasool Aqa had let up when he saw me stumbling. But the game went on and on; at least, it seemed that way to me. Apparently, I was the only one anxious to get it over with. In the end, I can say that the crowds, curious more than anything else about how I'd do, were more than willing to forgive my inaccuracies.

Yes, people were kind, *very* kind, and everyone was interested in my thoughts and impressions. The question of which place I liked better, Iran or America, came up again and again. When I'd come up with the same answer as before—that both places have their own charms—people seemed satisfied, even pleased with my response.

The feasting continued day after day, with Mahmoud's sisters' combined talents yielding richer, more elaborate, more delicious dishes than ever. At the same time, my gastrointestinal challenges grew worse, obliging me to make more frequent bathroom visits. Unlike the bathroom in Ahmad and Esmat's house, with its choice between the basic toilet in the floor and the model I was more familiar with (the "foreign toilet," or *toilet farangi*, as they called it in Persian), the village home offered only the former—outside, in a tiny, pungent corner stall on the cement front porch.

Now, it's one thing to manage your physical and mental balance when you're engaged in the "art of going." It's quite another when your knees are half-shot from too much bobbing and squatting, your cramping stomach signals urgency, and you're holding your own while waiting to use that one basin shared by thirty-five other guests. On top of that, there was still no toilet paper—only that lovely plastic red pitcher of water, not used for watering plants.

When I could camouflage my stomach pain no longer, my sympathetic sisters-in-law took me aside, offering me a soothing remedy of tea they had brewed with dried peppermint leaves and a special crystallized sugar called *nabat*. While the tea helped ease the pangs, what I really craved was a quiet corner and some solitude. When I thought about it, I realized I hadn't had a single moment by myself—or alone with Mahmoud— since one week earlier when we first arrived. But how could I hope to find any semblance of privacy in a house with just three basic rooms, no doors, and no less than a dozen visiting folks in any one room at a time? What a striking change of scenery for a person who'd spent hours of her growing-up years playing by herself, sitting quietly by herself, even dancing by herself, happily. Solitude, like a fine chocolate or rich cup of coffee, was a treat in my day, a morsel I always savored. It didn't take much to satisfy me, but I truly missed it if I couldn't get just a little. At some point it dawned on me that this missing piece, this daily lack of time alone, was beginning to ail me more than the stomach pangs.

Even at night when the lights were out, I'd hear the rhythmic huffs and snores of heaving bodies all around, each one on his or her own mat, but sharing the same cramped floor space with Mahmoud and me. It didn't exactly allow for a playful rendezvous under the bedsheets, but Mahmoud took it all in relative stride—with a sense of humor about our zero privacy, just like everyone else's.

"Goodnight, Mahmoud!" I whispered in his ear the first night we slept with this arrangement. "Will you be okay with this?"

He turned his face toward me with a blink and a grin, while under the sheet his feet played with mine.

"Not gonna like!" he quipped. "But life goes on!"

***

The morning came when I woke to the announcement that we were going to visit *Sarighayeh* for the day. "Who's that?" I wondered, struggling to remember the name, then quickly giving up. When I learned it was a *place* rather than a person and that we might even do some sightseeing there, I quickened my pace and got excited. Getting out of the house would afford a change in scenery, a chance to work my cramped legs and belly, and a temporary escape from the daily ritual of eating too much, meeting new faces, and flubbing another round of the name game. As a special treat, Mahmoud was back from several days away and would be able to join us. I decided it didn't matter that we'd have to travel ninety minutes or so in the arid heat before reaching our destination. After all, I told myself, it couldn't possibly be worse than that rocky ride we'd taken from Tehran to the village.

It was. *Much* worse. The inclines felt much higher and the dips much lower as we skipped, jolted, and slammed continuously over rocks, fallen trunks, and dry, crumbly matter that gave in to the weight of the Land Rover. Plus, my stomach kept reminding me of the much-too-rich dinner I'd eaten the night before. I closed my eyes for the rest of the ride to manage my equilibrium. When they woke me up from a hazy sleep, we were in *Sarighayeh*.

Sarighayeh: a name intimidating to pronounce but succulent and lyrical to the ear, evoking magic from the first time I heard it. Turns out to be a word of Turkish Iranian origin meaning "yellow rock," a name that Baba had decided to keep when he'd bought it years earlier for planting fruit and nut trees (even though many had urged him to rename it *Firoozabad*—after himself, Firooz Ahmadi). The place itself was a vast sweep of land in the middle of nowhere. A thriving orchard on sandy soil in a small gaping canyon, it was a collection of geographical contradictions. There were jutting bare bolts of mountain on one side, lush rows of fruit and almond trees on another, and on the path where we were standing, an infinite stretch of sunbaked rocks, occasional patches of tiny green plants, and sparkling ribbons of water flowing this way and that. One look and you were cured of whatever ailed you: feeling bloated, constricted, without solitude, without space. One look, one breath, and you thought you could go on endlessly, just like those wandering streams.

I spent the day playing—with my husband and his family— laughing, wading, clambering, exploring, and learning the taste of sun-ripened fruit. "No need to wear a scarf here," they told me, "It's just us," and so I didn't! Somebody brought me my first handpicked treasure, a nectarine: small and succulent, smooth and faintly green with a healthy pink blush. Exquisitely fragrant, it exploded in my mouth, a wet, delectable blend of sweet and sour with a lovely, subtle trace of bitter. When I asked them its name in Persian, they told me '*shaleel* [shaLEEL].' "What a beautiful-sounding word," I told them. "If I have a daughter one day, perhaps I could call her 'Shaleel'? "*No*," they told me firmly, "You can't name your kid after a fruit." It hadn't occurred to me that if a newcomer to the States had asked if she could name her daughter "Nectarine" or "Cantaloupe," I might have answered the same way.

The return home in the cool of the evening wasn't so bad. The day's memory lingered, leaving the flavor of mountain air, spring water, and bright, tangy nectarines in my mouth, and I wondered when we would come back. It wouldn't be until two years later, when I'd be toting a baby daughter in my arms. Her name (which wasn't after a fruit) was Parisa, meaning "like a fairy" in Persian.

***

The road to the village had been long, the road to Sarighayeh even longer, but the longest road of all on this two-week "look/see" trip was the one to Hamadan. Technically speaking, the road itself wasn't the problem. It was what happened once we got there that made the journey too long for me.

Mahmoud had business in the northwest city of Hamadan to visit the university there and explore the possibility of a future appointment. Having learned the joys of traveling with my husband as I'd discovered in Sarighayeh, I asked if I could join him. He said he'd be glad for the company and asked Esmat, Ahmad, and "name game" toastmaster Rasool Aqa if they would come along too. They graciously agreed, and we made plans to leave Tehran early the next day for the four-hour drive.

When morning came, Mahmoud dipped into his suitcase and handed me a long, lightweight coat I'd forgotten all about. We'd picked it up in Tehran for just-in-case occasions. It was a striking cobalt blue, an emerging fashion color in Iran's capital, and wearing it seemed a good idea at the time. Evidently, Hamadan, known for its religious, more conservative values, represented one of those places where wearing a bona fide coat made more sense than wearing my tan cotton dress. So, I buttoned up, slipped on a black *magnaeh* (hood), pulled on a pair of black stockings I'd brought from the States (the darkest I could find), and settled in the back seat of Rasool Aqa's car for the ride. I felt ready for the streets of Hamadan.

What I didn't expect was that Hamadan wasn't ready for me.

You wouldn't have known it from the face of things. With its serene, sweetly manicured streets and moderate climate, it felt welcoming — so much less intimidating than bustling, broiling Tehran. Besides, buttoned up in the security blanket of my first real manteau since entering Iran, I enjoyed the feeling of being "proper." As we explored the pretty buildings, the impressive historic sites, I felt happy, carefree, even proud that I had finally managed to blend in.

Looking back, I suspect it was the cobalt blue of my manteau, perhaps too intense for the local fashion of Hamadan at the time. It probably didn't help that with my relatively tall 5'8" frame, the cobalt was all the more visible from a distance. It didn't help, either, that I'd chosen to twist my hair into a topknot—extending the scarf at the top of my head to the glorious form of a bump, making me look that much taller and exposing my hairline in the process. If I'd wanted to draw attention to myself, I couldn't have done a better job of it.

Given my state of ignorant bliss, I never saw it coming. In fact, none of us saw it coming when two women draped in black, whom we'd first spotted off in the distance, headed closer and closer in our direction. Nor was I prepared when they stopped in front of me and, after greeting me with a smile, started a conversation about my appearance.

Soon recognizing that I couldn't understand their Persian and clearly wasn't from anywhere near, the women redirected their comments to Esmat, who had rushed to my side. From time to time one of them would look back at me, her face still smiling, and with lightning-speed hand and finger gestures delivered essentially the same message that Esmat had heard in Persian: that I should be careful to tighten my scarf over the hairline, and that in addition, I should select black stockings that weren't so sheer.

It was apparently a civil conversation, and it didn't last long.

One could even say that they had let me off easy. But my temples were pulsing and prickly, and I couldn't stop this searing sensation rising within my spirit. I glanced at Esmat, who paused, not knowing how to respond to my bewildered look. "*Eyb nadare* (It doesn't matter)," she finally managed to say, but the pain in her eyes told me differently. I resolved then for her sake to keep my feelings of shame and embarrassment under wraps.

Some "cultural expert" you are, I chastised myself privately.

Searching for the men in our group, we spotted them a few yards away on the other side of the street. They were conversing with two other men we had not noticed earlier. Later I was to learn the identity of these men by another name: as members of the *comité*, or "moral police." These were government-appointed citizens with the authority to uphold and enforce the prescribed moral codes of the regime, even to prosecute at will. Turns out that they were members of the same party as the women we'd just seen and were carefully conveying the same message about my appearance. Mahmoud told me later that one of the men, figuring Mahmoud to be my husband, pronounced each word, each syllable to him in simple Persian, with painful deliberation—as if he were speaking to an outsider.

"*Khanoom-e-toon na-ba-yad moo-ha-shoon bi-roon ba-shad—khob?* (Your wife must not let her hair show—okay?)"

"No need to slow down, Sir; I can speak Persian," Mahmoud said to him, bristling, before the official could take another breath.

Once we were left alone to collect ourselves, Rasool worked desperately to dismiss the incident. Esmat tried to talk out the details. Mahmoud clung to silence. Ahmad simply stood there and swore.

With a rushing urge to do a combination, I felt my bottle uncork from within as the others looked on helplessly. I, too, was powerless as the tears came swelling, surging, streaming down my face despite my best efforts to stop them. I knew that the pain of my new family hinged heavily on my reaction, that my silent, rolling tears might dissolve the only glue that held things together for them and kept their feelings in check. And yet there was nothing I could do to hold them back.

One side of my brain understood that the women had honestly tried to be gentle, recognizing me as a foreigner and newcomer who didn't know any better. The other side felt stunned, so misunderstood, to have been approached when I'd honestly tried my best. Rasool Aqa, who had the gruffest exterior, was having the hardest time of all as he told me to stop my crying and forget about it. I suspect he was hardly able to handle his own pain, let alone mine, over the shame and confusion that had overcome me.

We all made do with the rest of our visit, but it wasn't easy for any of us. With no one in the mood for a new adventure, Mahmoud simply took care of his university business as the rest of us trailed him from office to office. We all went home wounded and a little disoriented that day, perhaps taking far too much to heart. But my living out that scenario was simply too new and too raw for a different reaction.

For better or worse, Mahmoud and I left for the States just a few days later. I'd been touched by my visit in many ways, some of them heart-lifting, others unsettling, but more than enough for one trip. Between all the external sensory changes and the feelings for which I couldn't find words, I had reached my point of absolute limit—and I couldn't wait to board that plane. Frankly, I was too overwhelmed at the time to read or even notice the moist, glistening eyes on the crestfallen faces of my new Iranian family, especially Baba and Mamán, as they saw us off. Nor did I consider what my poor husband might be going through as the ill-fated bearer of each side's emotions.

So, the "look/see" trip was over and we went back to Columbus. Filled with my own whirlwind of memories and feelings to sort out, I'd need the two years back home to let them incubate before heading back to life in Iran.

Chapter Ten
In the Interim

During that period between my first brief visit to Iran and the big date of our actual relocation (1990-1992), life in Columbus went on, marked by events of both the rudimentary and land-breaking kind. I went back to teaching language courses at the university, but in anticipation of my likely career in Iran, I switched my focus from teaching Spanish to American students to teaching English as a Second Language (ESL) to international students—a change I found refreshing but with its own surprising learning curve.

Mahmoud, who'd been working as a post-doctoral research assistant at the agronomy department of Ohio State, put in another year before announcing to his supervisor that he'd be leaving his post in six months, the end of the 1990 -1991 school year. At that time, he'd assume the position he had just landed as Assistant Professor of Agronomy at the prestigious Isfahan University of Technology in Iran. It was our plan for Mahmoud to return to Isfahan six months ahead of me, allowing him to get established and start laying the groundwork for the new life we'd begin sharing in 1992.

To add to the flavorful transition in our lives, I also managed to become pregnant with our first child in December of 1990—not four months after I'd eaten my first *shaleel* (nectarine) in Iran and contemplated calling a future daughter by the same name. Mahmoud would be with me in Columbus for the blessed but harrowing birthing event when I and the baby, Parisa Rose Ahmadi, survived the complications of pregnancy-induced hypertension. He would then remain for Parisa's first five months before leaving us for Iran.

In Mahmoud's absence, I would be strongly supported by

Akbar and Esther Karimian, a lovely, feisty Iranian couple in their sixties who were the parents of one of Mahmoud's former roommates. In anticipation of his departure, Mahmoud had moved us next door to them, knowing they'd be glad to watch out for Parisa and me and to care for Parisa the hours I was teaching. It seemed fitting that Esther Khanum would speak to Parisa exclusively in Persian, feed her Iranian soups and stews, and warble happy Persian tunes while guiding her dainty arms into lively, classic dance-like gestures. It was also a curious parallel to me that Esther Khanum, an Iranian of Armenian ethnicity, had grown up a Christian in the Armenian Iranian church, and that her husband Akbar Aqa, of Azerbaijani Iranian heritage, was Muslim.

My last six months in the States were filled with the endless activity of working full-time and managing the challenges of being a new mom as a single parent. Not that I minded being insanely busy; still having absolutely no idea of how to prepare mentally for the move ahead or how to process what I had already experienced of Iran, I never found myself longing for extra time to reflect actively on these things. After all, from all indications we were moving forward with plans—ready or not, reconciled or not. Perhaps a side of me was still afraid to face the unresolved questions that I chose to keep out of conscious range.

At the same time, I cannot recall a single nightmare that would enter or haunt my sleep in that two-year interlude as the day of the big move drew closer. In fact, our last month in Columbus was marked instead by a mixture of joyous and bittersweet events: Mahmoud's triumphant return from Iran as "Professor Ahmadi," reuniting with his wife and daughter; the three of us celebrating Parisa's first birthday as family, smeared with frosting and cake crumbs; a relatively smooth process of pulling things together and packing up; and the last few days of spending time with family and friends to say our goodbyes.

Saying "goodbye" to my sisters, father, and Aunt Annise was in no way easy. I mean, how do you convey the idea "I'm not sure when or even whether I'm returning," to a family member and feel good about it? But Dad had a knack for understatement at poignant moments, and this time was no exception. "Have a safe trip and be successful!" he told us with a big grin. "Find a good place to raise my grandchildren."

And when it was time to go, we left—with a howling baby on the plane, a new life to build, and an uncertain future ahead, but somehow without the same angst as before.

I'm not sure how to account for the change in me —a change I could not fully understand myself. All I can say is that in those amazing first hours, weeks, and months of our relocation and of settling in with a thirteen-month-old baby, the angst simply continued not to be there. Whether it was because my cumulative experiences happened to be so much gentler than the first time around or because I myself had changed, I still cannot say. It's almost as if the initial exposure itself—the two-week "baptism by fire" from two years earlier—had mysteriously inoculated me from a future bout of culture shock, and I found myself in a position to discover, little by little, all that this intriguing new country had to offer me ... including the rekindling of some of my fondest childhood memories.

Chapter Eleven

Ready or Not:
Back to the Village

When I was about ten years old, I discovered the beloved children's book known around the world as *Heidi*. It starts as the story of an orphaned girl taken to live in the Swiss Alps with her reluctant and embittered hermit of a grandfather. There in the alpine pastures, Heidi discovers an amazing world filled with the splendor of wildflowers, pine-scented air and cloven-hoofed goats dotting a green mountainside. With the power of her innocence and tenderness, she helps her grandfather reconnect with life, beauty, and the people around him.

I loved reading over and over how Heidi delighted in eating off the land—how she savored each chunky morsel of bread, every slab of cheese, each warm, frothy sip of goat's milk in the company of her grandfather. Her connection with the Alps and her life there becomes evident when she is taken from her grandfather to be educated in the city, and her health and spirit quickly deteriorate until she is restored to him. In the end, she helps Clara, her wealthy but crippled friend from the city, by inviting her to their home in the Alps. There, in the wholesome ethos of Heidi's world, Clara overcomes her frailty and pain and reclaims the use of her legs.

What was it about Heidi's story that called to the heart of a Black American ten-year-old, who at the time was living in an urban setting of Dayton, Ohio? The answer lay in the life she had known for nearly her first five years (1954 – 1959) in her home of Rocky Hill, Connecticut, marking the era of her earliest and sweetest memories.

We lived in a small, secure community for medical staff working at the Veterans Administration Hospital. Dad worked there as a resident physician and enjoyed the convenience of his daily four-minute walk to and from the hospital, just a few hundred feet from our little red-brick house and sweetly "neighborly" neighborhood, populated by an eclectic combination of residents, White, Black, and Brown, including international neighbors. It was a time when a man in a starched white uniform delivered milk at your door every morning, when you regularly hung your laundry to dry in the sunlight while chatting casually with your next-door neighbor. It was a time when you could see stars clearly twinkling in a black night sky, smell the rain on the sidewalk, and frequently spot a rainbow. James Brown, Elvis, and Hula Hoops were all the rage among teenagers and children, cigarette smoking was fashionable both in and outside of the medical community, and milk and Kool-Aid were my favorite drinks.

Most of all, it was a time when I spent the better part of my days roaming in my favorite part of the V.A. property: an open field dancing with cabbage butterflies, yellow and white. There were also bumblebees, dandelions, buttercups, clover, and Queen Anne's lace. The field was juxtaposed against a fence-lined border of woods, filled with the lure of wildlife and the threat of poison ivy. On those special days when Mom would take her three girls for a walk through the woods, we'd frequently follow a "secret path" that led us through a hidden menagerie of woodpeckers, possums, toads, an occasional skunk or red fox, and other treasures we hoped to spot. On other days, she'd drive us outside of the V.A. limits and take us along another wooded path—where she delighted us by pointing out where a fairy might be hiding.

That period was the most magical time of my childhood.

Years later, when I was ten, I'm not sure I made a conscious connection between what drew me to the story of Heidi and my early life in Rocky Hill. A little town whose simplicity of life and boundless stretches of light, color, space, freshness, and fragrance called me to a place of both peace and yearning, just as the mountains had called to Heidi. All I knew was that whenever I read *Heidi*, something came alive in me—the same way it had come alive for me in Rocky Hill. The same way my whole being came alive in the village—the first stop in our transition back to Iran.

***

I had totally overlooked the charm of the village of Duzaj, my husband's birthplace, in the days of my original "look/see" visit. Brimming with the spirit of Heidi, it had been there all along, of course—dwelling in the well-swept crimson carpets of the three-roomed house, the welcoming floor cushions for comfortable sitting and leaning against walls, the magnificent natural tree trunks that formed the beams of the ceiling. It was present on the kitchen walls in the bright hand-painted images of carrots, radishes, onions, and tomatoes personified as ladies' faces with plumped-up lips and merry, long-lashed eyes. It was also captured in the other rooms within striking framed black-and-white photographs of past glories: Mahmoud's father and brothers on horseback, plus his beloved grandparents and grandparents in stoic poses.

On the house's thick cement windowsills and other corners were beautiful, polished brass items of unfamiliar designs—boilers, trays, and the like—for brewing and serving tea, the consummate emblem of Persian comfort and hospitality. Outside the windows, beyond the fresh-hung laundry drying in the sun, was a whole other splendid world of gardens, fruit trees, and starlit skies that I would not discover until this second trip—the trip of our relocation to Iran. The first leg of our transition would start here in Duzaj in the shelter of Mahmoud's parents, where two of Mahmoud's siblings also lived nearby and the other siblings frequently gathered on summers or weekends.

Mahmoud's leaving Parisa and me in the company and care of family members served a valuable purpose: allowing everyone a season to get acquainted. It also gave me a concentrated, undistracted period of getting better acclimated to a new language and culture. As fortune would have it, the members of Mahmoud's family proved to be charming companions and patient teachers in my husband's absence. Given its central importance to the extended Ahmadi family, the village home of Baba and Mamán was among the places I'd stay for extended periods in those first months.

What made my second experience of the village so different from the first? For one thing, I'd already been introduced to family and surroundings. Although it had felt like a whirlwind, it made all the sensory data much less overwhelming this time around. For another, we were bringing Parisa, our first child, at the tender age of one. I had juggled the life of a single parent for nearly eight months in the States while Mahmoud had gone ahead to Iran to make preparations. In the village, I quickly came to appreciate the benefits of coming into a family whose members, particularly aunts, were eager to claim Parisa, enfold her, and attend to her carefully whenever her mom needed or allowed it.

Our first visit to the village took place in the summer, which meant two things. We faced relatively high temperatures, which kept me mostly indoors and feeling shut in—although, over time, I came to prefer this arid heat over the humid heat of Ohio. Coming to the village in summer also meant we were there during the school break, making it easier for all of Mahmoud's nieces, nephews, and their families to gather for longer periods at a time.

In contrast, our second trip took place in the fall, when school was in session. The temperatures were more moderate, as were the frequency of visits and number of people who visited the village. This allowed me the ability, over time, to sort out and recognize individual faces and names—much preferred to perceiving a sea of faces as a single, indistinguishable mass as I had before. With fewer people there at a time, I could also enjoy the luxury of more one-on-one exchanges at a leisurely pace, the joy and fun of building relationships, a more comfortable rhythm for learning Persian, and periods of rest and renewal in between. In particular, I got better acquainted with two of Mahmoud's younger siblings, Parvin and Ali, who had established their own households nearby.

Parvin was the industrious and tenderhearted principal of the local elementary school, as well as a talented artist and homemaker. She often wore colorful Indian tunics and delighted Parisa with the musical videos of Bollywood. Her husband, Hossein, was a gregarious local shop owner with a deep and charming voice. He sold sodas, ice cream, cigarettes, and the like in a small, open structure just up the way, the place where neighbors liked to gather and gossip. On the walls of Hossein and Parvin's home hung samples of Parvin's artwork: acrylic paintings of women, children, or animals born of her fancy. The exception to that collection I couldn't help but notice was a classic style painting she'd bought in Tehran years earlier: a hauntingly beautiful piece of the Madonna (*Maryam*) and the baby Jesus (*Isa*). When I shyly mentioned my surprise at seeing it on the wall, she took my comment to mean I was surprised that the painting was in oil, not acrylic like the other pieces on the wall. She never suspected I'd find anything unusual about a painting of Mary and Jesus so tenderly displayed in an Iranian Muslim home.

Ali, the high school registrar in the village, was a charming combination of down-to-earth and dashing. Smart, mischievous as a schoolboy, and slightly flippant, he was also sentimental. He surprised me one day by pulling me aside to share a photograph he apparently had held onto for many years. It was a snapshot of *me* in Ohio, crouching in the high autumn grass, wearing simple clothes, and happily smelling a flower. Mahmoud had sent it to him years earlier when he knew he wanted to marry me. Ali had saved it because he liked the photo and "maybe the person in it." He glanced at me, and we exchanged a grin.

Ali's young wife, Ashraf, was a soft-spoken and gifted beautician. With her large mocha eyes, lush and dramatic brows, and rippling waves of hazelnut hair, she was a natural beauty herself. As shy as she was, she enjoyed my frivolous humor. I loved making her laugh with colorful accounts of my misadventures with Iranians, both there and in the United States. Like the first time Mahmoud and I drove to New Jersey together to see Fati and her husband

Mahmood. And how on day two of that visit, the chatter at the breakfast table went suddenly silent, then exploded into laughter when I tried to ask Fati for "milk" in Persian—but chose the wrong word and asked for "penis" instead. In exchange for my outrageous admissions, Ashraf would "beautify" me with her exfoliating thread, her pencils and color pots, and her lavish arts.

Ali and Ashraf had a single child, a daughter named Bahareh ("like spring"). She was just six months younger than Parisa and proved to be a loyal friend as the two grew up. Parvin and Hossein had three children, the youngest of whom was their daughter Ghazal (meaning "love poem"), who was similar in age to Parisa and Bahareh. The trio was constantly playing together: the "poem," "spring," and the "fairy" Parisa.

Most of all, my stays in the village gave me extended time to spend with Mamán and Baba, as well as time alone and with Parisa, to observe and soak in the pleasures of this world.

***

I came to love the morning hours during our stays in the village. Baba, Mamán, Parisa, and I would sit contentedly at a small round table in the kitchen, or at a pretty tablecloth on the carpeted floor in the next room. Parvin, Hossein, Ali, Ashraff, or any of the kids in combination might also join us. Together, we'd eat "the fat of the land," something I'd only read about in storybooks. On some days—my favorite days—the scrolls of flatbread were soft and hot, fresh from the earthen ovens used to bake this daily staple of the local residents. From these scrolls, we'd tear off generous strips of the baked dough, then slather them with our fill of honey, ground walnuts, fresh butter or cream, or the village white cheese. In addition, served in tiny ceramic bowls were homemade jams and jellies of every fruit, component of fruit, flower, and even vegetable imaginable: sour cherries, apricots, figs, quince, rose petals, carrots, and even watermelon rinds, all of them potently delicious.

On top of it all was the deeply satisfying, full-flavored taste of Iranian tea—so easy to empty, glass after delicate glass. There was an art to preparing it. First, you'd brew the loose leaves in an open kettle till they reached a deep hue and maximum fragrance. At that point, you'd pour the dark brew into a transparent tea glass—one-third, one-fourth, or one-fifth full, depending on how much hot water you wished to dilute the brew with from a larger teapot or boiler. Some drank it with loose sugar stirred in, others popped a sugar lump in their mouth and let the tea wash over it sip by sip, others would take a bite of bread dipped in something sweet and gooey and complement it with a swallow or two. Still others would pour some into a sugar-lumped saucer and wait for it to cool before sipping.

Although the tea had every bit as much caffeine as the coffee I had in the States, drinking it had an unexpected effect on me. Instead of revving me up for a fast-paced and demanding day, it seemed to soothe my body and spirit and actually "relax" me into focus, if that's possible. It wasn't long before coffee became only a remote memory for me, barely missed and frequently turned down when offered. (Of course, the fact that most coffee was *instant* coffee made it less appealing anyway.)

My first independent exploration outdoors soon turned into a daily ritual of walking outside after the morning shower, sometimes with Parisa, sometimes alone while Parisa napped or played with a family member. There was a high, dry wall of earth and clay surrounding parts of the property—who knows for how many decades. Crumbly and fallen in places, it had seen grander days. But it proved to be a welcome cocoon, shrouding me from outside onlookers and making it possible for me to observe a more casual version of modesty by wearing a long, loose blouse and slacks with a scarf. What a relief to be free of the tight tan dress and look more like the other female villagers in casual everyday wear, including the women in my own family. Fortunately, I had brought several articles of my own that would blend in with the local wardrobe landscape.

Within our walls, there was a pleasant, grass-worn pathway also encircling the house that was marked by logs to sit on, tiny, pebble-lined brooks to walk by, a few shady trees, and an open field along one side of the path. The field was full of high grasses and all manner of wild plants that seemed to attract magpies—the striking black-and-white cousins of crows. The path led around and behind the house, where there was the stable and a handful of sheep, chickens, and a milk cow were housed. At the high altitude of the village, the air was so fresh and inviting that on some days, the sun's intense rays would sneak up and take us by surprise.

On other days, I would depart from the path to an open area where a light overcoat would be required for modesty's sake. Depending on the season, my wanderings could take me through golden wheat fields or stretches of tiny, flaming red poppies that bloomed wild. A little farther out was a herd of glorious sunflowers. Had I gone in the other direction, I would have come across the neatly cultivated rows of vegetable crops and herbs from which our savory stews were made: carrots, potatoes, eggplant, dill, parsley, cilantro, basil, and mint.

Beyond the vegetables were the fruit trees, nut trees, and beehives that contributed to the condiments on the breakfast table. I was excited when asked one morning if I'd like to join the young nieces and nephews in picking ripe apricots off the trees. Head hurting, arms aching, and prickly with sweat three hours later, I was less enthused after the actual experience of picking. But it helped remind me that the luxury of eating never comes without someone else's sweat involved.

***

The most extravagant feasts came on weekends when big family gatherings were possible. Guests included up to seven of Mahmoud's brothers and sisters—along with spouses, twenty-seven of their children, half a dozen grandchildren, and any number of village friends or relatives. Conspicuously missing were Ahmad, Esmat, and their two daughters, our first hosts from two years earlier. They had emigrated to Germany a year before our relocation, and, as the Persian saying goes, "their space was empty" (*jaye-ishoon-khali*)—figuratively meaning their absence was acutely felt.

Mahmoud's mother, sisters, and sisters-in-law rolled up their sleeves regularly and proudly worked their magic, cooking up a production of fabulous food. Steaming mounds of rice dotted with yellow saffron and jewel-toned berries and bordered by hot, crusted slabs of potatoes. Juicy kababs of chicken or ground lamb glistening on skewers. Hot bowls of tender stews, where lemons, parsley, homemade tomato paste, and hours of simmering melded rich and subtle flavors into eggplant, celery, and succulent meats. Yogurt tasting like sour cream, flatbread to dip in it, herbs, and salad greens to nibble on. Tangy relishes, fruit and nut pastes, cucumbers, and tomatoes that tasted like dessert.

With a fairytale spread so visually lush, it was easy to stuff yourself—but knowing more was sure to come another day, I learned *not* to ... most of the time. My reward came in the form of a gastrointestinal system I could live with comfortably. Even so, I still remember the advice of Said, Mahmoud's uncle from Scotland who visited Iran every couple of years. He shared it in a confidential side comment one day, right at the start of the midday meal:

"Leslie," he said, his resonant voice laced with an Iranian version of Scottish brogue as he continued in English, "if there's one thing I've learned at these gatherings..." He paused as if to call my attention to the life lesson he was about to impart, "If there's one thing I've learned, it's that you had better eat quickly ... or you might end up not getting enough!"

Hmm. I hadn't expected this. I searched his face, looking for a sign of joking in his eyes—and in the end barely caught it in the faintest glimmer. I think.

***

Meals weren't always so luxurious. During the week when there were fewer of us, we might enjoy the simple fare of fried eggs with rice and yogurt, pinto beans mashed with potatoes and a few well-stewed chunks of lamb, or a village blend of whole grain pasta, herbs, and rice. In the village's fresh, clean air and peaceful space, meals always tasted good. It reminded me of how much I had enjoyed the simple fare of yogurt, walnuts, and green onions with Mahmoud back in his dorm room at Ohio State. Similarly, here in the village, whatever was served and whatever the occasion, sharing a meal was for more than just eating. It was a time when not only family members could gather but friends of the intimate village community as well.

There was Dr. Mahgerefteh, a village doctor of the Jewish faith, who was a lifelong friend of Baba and had circumcised all the Ahmadi boys according to the local tradition shared by both Muslims and Jews. I would eventually meet another of the village doctors, Dr. Singh, who was from India and of the Sikh religion, and a close friend of Baba as well. Baba and Mamán had lots of friends, evidently. I was amazed at how many of them had last names that also happened to be "Ahmadi." Apparently, it was not uncommon for a village to be populated by a clan of distant relatives.

After a heavy meal, Baba, Mamán, and other family members would provide their guests with light blankets or sheets to pull over their heads and snooze on a patch of carpet. Many would choose to sleep on the front porch instead, under a tent of mosquito netting. After naps would be hot brewed tea, trays full of grapes, plums, apricots, and the like, and leisurely conversations in Persian or *Torki*, the local village dialect. People could choose from any number of late-day activities. These included more chatting, playing cards, or backgammon. They also included singing, dancing Persian style, and storytelling with the help of a tambourine, drum, or headscarf to twirl. Sometimes, a group of twenty or so would circle around Baba and Mamán's tiny black-and-white TV to get our fill of a local comedy, a cheesy American or British film from a past era

(I still remember something like *Attack of the Army Ants*), or a video someone had brought to share.

Whatever we were doing, I was surprised by how delightfully little it took for a moment of joy to be birthed—how someone would turn an idle pot upside down and use a spoon to come up with a clanging metallic beat. The kids would run in with their rippling laughter—and lo and behold, Mamán would be shifting from side to side, waving a scarf of multiple brilliant colors above her head. Moments later, Hossein would be wearing the very same scarf, pretending to be an old village woman droning on and on about her aches and pains.

My own favorite activities involved walking or riding along new or familiar paths with family members, including little Parisa clasping somebody's hand. As late afternoon turned into evening, there were jackals to scout, bonfires to light, and hills to scale— like that special little hill beyond the giant wooden gate. In the cool of the evening, Mahmoud's sisters, sisters-in-law, and I would often clamber up, huddle at the top with our little ones, and survey the peaceful village under a flock of amazing stars. The teenagers had their own afternoon routine: clustering at Hossein's store for sandwiches or ice-cream bars before heading up the hill. Together, they'd sit there for hours, sharing secrets, daydreaming, and watching the motorcyclists below whiz by and out of sight till dusk turned to darkness.

This was the village where Mahmoud had grown up. Now I had become part of it—and Parisa too. My contentment was deep, quiet, and bright as the village stars.

One day, at an unexpected moment, a funny thought occurred to me. All the while I'd concluded that, due to my early days in Rocky Hill, what tied me to the village was my affinity with Heidi: how, despite our visible differences, I'd identified myself with her on a meaningful level. But when I thought about it, I had to ask myself whether the real Heidi was my *husband*, and whether somewhere along the way *I* had become Clara—the crippled girl from the city who needed the village to find restoration and walk again in new ways.

***

Over time, as Parisa, her baby brother Niki (who came along later), and their cousins grew up in the village, I saw the village change along with them. Unpaved roads became paved, Baba and Mamán got their own separate telephone line, and indoor plumbing along with glossy tiles, a modern shower stall, and a foreign toilet were installed. At the same time, the sweet, happy vegetable faces in the kitchen disappeared under a coat of fresh white paint, and the magnificent natural tree trunks in the ceiling got replaced—or at least sealed over—with plaster. On top of that, with the growing economic distress of the country and pressure to keep up, people had less and less time to congregate in the village on weekends and holidays. For the village, just like anywhere else, "progress," in addition to its benefits and conveniences, had its price.

Fortunately, I had yet to see the soul of the village disappear. It would take far more than a few coats of paint, some plaster barrels, or even economic stress to overturn it. No, the secret of the soul of the village lay in the muscles and sinews of its traditions— and in its vital organs, which were our family members. Most of all, perhaps, it lay in the *heart* of the Ahmadi family: in its matriarch and patriarch, Mamán and Baba.

Chapter Twelve

Persian Parents and Grandparents: Baba and Mamán

What I most remember from those early days with Mahmoud's father was how striking the physical resemblance was between him and my husband. Baba, twenty-two years Mahmoud's senior, appeared a more delicate version of his second-born son, although no less hardy. I'd always considered Mahmoud handsome in that rugged way—and the same with anyone who shared his likeness. Both Mahmoud and his father had deep, sparkly, and intense brown eyes beset with laugh lines. Both displayed distinctively prominent noses on long, narrow faces that were punctuated by a chiseled crease along each cheek. Both men were nimble, lean, and muscular—not afraid of hard physical labor, hunting, long hikes in winter, the harshness that life could hurl at them, telling a rousing story, or laughing heartily at someone else's. And just showing kindness.

It was also his genteel, seasoned speech and wordless, animated expressions that made it oh, so easy for me to address Mahmoud's father as "Baba," a term of endearment meaning "Daddy" in Persian.

As was true for so many youngsters in Iran, it was one of the first words that I, a woman of thirty-seven, had learned to say and write in Persian. No one ever corrected my rather childish but more intimate form of address. Years later, I finally noticed that out of deep respect for the stature and authority of their father, all his adult children called Baba *Aqa* ("Sir"). But even before I'd noticed the discrepancy, I felt privileged to be able to simply call him Baba, and Mahmoud's mother Mamán ("Mom"). Happily for me, those names of endearment were allowed to stick.

While Baba somehow always left me "recharged," Mamán had a way of bringing comfort. On the face of things, the couple, who had been happily married from the time Mamán was fourteen and

Baba fifteen, seemed polar opposites. While Baba was straight, lean, and energetic, Mamán was decidedly shorter, softer, and rounder. She moved slowly and took her time with things, which is why I was always amazed at how quickly a meal for twenty or so could magically materialize when prepared by her hands. She was comfortable remaining behind the scenes, and yet offered a substantial, reassuring presence with her soft hugs and pats, few words, dispenser of incense with blessings, gentle chuckles, tears of joy, and terms of endearment for her children, grandchildren, *great* grandchildren, *and* daughters-in-laws!

"*Ghisim, Ghisim*" ("My daughter, my daughter," in Turkish Iranian dialect). These are the words I remember her saying when she first laid eyes on her thirteen-month-old granddaughter Parisa and gently beckoned her to come. It was two years after my initial short visit to Iran with Mahmoud and also the historic first day of our relocation from the States. We were fresh off the wings of a somewhat grueling and sleepless twenty-three-hour journey from Columbus. And it was Parisa's first marathon flight, launching her into a world of endless new faces, including her grandmother's.

"*Ghisim*," Mamán gently beckoned again, and extended her arms to the brown-skinned toddler with exploding black curls on the other side of the room. I was astonished to see how quickly little Parisa broke free from her daddy's warm clasp, then lightly lumbered across the circle of family members—straight into her grandmother's arms.

The Persian language is brimming with apropos proverbs for every occasion, and Iranians are fond of saying them. Mamán contentedly uttered one of them for this occasion, speaking spontaneously, almost unconsciously, as if her soul had said it for her: "*Del be del rah dare.*" Mahmoud, sitting beside me, translated it as "A road can always be found between two hearts."

I would hear Mamán use the word *Ghisim* many, many more times, usually either to Parisa or one of her twenty-six other granddaughters, ranging from age twenty-five or so on down. She would often use it with me too, usually before or after any long separation. Although it would never replace the sound of my own mother's voice, it would always leave me feeling comforted. When Niki was born two years later, Mamán would likewise affectionately call him "*Oghlúm*," the Turkish Iranian word for "my son."

As both the children grew older, Mamán would consistently show the same degree of kindness and patience to them, as well as to their mother, even when it might not have been warranted for any of us. Even when Parisa was past the "terrible twos," she would sometimes turn down an entire array of elaborately prepared delicacies served at the large family gatherings and ask for homemade Iranian French fries instead. "What do you mean, you 'can't eat that'?" I remember saying one evening, trying to camouflage my annoyance with my daughter but recognizing my own mother's admonishing voice in mine. "You'll eat what they've already prepared for us, or maybe you'll just have to be hungry."

But Mamán recognized the tension in my voice and came not only to my rescue but to her granddaughter's. "Let the little ones have whatever they want," she said gently and matter-of-factly as she handed me a plate of French fries she'd somehow already prepared and set aside for just such a moment. "Later, they can and will learn what is expected of them, but in the first seven years of their lives, they must learn the most important lesson: that they are *loved*. If they learn this, they will learn to be loving too."

Slightly embarrassed and wondering if I had just been reprimanded, I paused, daring to glance a moment into Mamán's face. Her brown eyes were warm and understanding, without a hint of judgment or condescension. I could not resist the spirit behind those eyes, nor did I feel the need to, and Parisa feasted on French fries that night. How Mamán had managed in that boisterous crowd to appear with fries at that very moment—deciphering the situation between me and my daughter when she didn't know a word of English—I'll never figure out.

On rare occasions, she shared other thoughts as well—thoughts that would set me thinking and sometimes questioning too. There was the day I noticed her stroking Niki's curls as she rocked the drowsy toddler on outstretched legs.

"I'm thinking," she said of Niki with a claiming grandmother's pride, "I'm thinking his hair will go straight sometime … like my hair." Having said what was on her mind, she then stopped, neither inviting a response nor discouraging one.

As I weighed her words silently, I wondered how Mamán could possibly think that the child of both a wavy-haired father and a crinkly-haired mother would ever have straight hair. I knew I was no prize student of genetics, but I figured it was safe to conclude that Niki's curls weren't going anywhere.

His hair went bone straight by the time he turned three, and took its sweet time, maybe five years, before a single curl crept back in. When years later I finally owned up, confessing to Mamán how I'd doubted her prediction that turned out to be accurate, all she did was chuckle. I joined in, laughing mostly at myself. After all, how many children—and children's children—had she observed over a lifetime? What else had she observed, heard, or understood that I could learn from her, things I would never learn from a book?

***

People as understated as Mamán are likely to be misunderstood sometimes. I myself have felt misunderstood for a certain soft-spoken side of mine that can sometimes emerge, threatening to distort the full dimension of my personality in others' eyes. Remembering this makes it even more painful whenever I realize that I have misjudged someone else for the way he or she has communicated. Call it a "cultural disconnect," call it the "persecute the mother-in-law syndrome." All I know is I was caught off guard one morning when Mamán called out to me from the next room, "Leslie Khanum, come get these potatoes and start peeling them for lunch."

It wasn't that I minded helping with things that needed to be done. It was just that I had been raised to attach a "please" or "thank you" to any request, that to do otherwise was disrespectful, demanding, or short-tempered somehow. As I obediently headed to the next room and took the knife and basket of potatoes from Mamán, I felt a wave of resentment take over in spite of myself. *What had I done*, I asked myself, *to warrant my mother-in-law talking to me that way?* At the same time, I couldn't help but feel guilty for my sensitive reaction to a request, however terse, from a person who had opened nothing less than her arms, her heart, her household to me. How could I let her one-time statement throw me so much? Anyone could have a bad day, and Mamán of all people was entitled, I reasoned. But somehow, her words still left me feeling stung.

The experience was an isolated incident, with Mamán continuing to be the tender and unassuming soul she had always been. I had all but forgotten the event until one day, it somehow occurred to me that I had unfairly judged my mother-in-law in the same way a friend of mine had unfairly judged my husband. It happened one summer day at a lovely resort by the lake, where Mahmoud and I had joined another newly married couple for a carefree day together. We were getting ready for lunch when I heard my husband call out to me, "Leslie, bring me the cooler from the trunk of the car." Our companion Pam, who overheard Mahmoud's request, decided I needed someone to come to my defense. So, she interjected sharply, "Mahmoud, why don't *you* just go over there and bring it *yourself*?"

It was a comment that stunned both Mahmoud and me; Mahmoud and Pam had known and respected each other for years. Yet, as I looked into my friend's eyes, I could see that she herself seemed stunned and offended by Mahmoud's statement. All I could guess was that she had managed to let Mahmoud's words push one of her buttons—that in the moment, what she had perceived in my husband was a man ordering his woman around while not lifting a finger.

As for me, I was perfectly contented to get the cooler myself.

Unfortunately, flustered by Pam's directive, Mahmoud turned back and got it before I could. Perhaps my willing attitude had stemmed from knowing that Mahmoud would literally walk a mile to fetch one, two … or *ten* coolers for me if I needed him to, even without my asking. As far as I was concerned, he had done the equivalent of that for me in a thousand different ways, time and time again. There was such a closeness and understanding between us that there was no need for a formal "please" or "thank you" to be inserted in the request. We were simply there for each other, and both loyalty and gratitude were already understood.

So, as I was thinking back on the cooler incident, it suddenly dawned on me. Might I have viewed Mamán and her comment in the same unfair way my well-intended friend Pam had looked at Mahmoud? Mamán, after all, had raised this man who communicated in the same straightforward way as hers, at least to those close to him, and thankfully, I had always connected the dots. The irony was that I had read Mamán's words as disapproving—perhaps just when she was drawing closer to me in her own way. Her straightforward requests without the word "please" would not throw me again.

Not that she was always straightforward. Oh, the countless times over the years she had to cough discreetly to remind me not to show my back to anyone in a room during social visits (which were nearly all the time), as such behavior was considered a sign of blatant disregard. Oh, the times she had to tilt her face ever so slightly in my direction when she could hear me sniffling with a cold, viewed by Iranians similarly to how slurping is generally viewed in the States. I finally reached a stage where I could at least catch myself in the unwanted behavior and correct myself in the act. Then I'd anxiously look over to Mamán and note the merriment in her eyes, her quiet, deep-throated chuckling.

God knows all the careful, continuous listening and laughter offered by Mamán over decades—to both the rambling and reluctant speakers, the funny and forgettable stories—in the presence of family or friends. No matter who you were, Mamán always gave the same attention. I can only imagine what silent insights and secrets she owned as a result. To my mind, these are the unsung qualities that constituted her greatness, her mystery, and her strength. And if Baba's wisdom flowed to the surface through the words he spoke over the years, perhaps Mamán's wisdom—and legacy—were best revealed by what she chose *not* to say. Perhaps it also explains, at least in part, the secret of their happy, seventy-plus-year marriage.

Chapter Thirteen

History and Transcendent Mystery

Both Mamán (Shazdeh Amirhosseini) and Baba (Firooz Ahmadi) had been born in Khareghan, a scattered conglomeration of villages on the outskirts of Tehran belonging to the tribe of Iranians linked to a Turkish heritage. Both had spoken the Turkish Iranian dialect before speaking the national language of Persian, as had Mahmoud and his two older siblings. Distant relatives, they had seen each other at family gatherings from their early years. Baba recalled how she had surprised him with a stunning smile on one occasion as she passed him by. Mamán vehemently denied the account every time. Who's to say who was right? She was six and he was seven at the time. In any case, when they finally married eight years later, the seeds had already long been sown toward "a union of much love and affection" (Baba's own words, an assertion Mamán never denied). They would partner in giving life to twelve children, three of whom they'd bury shortly after birth, and in the nurturing of thirty-one grandchildren, including the great grandbabies. Over the years, they would also receive a continuous stream of friends, relatives, and neighboring villagers, as well as high-ranking officials and dignitaries both local and from abroad.

Born in 1926 (three years after my father), Firooz Ahmadi was a child of the feudal era, when tenants of land parcels would pay rent through a tribute, or a percentage of what they raised on the land. He was the son of a noblewoman, Morasseh Khanum, roughly the equivalent of a duchess. Perhaps it was his mother's noble bloodline that bent Firooz toward his genteel speech and ways. His father, Rahim Ahmadi, was in a high position himself, working in direct service to the grand lord as appointed tribute collector for the village of Duzaj.

By the time he was fourteen, Firooz was already developing the stout and discerning heart of his dad. One might even say that Firooz had unconsciously begun to take on his father's torch without usurping it. As he honed his literary and math skills under a tutor and grew in insight, maturity, and his natural charisma, he was soon noticed by the feudal lord, who placed him in charge of a village by his eighteenth birthday. He was quickly promoted from overseeing one village to fifteen, first as chief accounts auditor and then as executive manager.

As Firooz forged his own career in service to the feudal lord, his way of managing gained its own brand of controversy. In fact, news of Firooz's unique administrative style started circulating quickly—first in the village he'd been placed in charge of, then throughout the entire district. For one debtor, he'd postpone collection to make sure he'd be able to feed his family. For another, he'd collect only a portion and record that the debt had been paid in full. "You can pay me later," he'd tell them. So, not wanting any discredit to fall on Firooz, they nearly always did. For yet another person, Firooz would forgive the debt altogether. It didn't matter if you were young or old, highborn or lowborn, native or foreign, Muslim or not. What mattered to Firooz was you the person, the plight you were in, and your family's welfare. For decades to come, the people of Kharegan and their progeny would welcome Firooz Aqa into every circle and every ceremony, entreating him to join them as an honored guest or to serve as arbitrator over a dispute.

Back in those early days, word of Firooz's management style with some of the indebted villagers also reached the ears of his rivals. They accused Firooz of both fraud and treason and brought their complaints to the feudal lord, who, in turn, asked Firooz for an account for his actions. Firooz freely owned up to his way of doing things, stating his motive to execute both justice and mercy within the authority that had been given to him. The lord, who had liked Firooz from the start and trusted him implicitly, asked him if he'd like his accusers disciplined for their clearly malicious intentions.

"Why should his lordship trouble himself?" Firooz was reported to say. "Their intention to harm was not against you. Why not let things stand as they are?" And so, things did stand—until one day, many years later, Firooz was surprised by a visit from one of those former accusers. Without a clue as to how much Firooz knew of his earlier treachery, he now voiced respect for his longtime opponent, a man he'd come to love as a friend.

***

"But how could that be?" asked some of the older children after hearing the same account about their *baba bozorg* (grandfather) from their parents, namely Mahmoud's brothers and sisters. Admittedly, even to me, it sounded a bit like the stuff of ballads and fairy tales: "too good to be true." Even so, I always trusted the accuracy of his account, just as I believe his grandchildren did. I don't think their question was so much about whether the reported events had taken place as how Baba had managed to beat the odds in a world that could be so cynical.

If Baba ever happened to be within earshot of his grandchildren's question, he was happy to offer his perspective. "Because I liked people, they liked me back," he'd say simply with a smile, then after a pause, added something else to think about: "When you want to bring about people's happiness, you become happy too."

I eventually found a way to ask Baba a variation of the same question. One day, after a discouraging dose of the news on US-Iranian relations, I asked him what he thought the secret of working through conflicts and barriers with others was—where "others" could refer to either individuals or governments. I will never forget his unfaltering response:

"Leslie Khanum, the secret to getting along, to getting past barriers in relation to others, is to *want* to. If you truly want it, it can be accomplished." To my mind the comment called for no more than a silent acknowledgment, like the day Mahmoud shared, "We

(Muslims) like Jesus too." As I silently sat, taking in Baba's statement, my eyes began scanning along the back wall, where Baba had hung the framed black-and-white picture of Dr. Martin Luther King Jr. and Malcolm X, formerly bitter rivals as civil rights leaders, sharing a moment of laughter together.

And as I looked back at Baba, there was hope in his voice and brightness in his eyes, and he leaned slightly forward to complete his advice:

"And hope in God; hope only in God."

I knew Baba was referring to our first theological discussion from one year earlier, following one of those wonderful family gatherings in the village. From oldest to youngest, the gang had surrounded the tiny television screen to see which video "Uncle Mahmoud" had brought them from America. On this occasion it was a Dreamworks animation, a favorite of mine, titled *Joseph, King of Dreams*. The film focused on the life of the man named Joseph ("Yousef" in Islamic circles) whom Jews, Christians, and Muslims all recognize as God's chosen servant. This Semitic youth, also known for his "coat of many colors," had been favored by his father, beaten by his jealous brothers, and sold as a slave to Egyptian neighbors. He was quickly promoted to attend Pharaoh's first officer Potiphar, only to soon be falsely accused of taking liberties with Potiphar's wife. He was thrown into jail until his God-given ability to interpret dreams came to Pharaoh's attention.

The viewing of the animation was a categorical success. The family was fully absorbed by the story unfolding artistically on the screen, and the English narrative seemed to pose no problem at all, in light of the familiar plot displayed in colorful images and decisive actions. Even so, once the final scene had concluded, the lights were turned back on, and shouts of thanks were offered, the room quickly cleared. No one except me, evidently, had felt the need to linger a moment, digest what they'd seen, or engage in a meaningful discussion. Upon second glance, however, I suddenly noticed Baba, relaxed and seated calmly in place, almost as if he were waiting for me. Drawn by the receptive expression on his face, I accepted his nonverbal invitation and sat down beside him. I barely noticed the fragrant cups of tea being served us by one of the children as I asked Baba the first question that came to my mind:

"Baba, why do you think God permitted Yousef to endure so much suffering under the unjust treatment and neglect of others?"

It looked like Baba, a scholar dedicated to sacred texts, had contemplated the question before, possibly many times. I could see he was open to sharing his thoughts, and I was anxious to hear them. I'd forgotten, however, how our past few attempts to discuss deeper topics without the help of an interpreter had turned out. Between my basic textbook Persian and Baba's eloquent speech, full of literary language birthed from a lifetime of contemplative readings, we generally weren't all that successful in understanding each other. It seemed like every other word that Baba spoke was generally met with my blank expression, and the rest of the spaces were filled in by our laughter. But this time Baba seemed to choose each word especially carefully, determined to honor my earnest question with an answer I could understand with my own ears.

"Leslie Khanum, the reason Yousef suffered for so long, I suspect, was that he had chosen to lean too much on the goodness and resources of men rather than on God first. After being thrown in jail for a crime he didn't commit, he counted on a fellow prisoner who was about to be freed to put in a good word to Pharaoh. And so, he failed to trust in God for his freedom. When we turn to people and not to God for solutions, well, we shouldn't be surprised by a disappointing outcome."

He didn't use the exact word for "disappointing." If he had, I wouldn't have understood him, as in past conversations. The word he chose instead was *kharab*, literally meaning "broken," but carrying the colloquial connotation of being "messed up." So, I looked at Baba for his uncharacteristic choice of words, and we burst out laughing together, both of us recognizing how determined he'd been to make his point clearly understood.

***

After that successful exchange with Baba, other memorable conversations followed, sometimes with the help of an interpreter, sometimes not. One day I felt brave enough to ask Baba if Islam really did permit a man to take on more than one wife at a time ... even up to four. "Well, yes," he said with a tentative sound to his voice, "but the Qur'an also clearly states that this can be permitted only if the husband can keep each wife completely satisfied." He paused, then added with a wide grin and tilt of his head, "And who can possibly achieve that?"

I was grateful for the wit that so complemented his dignity, his proclivity for seeing humor while somehow managing to keep everyone's dignity intact. Who cared if I had introduced the family to the American tradition of Thanksgiving with a turkey baked so crispy (in that blasted, unfamiliar Iranian oven) that you could hear the crunches soundly around the table between lackluster choruses of *Mmm ... very good, Leslie Khanum ... yes, very good ...*? Who cared if the flan dessert, known by Iranians as the firm and elegant *crème caramel* that I'd just prepared and presented, lay a flat, yellow mass in the shallow serving dish as if someone had cried into it? Baba would somehow find something kind to say, and we'd just laugh about it later. It seemed there was nothing I couldn't take to Baba that he wouldn't approach with wisdom, grace, and a little bit of "salt," as the Iranians say.

Still, it would be three years or so before I'd bring myself to ask the "ultimate question": how God looks at people who aren't Muslim. Perhaps subconsciously, I wasn't so sure I'd be brave enough to hear an answer that might leave one or both sides regretting that the subject had been raised.

But with the passage of time and no one planning it, the opportunity came on its own. It happened in a conversation over tea one day, when another family member incidentally brought up a topic for me to chew on—what God expects of all Muslims. So, the question bubbled up from inside of me, though I paused for a moment before I let it come out:

"And … what do you think will happen to others—those who are trying to follow God but not strictly Muslim … what do you think will happen to them in the end?" I tried not to sound challenging.

The person's response, which didn't come right away, was no less gentle. Curiously, it had a familiar ring to it. It reminded me of the explanation I'd heard from some Christians of how God looks at people who seek Him, but not necessarily as a Christian.

It went something like this: "Suppose God were a manufacturer of cars, and at some point in your life He gave you a certain model to drive and said, 'This is my gift to you. Drive it.' You would love it, and you would drive it, wouldn't you … for as long as the manufacturer still wanted you to have it. But suppose that one day, that same manufacturer told you that He had designed a newer, better, more updated model for you and that He wanted you to drive that one instead? That would mean that in order to stay obedient and faithful and to remain on His chosen path, you would need to abandon the old model and accept the new. And if you were to decide *not* to abandon the old model, well …" That's where the voice trailed off, leaving me to conclude that the person thought it kinder not to spell out the alternative. Evidently, from this person's perspective, the model of faith I was driving needed an update. What an odd and humbling sensation it was to be on the receiving end of that argument.

Now that the proverbial box had been opened, there was no shutting it, at least not yet. Throughout the day, I looked for a moment when I would find Baba alone, when I could pull him aside and ask him the same question. I wanted to know what *he* thought.

His answer to me was simply stated and unhesitating. "Leslie Khanum," he said in warm, emphatic tones, waving his hand gently, "You shouldn't worry about such things. God, on whose mercy we all depend, looks at the intention of people's hearts. Don't worry about such things," he repeated, *"at all."* End of discussion. But his words, once more, had a compellingly familiar ring, reminiscent of exchanges long past in the States, only now delivered in a whole new context I would not have imagined.

Baba had that rare and genuine gift—the ability to make you feel so safe, so valued, and accepted unconditionally. Yet all of us in the family recognized that Baba's gracious way of responding was born out of a deeply generous spirit. At the same time, he was not one to take things lightly. He was, after all, the same Firooz Aqa who had been appointed and trusted to oversee the affairs of the grand feudal lord. He was not a man to be trifled with or someone you ever wanted to face under compromising circumstances. His standards were high, and his internal convictions were even higher.

***

Both *knowing* that about him and *loving* him, Parisa told me one day, left you never wanting to let Baba down—and feeling absolutely terrible if you did. She was a teenager when she told me that—a young woman straddled and torn between two worlds where it came to acceptable standards of modesty. It wasn't as much a big deal being talked to by Mamán, who'd simply say something like "Parisa, I can see your cleavage," in the same matter-of-fact way she might have said, "Let's have some fruit,"—then nothing more was said about it. Mahmoud, a curious balance between his mother and father, would playfully gesture with his hand to Parisa to lower her neckline for an even better view—making his point while still making her laugh (I often marveled at how Mahmoud could get away with actions and words that no one else could, a trait I found both admirable and annoying.) But with Baba, it was evident how painful it was for him even to have to say something about the topic, and *that* made the exchange hurt all the more. I was touched by my daughter's struggle and her choice to confide in me about this, and I tried to offer a compassionate ear in return. But little did she know how well I related to parallel issues, even if my direct encounters with Baba had (perhaps) been fewer and further between. Evidently, any moment of truth—a moment where a call to some standard was on the table and you wondered if you'd make the cut—could become a memorable moment for either daughter *or* mother.

For me, the most memorable day of testing came one summer afternoon after a midday meal, a time when guests would generally not be expected at the village home. Yet the guests showed up anyway—three gentlemen from the neighborhood suddenly appeared at the door, searching for Baba.

Within seconds of the male voices sounding from outside the door, all the women in the room who had been without headscarves had put theirs on. By this time, I understood the local protocol—the Islamic code for women to be covered in the presence of men not counted genetically as family. On similar occasions in the past, with a single, subtle glance, Baba had communicated his wishes for me to follow suit, and I would always comply by covering my hair. On this occasion, however, my scarf was hanging somewhere on a remote hook or under a pile of clothes. Retrieving it would mean having to plow through or stumble over a pile of people, not to mention bringing to everyone's attention that I was holding things up. For whatever reason, my emotional state at the time made it a vulnerable moment; I felt somehow self-conscious and embarrassed to have been caught off guard. At the same time, I was uncertain of what to do, yet equally afraid to meet with Baba's gaze, however gentle. But in the face of limited options, and before the cloud of eyewitnesses who were my family, I looked over at Baba, and our eyes met.

In retrospect, I suspect that at that moment all eyes were fixed on him, the patriarch of the family. How would he handle this situation and his foreign "bride"? As I awaited his direction, I noticed a rare moment of vacillation in him. Perhaps he was struggling with the same question, with a series of questions. Would he protect the integrity of his faith and the reputation of his household by gently relegating me to the other room? Yet, as I noted a subtle shift come over his face, it seemed to me he was looking at something else, *someone* else in a vulnerable moment, hanging in the balance … and that person was *me*, his daughter-in-law.

He glanced at the door where the guests were waiting, then glanced back at me, then shrugged as he let his tense expression dissolve into a relaxed smile. With one hand, he waved at me in a way I clearly took as a canceling motion—a motion I somehow understood to mean, *Let it go … let it go, Leslie Khanum. You let go of it, and I'll let go of it too.* With the other hand he reached for the door and invited the guests in. At this time of day, Baba had evidently decided that the impromptu guests would have to deal with being received by his family, *all* of his family, just as they were. And so, they did.

My heart was moved with gratitude for this man who, scarcely having been outside of Iranian borders for the nearly seventy years of his life, had placed his deep-rooted traditions aside for the moment on his "bride's" behalf. How could I not respond in turn? As soon as I saw the opportunity, I slipped into the other room and returned with a scarf carefully draped over my head.

I admired Baba for his refreshing blend of honesty, diplomacy, and conviction, mingled with that humor toward himself and others. It gave me a firsthand appreciation of how he had become so favored and trusted in the eyes of so many from all walks of life. Although he was always open to theological discussions when invited to enter in, I noticed that he was not so much one to talk about his faith as to live by those convictions in simple and great ways.

What was faith to Baba? Among other things, it was his unfailing visits to villagers who had lost a family member—and it seemed like someone was always dying. It was the fuzzy gray donkey he would arrange to bring to the farm certain summers for little Niki's sake.

In an earlier era, it was purchasing *Sarighayeh* ("Yellow Rock"), that vast sweep of land in the middle of nowhere, with its soil strewn with stones and jutting peaks, and turning it into a lush orchard of all manner of fruits by planting one tree at a time. And when the boughs were heavy with fruit, it was the extra bushels upon bushels of apples and other fruit that he distributed among the hires who had helped him to tend it.

It was the attentive way he would include me in the ceremonious breaking and sharing of a glistening red pomegranate, one of Iran's glories and perhaps Baba's favorite fruit. It was the heartfelt, reflective walks and talks with his son Mahmoud, or another of his children, through flowing white wheat fields, or the hand-in-hand strolls with a grandchild or great-grandchild along garden streams in the cool of the day.

Perhaps I saw it most clearly in the way he and Mamán chose to love and embrace their American "bride" with no strings attached. Knowing full well the stakes involved with a son whose wife still had ties to her homeland, they lived in the shadow of our uncertain future. Yet they never tried to exert any pressure or demonstrate any sense of entitlement. As much as he longed for us to remain with them, Baba would stand by what he believed in. He'd trust in God, and God only, for his future and ours.

Chapter Fourteen

Khanumeh Doktor: "The Doctor's Wife"

It was time to enjoy tea after lunch at Maman and Baba's house in the village. Already settled on the carpet, I was waiting for my savory brew to cool when I sensed somebody looking at me from above. It was Zahra. Her gorgeous dark eyes were warm and coaxing with a hint of apology, but her voice was uncharacteristically directive.

"Get up, Leslie Khanum! Get up, shower, and find something chic to put on. Dr. Shams is coming to meet the doctor's wife."

I stared blankly at my young sister-in-law while I translated her Persian in my mind. Someone coming to see the doctor's wife. "The doctor's wife"? *I* was "the doctor's wife"!

That was how Zahra and all the family members introduced me whenever I had to meet just *one more* person—anyone who knew my husband as *Aqayeh Doktor* ("Mister Doctor"), the one who had gone away to the States and returned to Iran with a PhD. And I was the *Khanumeh Doktor* ("the doctor's wife"), his relatively new wife from America who was still to be presented and welcomed—and subjected, I feared, to whatever other surprise might come with the welcome package.

Zahra's delicately manicured hand entered my field of vision, ready to pull me up to my feet. Away from my cushy space on the intricate carpet. Away from the steaming tray of exquisite tea glasses still waiting to be emptied. Away from the shining saucers of fragrant pears, cucumbers, and nectarines still waiting to be peeled and tasted. "*Boland Sho* (Get up), *Leslie Khanum*—get up and get ready! Dr. Shams is coming soon."

Resisting her message, I stared at her blankly. It was only two-thirty in the afternoon, that sacrosanct time of day following a heavy, elaborate lunch and laborious cleanup of all those pots, pans, and plates. Fortunately for me, Zahra, the youngest sibling of my husband's eight brothers and sisters, was eleven years younger than me, giving me some leverage to resist her orders. "Who is Dr. Shams?" I demanded.

"He's one of the village doctors—a longtime friend of the family and a great man. And it's only proper that he should meet you," she added with a serious air. But the look on my face got her laughing. "Leslie, get up already! Do you want help finding something suitable to wear?"

"What's wrong with what I'm wearing, Zahra?" I protested. After nearly one full month in Iran, I still hadn't figured out the standard for what constituted "suitable," let alone "chic" for different occasions. To my mind, I was modest enough and certainly appropriately dressed for company, with my loose, long-sleeved blouse and full-length floral-print skirt. In fact, I reasoned to myself, I didn't look so terribly different from the other female family members in the household. All I'd probably need was a fancy headscarf to dress things up.

"Come on, I'll help you find something," she answered, finally succeeding in pulling me to my feet. There was a soft place in my heart for Zahra. The natural elegance and glamour of her persona charmed me, and although to me she was a stunning beauty, she never took herself seriously. A kindred spirit to the flamenco dancer in me, she was always the first one to find an opportunity for fun, to whirl gracefully around the room to the tune of Russian or Turkish-style music, sash in hand flying above her sleek waves of black hair. And yet she was also the first to listen, to offer a laugh of sympathy in response to my woes or moments of feeling awkward—whatever I needed to help me put it all in perspective.

I certainly felt the need for her sympathy now. As Zahra led me to the back room, I imagined myself being led to the slaughter of my self-determination—at thirty-nine years old on top of that. I figured I knew which outfit Zahra would choose for me to wear: the pleated skirt and ruffled blouse ensemble in polyester, meticulously designed and hand-tailored for me by a senior family member. It was the outfit whose swirly design and iridescent colors rivaled those on the fruit plates.

Zahra took me to the backroom closet, where many of my outfits were hanging. She flipped through the inventory on the rack, one outfit at a time; there weren't that many to flip through. When she got to the polyester outfit, she paused for the briefest moment, then pushed past it compassionately. After all, the one who had so proudly sewn it was not present or likely to show up.

Finally, Zahra pulled out a simple silk red blouse with stylishly cut sleeves and a graceful neckline. This too had been hand-tailored for me by another family member. Next, she selected a long sleek black skirt with a delicate inlay of black lace along the hemline. "Here you are, if you please," she said courteously. "Will this do?"

"Okay," I agreed, then dared to add, "It's just that I really am not fond of the idea of someone I don't know coming to 'check out the doctor's wife' to see if I 'measure up,' if you know what I mean." Assuming the role of this Dr. Shams, I sidled alongside Zahra to demonstrate how it might feel to be scrutinized, giving her a thorough once over through my narrowed eyes. I addressed her as I imagined Dr. Shams might address me, in subtly accusing tones and a lofty, "So you're the doctor's wife, eh?" topped off by varying inflections of, "Hmm … Mm-hmm?" and "Uh-huh!"

Zahra said nothing, but her eyes reflected both empathy and amusement.

I took my shower, dressed myself in silk and lace, plucked out the stray hairs in my eyebrows, made up my face tastefully, and artfully donned my gold necklace and earrings. By that time a whole hour had gone by, and I could only hope that Dr. Shams was not waiting for me in the guest room, wondering when I would finally make my appearance. I grabbed an ornate scarf of fine material hanging on the wall and hurried toward the room where the guests were generally received. I would need to find Zahra to help me drape the scarf around my head and neck just so, but I didn't find her. Instead, I found myself stepping around sleeping bodies covered in sheets and camped out along the floor as I passed from room to room. Finally, turning to a small mirror on the wall, I made my best effort to drape the scarf for myself.

In the mirror's reflection I saw Mamán walking slowly toward me with a tray of steaming tapered glasses. "Come, Leslie Khanum," she beckoned with a soothing voice that had no trace of demand. "Come, sit down and have some tea."

I sat down gratefully on an unoccupied patch of carpet and let her serve me. Evidently there had been no need for me to worry about keeping Dr. Shams waiting, or holding up anyone else for that matter. Nursing a homemade sugar lump in my mouth, I finally took a sip of that wonderful, comforting tea, then asked, "Mamán, do you know where Zahra is?" I tried to sound casual.

"Zahra?" Mamán answered, moving on to serve the next person. "Oh, she went out to bring back Dr. Shams. Don't worry, they're coming." So, dutifully, I waited.

Over the next forty-five minutes I saw the room clear of napping bodies, resume with the comings and goings of family, and give way to the mellow shadows of evening. But I saw no sign of Zahra, Dr. Shams, or anyone else concerned about it.

I was helping to set the tablecloth on the floor for dinner when Dr. Shams' presence was finally announced. At that point I no longer felt physically or mentally prepared to be introduced, and Zahra was still nowhere to be found. When I heard my name being called to receive Dr. Shams, I was crouched on the floor, spooning plain yogurt into tiny serving bowls. Barely had I straightened up and turned toward the receiving room when I saw a slight figure walking right toward me. He was moving so rapidly and deliberately, as if he had known me all my life, as if he needed no third party to introduce us. When he stopped in front of me, I couldn't help but notice in horror that I towered over him, and I took a step back in spite of myself.

"Madame Doctor, the doctor's wife?" he asked me in Persian (and with a touch of melodrama).

It starts, I thought, resenting my situation and this diminutive but assertive man. His beard and mustache were much thicker than I was accustomed to seeing, with almost a layered appearance nearly overpowering his face.

"Yes, I am," I responded politely, glancing awkwardly down at him. Resigned that this visit was going to be even worse than I had imagined, I waited for the next disaster to strike.

It *did* strike, and horrifyingly, eerily enough, it struck in just the same way I had jokingly predicted with Zahra: with his penetrating sidelong glance assessing and measuring me, the "hmms" and "mm-hmms" that accompanied the glance, the raised arched eyebrow framing the intense dark eyes, unusually lovely for a man …

It took a few more seconds for me to sort out the strange, juxtaposed images of face and figure standing before me, to realize that I had seen those eyes sometime, somewhere before. All at once, in a cataclysmic moment, my eyes were opened and I recognized that it was *she*: Zahra, in all her glory, dressed up as Dr. Shams! I let out a howl, half in amusement and half in righteous indignation.

"Zahra? *Zahra*! How *could* you??!"

Zahra said nothing, but amid the gleeful laughter of the surrounding family members sharing in the joke, her kind eyes met mine sympathetically, while still revealing a fiendish gleam.

Dr. Shams never came that night. I would be meeting him not long afterward, and a more charming, gracious man I could not have met (he didn't give me the once over, either.) I never did find out whether he knew anything about the outrageous scenario he had partly inspired. Of course, the joke had never been about Dr. Shams to begin with; it was all about me and my social anxieties. I don't know if Zahra's elaborate prank was born out of circumstances once Dr. Shams' visit fell through, or if she had simply cooked the whole scheme up. Was the male attire supplied by her father? A brother? Or did Zahra's resourcefulness know no bounds? As for the beard, I later heard that Zahra had reconfigured a wig that had seen better days. All I know, and what I'll always remember, is that Zahra was the mistress behind the magic.

Chapter Fifteen

City Living with Siblings in Tehran

When the time came to pack up and leave the village for business in the city, Tehran was our first stop, and Badri, around my age and the second of Mahmoud's five sisters, was right there waiting for us. It was dark when we pulled into the narrow, well-worn alley on the city's south side, where Badri's simple two-room, two-story house and a weathered string of others sat in an uneven, tightly knit row. A water duct that supported the city's drainage system ran the length of the alley, its trickling stream revealed in the moonlight.

"Careful, *Zan Daee* ('Uncle's Wife')," her little sons Amin and Abulfazl warned as they grabbed my hands and directed me to lift the hem of my manteau while stepping over the water. Although it was well after ten o'clock at night, there were still a few silent onlookers to witness the spectacle of this tall and curious-looking woman stepping into their world.

Badri, all of four feet, eight inches tall, was modestly cloaked in her black chador as she stood expectantly, a petite silhouette at the doorway. Her round face was bursting with a resplendent smile as she kissed and welcomed each one of us. Besides Mahmoud, Parisa, and me, there was Jamshid, the eldest brother who had driven us up from Duzaj, and his sentimental wife, Mahmonir. Tiny Parisa, sleeping soundly in her daddy's arms, did not hear Badri's spontaneous coos of delight over her young niece. She and her family would be hosting Parisa and me for the next two months while Mahmoud commuted to and from Isfahan in preparation for our move there.

She was magical, or amazingly clever, or both. She had to have been to transform a single room without furniture and no larger than a one-car garage into a receiving room, a banquet hall, a nursery/playroom, a TV room, a food-chopping station, a seamstress' corner, a community bedroom … each in its turn, all in one day, day after day. From the moment I entered her narrow gateway, crossed the open courtyard, and pushed past the curtain to her beautifully laid out meal, I marveled at this woman's willingness to serve. How could it be that for two solid months, such an insanely busy woman and a ridiculously leisurely one by comparison could share the same small space with a husband and four children (hers), a fifteen-month-old baby (mine), and an array of visiting family and neighbors? How could we find so much to enjoy with each other and talk about? How was this even possible when we were from such different worlds, and where one of us was still a fledgling in the Persian language?

We were both homebodies, for one thing, preferring the comfort and familiarity of Badri's four walls to the urban activity and madding crowds outside. In our late thirties, we were both mothers. I was a relatively new mom, and Badri the seasoned parent of a teenage son, a preteen daughter, and those two adorable boys Abolfazl and Amin. Badri took care and pride in her cooking and serving, and I had no trouble appreciating her incredible soups, stews, pickles, jams, rice dishes, and crisp green salads prepared daily. Exceptionally attuned, she'd serve me an extra portion of stew if I so much as glanced in its direction. She also had a knack for speaking Persian at a pace and diction I could follow with relative ease. Plus, her vocabulary focused on the concrete, day-to-day subjects of our shared space and interests: fruit, tea, cooking, formula, diapers, and most of all, Parisa. Carefully choosing her words as she demonstrated, she shared the secrets of her flavorful stews, how to rock Parisa to sleep on my outstretched legs, how to slice, salt, and enjoy a cucumber, or how to turn a bundle of fabric into a stunning silk blouse (it was a gorgeous crimson red, fell gracefully in all the right places, and I wore it for years till it fell apart.) This was a period when I'd hear her use the strange terms *masalán* and *injuree* time and time again. Triumphantly, I finally figured out one day that she was using them to say, "for example," and "like this," as part of her explanations. So, on top of everything else, Badri's little chamber became the ideal "language laboratory"—a place where I could listen to natural Persian, observe, ask questions, and imitate for hours at a time.

This period I spent with Badri and her family felt much like my early childhood revisited. A period when I could help to some extent, but when someone else took charge of meals, shopping, and laundry. A period when each day I experienced or learned something new. A period when I struggled with language but could also feel new language skills emerging, much more so than in the village somehow. Besides Badri, there were other teachers to listen to and learn from: her husband Rasool Aqa with his dry and blunt humor, and the children with their lively conversations, occasional squabbles, and affectionate interactions with Parisa.

There was also the wonderful world of children's television that my baby daughter and I took in together. Again, it took me back to my early days in the fifties, when I was a four-year-old girl sitting cross-legged on the floor for my daily dose of the kiddie show *Captain Kangaroo* on black-and-white TV. Now here I was again at nearly forty, sitting cross-legged on the carpet, eating fruit with Parisa, and getting my daily TV dose of *Kolah Ghermezee* ("Red Cap"), the nationally known puppet character whose clothing and overall appearance reminded me of Ernie, from the popular American children's TV show *Sesame Street*.

After a steady daily fare of language practice with Badri, her family, and the television set, my Persian got stronger week after week, and with that my conversations with Badri grew more interesting. She shared photos and stories of her growing-up years with her siblings, especially Mahmoud. She told me how she had come to know and marry her own husband Rasool and about the birth of their children. She shared some of her joys and heartbreaks, and despite my faulty grammar, she listened carefully and soulfully to mine. Sometimes, as we sipped tea or chopped vegetables together, references from our Muslim or Christian heritages would spontaneously spill into our conversation, stories that often rang delightfully familiar to us both: like about Abraham (*Ibrahim*), Moses (*Musa*), Mary (*Maryam*), and Jesus (*Isa*).

I was grateful for those common stories and characters. They allowed me a way to express to Badri both my gratitude (for her endless giving) and my guilt (also for her endless giving) with spiritual references we could both relate to. "If you get to Abraham before I do, please put in a good word for me," I used to tell her. Badri would always laugh with her husky laugh and just shake her head.

In the intimate space of their tiny house, Badri, Rasool, and their four children had created a world—and a home—for Parisa and me. As sunrise inched toward sunset each day, we scarcely noticed how light and shadow, setting and characters shifted from hour to hour in that same tiny space. I almost forgot that the *rest* of Tehran—that huge, historic, polluted, magnificent, and rather intimidating city—was just outside of Badri's four walls, waiting patiently to have its turn with me.

***

I'd already had limited exposure to Tehran, some of which had not been pleasant. There was the day Mahmoud arrived from Isfahan to take me to this office and that, so I could be issued the Iranian citizenship automatically granted to foreign spouses and get my legal working papers in order. Without access to Rasool Aqa's car during the day while he was at work, Mahmoud and I had to depend on public transportation. Riding the taxis felt familiar enough. But Tehran's traffic was so congested at certain times of day that the only transportation permitted in the heart of downtown was the city bus. I remember riding that bus maybe once or twice, but those times were enough to last me a lifetime.

I'm guessing that in those first moments when the bus suddenly pulled up to the corner and opened its doors to us, even Mahmoud was caught off guard. Maybe he just couldn't bring himself to tell me directly that there would be *two* separate entrances for bus passengers: one in the front for males and one in the back for females. Then again, a newcomer to his own country following the revolution, perhaps he hadn't anticipated this new seating setup either.

For me, the minutes that followed brought a disorienting, strange sensation. The disorientation came from being cut off from my husband and herded into that narrow unfolding rear door before knowing where we were going or when we would be getting off. The strangeness came from a vague sense of both identification and displacement. *Here I am*, I thought, *a Black woman in Iran—standing at the rear of the bus in a segregated setting. Great. Here it's because of my gender; there it would be because of my race.* It was something that had never happened to me personally in America, but it *could* have when I was growing up. Just sitting there instantly stirred up powerful, collective memories from my Black American consciousness. In a strange way, I could be grateful for the chance to connect with that side of myself, to share that psychological space of segregation with the people of my heritage. At the same time, here I was in a totally different time, place, and context, now sorted by gender. I didn't know how to name my feelings, how to make sense of them, how to rank them, how to draw parallels, or whether I should even try.

It was just as well. Standing at the back of that overcrowded bus, I was occupied with more urgent matters, my eyes desperately scanning the front of the bus for signs of Mahmoud.

It felt like an eternity, but I finally spotted him, just moments before I needed to, when the bus pulled to a sudden stop. Mahmoud, straining on tiptoe to catch my eye, flagged me with his arm and motioned for me to exit the rear of the bus—*now*. Wedging myself through a standing crowd of women, I beat a path down the stairs at the rear, fairly stumbling as I went. As I recomposed myself, I felt every eye on me, the awkward foreigner wearing the only forest green garment on the bus. But that didn't matter to me at the moment; at least I had made it out of the bus and back to Mahmoud. As I reached for the reassuring touch of his hand, he grasped my fingers gently, held them for a moment ...then let go.

"We can't do that in public," he said, a tone of regret in his voice.

I don't care about the rules, I shot back with my eyes.

Not that the incident devastated me, but I was deeply annoyed. There had never been a time I had reached for Mahmoud's hand and he hadn't reached back—not until then. *So, is this the start of a new way of not interacting with my husband because of "the rules?"* I wondered as I felt my stomach shift. *Is this the way it's going to be? This isn't what I signed up for—or, by virtue of agreeing to come here, did I? If so, what else did I sign up for that was on the horizon?*

I was the type who usually felt the onset of strong emotion take over gradually, like a spill that slowly takes over a sponge. So, together, Mahmoud and I walked quietly, our thoughts to ourselves, our hands by our sides. By the time we got back to Badri's, the burning sensation in my chest was beginning to well, but I just managed to squelch the memory of the entire, distasteful bus affair. Especially the part when Mahmoud withdrew his hand.

Mahmoud asked if I wanted to talk about it. I didn't. Perhaps part of me thought that if we didn't talk about it, it hadn't happened ... or at least it would be easier to forget. So, Mahmoud and I put a pin in it and didn't revisit the subject for a long, long time. Not until almost twenty years later, when my children and their cousins had newer, less restrictive versions to share of traveling the Iranian public transport system or the streets of Tehran. Only then could I admit how complicated and emotional it was for me to be relegated to the back of the bus—not only as a woman, but as a *Black* woman.

***

But even if I hadn't had a brush with the bus system or walkways, I still might have resisted exploring the big city of Tehran, home of six and a half million dwellers even in 1992. In addition to being a homebody, I had recently come from the tranquility of the village, with its clean open spaces, easy pace of living, and relative freedom from the public eye. Despite my private reluctance, Rasool Aqa, the four children, and even Badri would see to it that, like it or not, I'd get out of the house for a better, fuller taste of Tehran.

Of course, viewing the city in the company of family from Rasool's familiar sedan felt totally different from a view from the bus. It wasn't long before riding the chaotic streets of Tehran left me exhilarated like no other moment did. A trusting backseat passenger, I'd stare out the car window and soak it all in: the hot wind that pleasantly grazed my face, the flowing black script of Persian on green street signs, the sculpted gardens and old-world fountains. There was the high rise of modern buildings and towers, the worn-down buildings of yesteryear, the remnants of history and old glories. Beyond the buildings was the smoky haze of heat and pollution, drifting above the surrounding stark blue mountains. Over time, my eyes would discern a subtler, deeper beauty beneath the blue: a mosaic of purple, gray, green, pink, and golden tones. Arrested by all these new sights and sensations in the middle years of my life, I felt the wonder of my childhood return to me. If only I could capture these memories and keep them alive on paper, I thought. It was in one of these moments on one of those rides that I promised myself I would someday write a book.

Like most other cities, Tehran was a city of contrasts. There was the wealth and exclusivity of the north, the squalor and poverty of the south, the historic grandeur of tree-lined palaces, the forgotten litter down back ravines. On our driving sprees we'd pass entire blocks of shopping malls, their windows gleaming with jewelry in deep gold tones. We also spotted their loud print dresses, dramatic gowns, ruffled blouses, leather belts, and spiked high heels all on display, but not on mannequins. *Who is actually wearing these things? Is anyone really? If so, where are they?* All the while, women on the street would pass by in their flowing black chadors or, on the flip side, their fanciful, fashionable, bright or pastel-colored manteaus.

Turn the corner and our eyes would suddenly meet with a towering portrait of the late Ayatollah Khomeini ascending the side of a ten-story building. The image of his successor, the Imam Khamenei, likewise ascended the building across from it. A block later our eyes would be drawn to the candy shops, pastry shops, pizza and hamburger shops—like Tehran's famous "Big Mac" restaurant, whose burgers didn't taste much like the name. Especially nice were the shops that sold double-decker cones topped with bright yellow saffron-flavored ice cream, all dotted with green pistachio nuts.

I remember the night we parked, piled out, and sampled their wares. It felt fun, whimsical, magical, and delicious. A melting green and yellow blob slid off my cone and splotched miserably on my foot in plain view. With three-year-old Parisa on one arm and eleven-year-old Afsaneh on the other, I laughed out loud.

"*Zan Daee: ZESHT-eh* (That's *not* becoming)!" my young niece admonished me instantly under her breath, responding to my laughter with a shocked expression.

Startled by her knee-jerk reaction, I asked myself where this taboo against laughing in public—just for women, I presumed—had come from, and why it persisted. At the time I had not remembered that somewhere, somehow, in my own growing-up years, I'd picked up the habit of cupping my mouth with my hand whenever I felt a giggle coming on. *Where did that come from? I asked myself once I did remember. Could it be that this gesture I'd picked up was historically linked to the same social taboo? Still, the fact that I had never seen a *man* cup his mouth under similar circumstances made the question even more compelling.

Despite my little slip that night, our outings continued to be magic. I was happy that Afsaneh had not yet concluded that I was too embarrassing to be seen with. And in exchange for her trust and delightful company, I kept my exuberant laughter to myself, at least when in public.

We had other reasons to surf the streets of Tehran. A host of other relatives and friends were scattered throughout the city, and in keeping with the practice of Persian hospitality, each household had invited Parisa, me, Mahmoud when available, and our host family to join them some afternoon or evening for a meal. Among those who had invited us were none other than Mahmoud's and Badri's baby sister, the lovely Zahra herself, who lived on another side of the city with her husband, Yousef, and their two-year-old daughter Rokhsareh. Mahmoud's brother Ali also joined us that night.

I will never forget the way Zahra looked that evening as she warmly welcomed us into their charming, two-bedroom apartment on the eighth or ninth floor. Dressed all in white in a gauzy material and with her sleek, black hair brushed down her back, she looked almost ethereal—hardly the same rascal I'd seen earlier parading as Dr. Shams or smugly strutting in her father's trousers, brown plaid jacket, and signature gentleman's hat.

The apartment was equally lovely, illumined by candlelight and dimmed chandeliers. In contrast to Badri's house, the apartment was adorned with a few choice pieces of walnut furniture, upholstered in what looked like tapestry and brocade. I felt intimidated to sit on it, and when I did, there wasn't a whole lot of give to it. The dinner itself was both simple and elegant: *salad olivieh*, a rich chicken salad garnished with sprigs of fresh parsley, bright carrot slices, and sliced pickles arranged in a fun floral design. Although it was served at a fine glass-top table where I sat properly on one of their chairs, by the end of the evening I found myself down on the crimson carpet, where I'd grown accustomed to being comfortable and at home. Lazing against the floor pillows with the tea glass in my hands, I glimpsed out and lost myself gazing at the balcony clothesline, where sheets were blowing gently in the autumn breeze.

It felt good for our families to be reunited since our earlier gatherings at the village. We'd met there regularly over the summer. And I missed our big extended family with the community laughter, the group conversations, the spontaneous rounds of dancing where I'd get dragged in. Still, here in the absence of the larger group, I felt free to speak in English for a change. Zahra's dashing husband, Yousef, was an engineer with laughing eyes and an amazing talent for language. After studying for his master's degree in England, he had returned to Iran fluent in British English, complete with an accent and a few English mannerisms. So, for part of the evening, he and Mahmoud translated some old time Iranian jokes for me, just for the fun of it:

"A burglar broke into a home one night," said Yousef, translating a joke that Ali had just shared. He was already chuckling, his hazel green eyes twinkling.

"Yeah?" I said.

"He looked all over the house and didn't find a single thing worth taking."

"Okay ..."

"It made the chap mad, you see. So, he picked up a child's homework that he saw on a table and crossed out all the answers with a black marker!" With that, the engineer started laughing.

"Ah-ha. And then?", I said.

The engineer kept on laughing.

"That's the end?" I asked in Persian, turning alternately to Yousef and Ali. "He marked up a kid's homework? But—why is that funny?"

"I don't know," said Ali, "It's a joke!" And he started laughing too!

I manufactured a sort-of smile, then forced out a pathetic "Oh ... hoho!" I wasn't one bit convincing, but it was the best I could do.

In any case, it was then *my* turn to entertain. I decided to share a short joke with Yousef in English and let him translate it for the others:

"A mother was talking to her little boy at lunchtime. 'Eat your spinach, My Love,' she told him, 'It will put color in your cheeks.' But the little boy protested, 'Who wants green cheeks anyway?' (*Okay—maybe it's not **that** funny, but at least there's a recognizable punchline*, I thought.)

Immediately Yousef laughed out loud, then shared the translation with the others. They started laughing too—I mean, *really* laughing. Like Yousef, everyone's eyes were sparkling. I felt myself swell up with pride.

"So, you think it's funny?" I asked Yousef and the rest eagerly.

"Well—you see, Leslie," said Yousef, with a British cadence to his speech. "I should say—well, we can see *you* think it's funny, so *we* think it's funny too." His eyes were still warm and sparkling, without a hint of sarcasm.

I thought back on my first day of arrival to Iran, on our first gathering, and how everyone laughed at my best attempts to answer their impossible questions. Now, once again I was asking myself: *Did they laugh at what I said because it was genuinely funny, or because laughing is a love language all its own?*

"Yes, okay, but hey—my joke *was* funny!" I quipped, sporting mock indignation.

And everybody laughed *again*.

I got it. My joke wasn't funny. But it was still funny. Maybe.

Chapter Sixteen

City Living with Siblings in Saveh

Having stayed, laughed, and played with parents and siblings in either the village or Tehran for the past three months, we next headed two hours southwest for the smaller city of Saveh, where the rest of Mahmoud's siblings, along with their families, were waiting for *their* turns to host us. It would be two more months before Mahmoud, Parisa, and I would be able to move into our own house provided by Isfahan University of Technology for the coming term. And Mahmoud's family members in Saveh seemed not only willing but *eager* to accommodate us. From their perspective, we owed each of them equal visiting time.

These family members in Saveh included Jamshid, Mahmoud's big brother; Ozra, Mahmoud's big sister; and Nadereh, one of the younger sisters. They, along with their spouses and children, had long lived in the city of Saveh, home of 120,000 residents and known for its blistering climate, salty drinking water (at the time), and big, red pomegranates.

Once Mahmoud, Parisa, and I arrived, it was touching and terribly humbling to be the object of such attention from such well-meaning people. It was also disconcerting. To my knowledge, I'd done nothing to deserve all they wanted to do for us—wash for us, cook for us, take us sightseeing—nor did I have anything other than gratitude to return their kindness with. For another, it was hard to keep track of how we were dividing our time between the three families and what, to *their* mind, constituted a fair distribution of "visit time." Frankly, neither Mahmoud nor I wanted the responsibility of juggling and protecting everyone's feelings. It was too easy to get it wrong, too easy to blow it. Besides, without our own car and with Mahmoud in Isfahan most of the time, Parisa and I were wholly dependent on others to get us from one family to the next. In the end, that circumstance was the saving grace for all of us. With Mahmoud out of the picture and me out of the loop, the siblings would have to work out their own system to "take turns" hosting Parisa and me.

Imagine that. Instead of fighting over *who'd have to keep us*, they had worked out a plan on *how they could share* us.

But every now and then, I wondered how the saying I'd once learned in Spanish class, *Los huéspedes y los peces apestan después de tres días* ("Guests and fish both stink after three days"), could apply in Spain and the USA, but not in Iran?

***

Being at brother Jamshid's, then sister Ozra's, and then sister Nadereh's homes on a rotating schedule turned out to be a re-markably good fit for me in Saveh. Maybe I still wasn't ready to take on the status of a settled-in resident, so I *liked* the change in routine and surroundings, and I didn't mind the short notice. The ongoing activity kept my mind occupied—away from the street, heat, and dress code I preferred not to think about—and focused more on family and "life on the inside." It gave me a chance to see Saveh's face and make ongoing comparisons between parts of the city. But the best part by far was getting to know the unique per-sonality of each household.

At Jamshid's and Mahmonir's home, it was the elegance and etiquette—from the ornate curtains and fancy china to the elabo-rate menus that Mahmonir, a master instructor of cooking and sewing, planned for us. It was the fashion journals from France; the scraps of beautiful fabrics left over from the exquisite gowns she had created. It was how Mahmonir giggled with her children, how tears filled her eyes when I sang in Spanish on the guitar, how she held Parisa spellbound with the story of *Shangul, Mangul and Habeyeh Angur*, three little goats who escaped the wiles of the wicked wolf. It was witnessing the adults pray to God three times a day (in keeping with Shiite Islamic practice): Jamshid on his prayer rug, facing southwest toward Mecca, and Mahmonir in her white cotton chador with a delicate blue floral print.

The home of Ozra (or "Abjee" [pronounced *Objee*, which means "big sister"]) and her husband Forghani was the haven for pomegranates, those succulent spheres that ripened in their orchard. At Ozra's house, I learned what to look for in a pomegranate, how to crack it open and gobble up the pretty insides: red, pink, or almost colorless. Every day, after lunch and a nap, we would watch stunning footage of Iranian wildlife filmed for TV by her grown-up eldest son.

There were other distinctive markers of Ozra's household: roosters crowing in the courtyard, Ozra mixing her own blends of henna or eyeliner, Ozra offering to come into the shower where I was bathing and scrub down my back (I always politely declined), and also not to forget her masterfully whipping up one of her rich and savory *ashes* (pronounced *oshes*) for us. These were thick soups full of good things like beans, beets, and noodles with a special clotted cream, or fresh herbs with meatballs and pitted plums, and a dollop or two of her own homemade pomegranate paste. When Mahmoud was in town, there was plenty of gutsy laughter and camaraderie shared between him and the no-nonsense sister Ozra, who'd been like a second mother to him. There were also those lively, and not always lighthearted, political debates between Mahmoud and Ozra's husband Forghani, who'd been a teacher to Mahmoud when he was a boy. I would never have imagined two Iranians having such opposing views on which US presidential candidate would be preferable for the times: George H. W. Bush or Bill Clinton.

Then there was the household of Nadereh, the youngest Ahmadi sister next to Zahra. Full of laughter, energetic, curious, and sentimental, Nadereh was all about embracing life and nurturing it. She loved all things small and sweet and was always ready to take them in: the stray kittens in the courtyard, the bird with the broken wing, Parisa and her fledgling mom in a new country. She had a growing collection of pretty dolls and stuffed animals she was saving, she said, for her children's children one day. She adored Parisa, primping and dressing and fussing over her as if she were the favorite doll in her collection. She fussed over me too, artfully adjusting the collar or cuffs of my manteau or draping my scarf just so before taking us out on the town. To the park. To the ice cream shop. To the old end of Saveh with the antique flea market that sold exquisite metalwork, woodwork, and handwoven cloths.

When we got back home and put Parisa down to nap, we'd rest our bones from the blistering heat and chat over tea with a salty edge that would take getting used to. As I grew more accustomed to her speech, I'd answer her questions about life in America with my sisters, my father, and of course, her brother Mahmoud. My Persian wasn't great. It didn't matter. We laughed a lot.

Laughing was what we as a family came to do best together, especially when all three households in Saveh would gather in one of the homes to eat, swap stories, play cards, or dance. It felt wonderful, like the "good old days" at the village, a whole two or three months back. On special occasions, someone would bring a video to share, frequently featuring some popular film they'd gotten hold of from America. They surprised me one night with a special selection.

"Come on, Leslie Khanum!" they called from the other room. "Come and watch with us! Have you heard of a film called *Not Without My Daughter?*"

Wait—what? *Not Without my Daughter?* **Anything** but that! What a cruel, ironic twist of fate. Evidently, Mahmoud's family knew the film was based on a true-life story and wanted to see it. But up till then they knew nothing of *my* history with the story, and I had every intention of it staying that way. How could I possibly sit with them through a film that, to my mind, presented an Iranian man and his family members in the worst possible light—especially regarding how they treated his American wife and her daughter in Iran? Although I also understood the basic storyline of the author's abduction to be true, how could I answer to my in-laws for this seemingly blanket negative portrayal of Iran, its culture, and its people, with virtually nothing redemptive to say about it? At least that's how I saw it. And if that was the case, what could I possibly say to fix it?

"Leslie Khanum!" they called again. "Hurry up, you'll miss the beginning!" Two or three of them came in and grabbed me, pulling me by the hand. It was clear they were looking forward to an evening of entertainment. *Oh boy*, I thought, *are they ever going to be disappointed, and possibly far worse than that*. As for me, I could see there would be no getting out of this. Better just sit through it, take a breath, and get it over with.

When the video started and the dialogue, dubbed into Persian, kicked in, I knew I was done for. I must have been wincing for nearly half the film. *Mahmoud, why can't you be here when we need you most?*

The video finally ended; the lights switched on. I waited for the heavy silence, the stunned pause. I had no idea what I'd say when they asked for an explanation.

What do you know: they never asked me. Instead, they broke up the same way they did after any other film—standing, stretching, and making comments to each other as they dispersed. "Boy, what a jerk!" they said, referring to "Moody," the Iranian husband. "But wasn't the escape scene exciting?"

"Mmmm …" I began hesitantly before taking the plunge. "So, what did you think of the wife—I mean, Betty?" I recalled the author's dire portrayal of how she and her daughter had fared in the country, and how those images had come to life on the screen.

"We were scared for her—she and the kid almost didn't get away!" was their decisive response. At that moment, I realized my family had not taken the film as a negative commentary on Iranians at all, just the story of a poor woman married to a guy who had turned out to be a maniac. The fact that he was Iranian, or that she was American, had absolutely nothing to do with it in their eyes.

I knew there was a lesson in there for me. There's an Iranian expression one generally uses in response to generous comments such as, "You're so kind," or "You're beautiful." The response in the latter case would be, "Your eyes *see* me beautiful," comparable to the sentiment expressed in English, "Beauty is in the eye of the beholder." If the story of *Not Without My Daughter* had been intended as a charge against Iranian people, as I had taken it to be, there was simply not enough cynicism in any member of my Iranian family present that night to *see* it as such. Or perhaps they were willing to give the author the benefit of the doubt? I just didn't know enough to draw a conclusion.

What I *did* know is they had given me their best in every way: my family members in Saveh, Tehran, and Duzaj. I wouldn't realize how much till after the next move ahead.

Chapter Seventeen

"Half the World" Under the Moon: Settling into Isfahan

That long-awaited day in November finally came when Mahmoud, Parisa, and I arrived at what you might call "our own doorstep": the living accommodations Isfahan University of Technology provided for its faculty members and their families. Five hours by car from Saveh, eight hours from Tehran, and ten full hours from the village, Isfahan was a long way away from the comforting homes we had known until then.

Mahmoud's brother Ali and his young family had borrowed the family jeep in the village, picked us up in Saveh, and driven us with our scant collection of belongings to our new location. Before this day, Mahmoud had been staying at a simpler unit in the university complex, where some of our furniture, boxes, and other packed items had been shipped from the States and were waiting to be brought to this roomier, "homier" setting in the *kuye ostadan*, the faculty residence area.

As I surveyed the lovely two-story home with its large-framed windows, charming balconies, and dated but elegant "house suburban" design somehow reminiscent of the USA, part of me felt thankful and excited. It would also be the first time in the four months of our relocation that we, the three members of our tiny nuclear family, would have a place of our own.

But so much had happened since we'd first planned our life in Iran while still living on US soil. I'd been at such a different place then: mobile, resourceful, largely dependent on myself to get things done, *liking* it that way, and supposing that once in Iran, we would "need our own space" just as much as we had while living in America. And yet, as we passed through the iron gate, crossed the threshold, and stepped into the front hall, I felt a startling urge to turn around and beg Ali to drive us straight back to Saveh, which we had said goodbye to hours earlier.

Putting my emotions in check, I took a quick survey around and above us. Along the hall to the left was a small utility/washroom with a squat toilet installed in the floor. At the end of the same hall was a moderately-sized kitchen with a refrigerator and oven range. On the other side of the glass doors facing us was an elongated room with two separate areas that would serve as a living room and dining room. A winding staircase to our right rose to the second floor. On top were two bedrooms and one full bathroom whose tub, shower, and "foreign toilet" were similar to what I knew in America.

To my disappointment, the charming balconies I'd spotted from the outside seemed to have no doorway to allow access to them. But behind the house, just a few steps down, was a small patio and inviting garden surrounded by a high stone wall. In that intimate space was a lush array of miniature trees, whose fragrant boughs, I later discovered, would grow full and bright with blossoms in spring and yield apricots in summer or walnuts in fall.

Four months earlier, when I first entered the country, I would have considered the place an adequate size for a family of three. Now I was asking myself what two average-sized people and one small child needed with *so much space*. The feeling of endless expanse was accentuated even more by the lack of furniture, floor pillows, or any décor, and most of all by the stark brown "American style" carpet that stretched wall to wall.

"Leslie Khanum ... it's *nice!*" Ali's design-savvy wife Ashraf said, poking about excitedly and knowing exactly what she would do with every nook and corner.

As for me, wonder of wonders, the place felt "foreign"—as "foreign" as life with Mahmoud's family had felt in the first few weeks, but not so much now. As it turned out, most houses in the *kuye ostadan* ("kuee" for short) had been built in the early seventies, a few short years before the 1979 revolution. At the time, they had been designed with the tastes of non-Iranian visiting professors in mind, including the Europeans and Americans who used to come regularly. How could it be that it felt so strange to be back in a setting that should have been "familiar"?

Had the house been set in Columbus or another US city, I would have known how to set things in motion. Here, all I could do was stare at this blank slate of a house, a perfect match to my blank-slate mind. What was I to do next, and how was I to fill up the time? I had no idea, for either the short or long term.

And yet, in the months to follow, we would have to reconstruct an independent life for ourselves. Apart from my learning to buy groceries and cook again, there were boxes to unpack, furniture to buy, and this great big house to set up and maintain. There'd be colleagues to meet at the Language Center where I'd soon be teaching, childcare to plan for, neighbors to meet, a local community and city to explore. And all this without a car at this point. For the moment, it was all I could do just to stay standing there and face our big, empty, lonely new house.

I took a silent breath and headed for the kitchen, the space of my greatest domestic insecurity. Facing the bare shelves and empty refrigerator, I stood there alone, quietly ruminating. There were no staples, no spices, no cooking utensils. No doubt we had a pot or two packed in our boxes somewhere, but what would I put in them once I found them? Since coming to Iran, I'd washed plenty of dishes and helped prepare salads, but I hadn't bought a single food item, nor had I cooked a single meal. Still, I'd seen enough to know that meat didn't necessarily come already neatly processed and packaged in a tray wrapped in plastic, and that herbs and vegetables didn't always come washed, sorted, and without their roots attached. I suddenly pictured the tight sinews in the arms and thighs of my hardworking sisters-in-law, who could always sit so easily on their haunches and hack up a slab of meat and bone in no time flat. Was this the direction I was headed for? I didn't want to think about it, and yet how could I ignore it?

Ali, Ashraf, their three-year-old daughter Bahareh, and my own child and husband were tired and hungry after five hours of traveling, and there was nothing to eat. In this new scenario, *wasn't **I** the hostess now? Didn't the buck stop with **me**?*

My thoughts were suddenly disturbed by sounds from the

entrance hall: Persian mixed with hearty laughter, and Mahmoud calling my name. My anguished moments of panic and guilt would have to wait till after I'd meet some neighbors who apparently had come to call. As I entered the hall, attempting a sociable smile, Mahmoud introduced the visitors as Dr. Mehdi Karimi, a colleague and long-standing professor from the agronomy department, and his wife Nasrin. They lived just a few doors down, Mahmoud said.

"*Hale shoma chetore*?" I said in the standard greeting, inquiring about their health.

"Oh, no, Leslie!" Nasrin interrupted with a friendly laugh, speaking English as naturally as you please. "It's not necessary to be so formal with us! Welcome to the university." She and her husband had obviously spent time in the States.

Surprised, I smiled and glanced over to her husband, who greeted me with bright eyes and a happy chuckle. Grinning like a proud uncle, he had Parisa tucked under one arm and Bahareh under the other, and, with a cigarette suspended from his mouth, was talking to them affectionately in Persian. To my surprise, both girls were beaming, secure in his grip. "Let's go," he then said comfortably in English, not bothering to explain where.

Not thirty minutes later we were sitting with our neighbors at their dinner table—Ali, Ashraf, Mahmoud, and I—exchanging words in Persian or English (depending on who was talking with whom), laughing up a storm, and eating our fill of Nasrin's delicious chicken kababs, cucumbers minced with tomatoes and onions, and her beautiful saffron-laced rice. Their three school-aged children joined us, and consistent with what I had observed with Parisa's older cousins, they took it upon themselves to show their youngest houseguest a good time. That was the night that Parisa discovered *albaloo*, a popular variety of Iranian cherries that, in my opinion, someone had apparently forgotten to add the sugar to, big time. Maybe Parisa and Bahareh didn't know that yet, because they kept gobbling cherry after cherry, just as fast as eleven-year-old Pegah was able to pinch out each pit and pop the impossibly sour morsels into their mouths.

It seemed clear in those moments that Parisa had found a point of connection in her new surroundings. I relished the lively adult conversation, the children's rippling laughter, the Karimis' downright neighborliness, and the look of ease and contentment in Ali and Ashraf's eyes. And I couldn't help but hope that I had found a point of connection with Nasrin and her down-to-earth, English-speaking, and good-hearted family from Isfahan.

Isfahan, nesfe jahan, so the Persian rhyme goes, meaning "Isfahan, half the world," and suggesting that half the world's beauty is contained there. Famous for its stunning ancient structures, fancy bazaars with exquisite handicrafts, a large population of Christian Armenians with their own magnificent center of worship, and the people's colorful, lilting way of talking, the city beckoned us to sample as much as we could while we still had access to the borrowed jeep.

***

I had not understood that the city of Isfahan proper would take a good forty-five minutes to reach from the university campus, which was actually set in the small neighboring province-town of *Khomeini Shahr* (literally meaning "Khomeini's City"). In the last full day that Ali, Ashraf, and Bahareh were with us, we drank in the wonders of Isfahan together, beholding the face of a 2,500-year history.

It's one thing to admire a landmark in the flat, two-dimensional space of a photograph; it's quite another to stand at the foot of a mosque's massive dome, a towering, gleaming mosaic of aquas and royal blues. This was my first memory of Isfahan as we entered the city and stepped onto its pavement. As I dared to stare up into the mosque's soaring structures, I lost myself in its hollows and archways, its marble concaves chiseled into lace, and its hypnotic geometric designs. And I felt like a mite in a lofty world.

Bearing the weight of centuries, the city was also the keeper of many secrets — or so bragged the locals, friendly and curious, who had spotted us and pegged us as tourists. Was it really true that, by the genius of a Persian engineer, there was an ancient bath-house that had once been kept heated by a single candle—only to be snuffed out by some nosy foreign engineer who tried to discover its secret, and ruined it in the process? Was it true that the old royal palace in Imam Square had a chamber that could store music from a concert the night before, and release it again at the king's pleasure? And was it true that the old mausoleum near the Street of Four Gardens had a genuine pair of "shaking towers," where if you climbed up and shook the one, the other would start shaking too?

"I don't know. Maybe," Ali responded to my Persian in English with a grin and shrug each time I asked him. As evening approached, we strolled along the illuminated *Siosepol*: thirty-three ancient arches that formed a bridge over the gently coursing *Zayande Rud*, whose melodic name means "river that gives life." We huddled on its water-fringed steps and let the currents lap over our toes. When the air turned cool, we sought shelter in a tiny teahouse nearby, attached to a pier and surrounded by water. We ducked inside and filled ourselves with cardamom-spiced tea, the watery moonlit view, and the serenity of a cozy space. Sheer magic. I vowed to myself I'd be back many times.

We came back to our empty home that night, knowing that the next day Ali, Ashraf, and Bahareh would leave it emptier still. Their return to the village would not only leave me sorely feeling their absence; it would also mark the end of the phase in Iran when "home" meant being *with* family members, not in some far-away space by ourselves. Whatever had we been thinking when we decided on Isfahan? That was back in Columbus when Mahmoud's family was still a scary idea to me, before any of them had been written into my heart.

Ashraf and I spent the following morning stringing Parisa's many dolls and stuffed animals across her bedroom wall. Then, after a final meal together with the Karimis, Ali, Ashraf, Bahareh, and our family said our goodbyes. I had not imagined it would be this hard. We knew we'd see one another again, of course. But since Mahmoud and I didn't own a car, or the means to buy one at this point, it was hard to predict just when or how.

***

It didn't take long to set up the house. The large items we'd shipped from the States amounted to no more than a queen-sized bed, a chest of drawers, a crib for Parisa, and the comfy green armchair with sentimental value. They presented no challenge as to where we should place them. A box or two held more dolls and toys; another, a meager assortment of pots, pans, utensils, and dishware. The rest contained mostly books: textbooks that Mahmoud or I thought "might someday be useful," photo albums from our earlier lives, and a handful of personal books we couldn't or wouldn't let go of, including some of Parisa's favorites. It wasn't long before the albums and favorite books found places on built-in shelves, where we could find comfort in just looking at them.

To my surprise, one of Parisa's books kept drawing my eye: a picture book classic called *Good Night Moon* by Margaret Wise Brown. A vibrant depiction of saying "good night" to familiar objects in a small child's world, *Good Night Moon* was a longtime favorite of Parisa's, though not particularly of mine—at least not until then. Suddenly the pictures of a roaring fireplace, a braided rug, a bedside lamp, and a rocking chair became strangely compelling. They were calling me back to a time and place I'd almost managed to bury from consciousness while in Saveh, Tehran, and the village. It wasn't as easy to shut them out in this Western style house, just empty enough and suggestive enough of "home" to inflame my longing for everything I'd left behind: the household items, my sisters and their families, my father, my friends, my faraway homeland.

While *Good Night Moon* tugged hard at my heartstrings, it also helped somehow. It helped me air those feelings honestly and to do so in the safest possible space: alone with my daughter, with her book at bedtime. We'd find our favorite nighttime spot: the top step of the outdoor patio. There, with Parisa resting quietly on my legs, I'd read the bedtime incantations—sometimes under the moon itself.

"Good night room, good night moon, good night cow jumping over the moon…"

On especially beautiful moonlit nights, I found comfort in knowing that the moon whose light we spotted in Isfahan might also be watched several hours later by our loved ones in America.

And yet, I still could not bring myself to face the empty spaces of those relationships, which at that point felt lost to me. In those days, telephone lines and mail delivery were expensive and unreliable. And still there were no platforms like Zoom, Skype, or WhatsApp to help keep my two worlds connected. Even so, the loss of communication between those worlds wasn't for lack of my being remembered. I'd gotten those faithful, loving phone calls, postcards, letters, and the birth announcement with the precious black ink footprints. To this day, I hold on to that cherished collection. But the problem lay in how these things served to remind me of a time, a place, a *life* now cut off from me. How could I consciously manage this lifelong commitment to one reality at the cost of another? What end would it serve, other than *torment*, to cling to people and settings I might never see again?

I'm not proud of this, and it's hard to admit, but the only way I knew how to "hold things together" was to dim the reality of my cherished past. For me, that meant trying to forget the reminders, to quell the source of those inner stirrings. It resulted in my leaving those past ties "suspended" in a limbo that kept me from calling or writing. Those ties were still deeply held in my heart, but it hurt far too much for me to think or act on them. This worked for a while to help ease my pain, but it haunts me to think of what it must have felt like on the other end.

Pat. Sylvia. Dad. Evelyn. Judith. Debbie. Aunt Annise. I'm talking to you. Thanks for forgiving.

Chapter Eighteen

Breaking New Boundaries at the Kuee

There were other ways of easing the fever of homesickness, like exploring the local world of the kuee, the surrounding faculty residence grounds. In the coming weeks, I would occupy myself by exploring every inch of it. Not that there was all that much ground to cover. The kuee was a small squared-off area, no more than two blocks long on each side. With little Parisa as my daytime companion while her dad was out teaching, we'd spend mornings walking the length of one side, where the small, pebbly lot of a lonely playground awaited us at the end. Unlike her mom, by now Parisa was speaking Persian almost effortlessly to just about everyone. But when it was just the two of us, she'd chatter on endlessly in English about what we saw along the way. She'd point out the fancy street lanterns, the pretty houses, the brown autumn leaves raked into piles, the tiny pine forest off to the side, the thick black ants with a fearsome bite and whose "butts" were always "sticking up." (I didn't correct her last description. That's pretty much what they looked like to me too.) Once we reached the empty playground, there was a seesaw, a swing set, and a gigantic metal slide that looked decades old. Painted yellow and pink, it was chipped and faded, rusty in places, and frequently, way too hot from the sun. But we'd clamber up just the same, Parisa and I, child and mother, both of us rookies in a brand-new world.

When Parisa was with her daddy or playing at the Karimis', I'd find solace in traveling the kuee alone. Strolling to the end of the street and back, swinging by Nasrin's for tea and a chat, trailing the circumference of the whole neighborhood, I discovered the pleasures of walking again—just as I recalled my father had, back in the days of Rocky Hill.

Whether it was Isfahan's milder climate, my emerging confidence amid budding relationships, or less of an angst about wearing the overcoat that had something to do with it, I'm not sure. All I know is that claiming the outside world felt good again.

***

I discovered the local *madeh kudak* (daycare center) across from the playground, where Parisa would be going once I started teaching. From the street I'd cast quick side-long glances into the large windows of the school building. In those moments I'd catch the images of three or four women in manteaus and a surrounding flock of children: tiny girls clad in adorable, smart-looking black-and-white plaid uniforms.

One of the teachers drew my startled attention. She had skin the color of dark chocolate, with a nose and lips similarly proportioned to mine. I would eventually meet "Miss Farideh" face-to-face, and I wondered if we'd somehow acknowledge each other as two Black women. She would always be formal, kind, and professional, but in the end she would be no different in her interactions with me than she was with the other mothers, except that she'd speak Persian more slowly to me as a foreigner. Emotionally, I felt snubbed, but I talked myself through it. Born the daughter of an Iranian father and a Nigerian mother who had raised her in Iran, as I learned later, in some ways, she had more in common with Parisa, another child of two cultures, than she had with me.

I discovered the path beyond the kuee, on the other side of the entrance gate. It would lead me on a scenic six-minute walk through a delightful rose garden, still blooming in November. There was nothing more intoxicating than the natural perfume of roses in the air at that time of year.

From the rose garden, I would go on to the Language Center, with its eight-story aerobic climb. At the end of that climb, I would see and greet any of six faculty members—all Iranian, all men—who would be my colleagues at the center, and who taught English language skills to 8,000 of the country's best science, engineering, and agricultural students. All of them had a stunning command of English; two even sounded like native speakers, as if one were from England and the other, America. None of them were ever willing to speak Persian with me. When I suggested to the one who sounded American that I was in a Persian-speaking country—and therefore the one in need of more language practice—he grinned at me and replied, in English, "Yes, you *should* practice Persian. Just not with me."

Back at the kuee, I discovered Mr. Amin's corner store. As tiny as it was, that's where everyone went to buy dry goods, produce, dairy, bread, meat, and condiments like pickles and jams. The real gems were the things I never expected to see: a lone can of tuna here, a jar of yellow mustard there, a stray box of cornflakes, a "conventional" loaf of bread they called "toast bread," a few packages of spaghetti, a familiar-looking candy bar. Wrapped tightly in foil and a red-orange wrapper, its color, packaging, and piano key-like structure instantly reminded me of those crispy, mouth-watering, chocolate-covered wafers I'd grown up with in America known as "Kit Kat" bars. The best and most fun surprise was what I noticed at second glance: the words "Tik Tak," which, wouldn't you know, was "Kit Kat" spelled backward, printed in both Persian and English on its red orange wrapper! I hadn't tasted chocolate in nearly six months. Upon opening it up and eating its contents, I'm happy to say it didn't disappoint. It looked just like a Kit Kat and tasted like one too.

Speaking of food, I needn't have worried about me and the kitchen. Over time, I figured out what to put in those pots. I just needed time to discover my resources, develop my strategies, ease back into cooking, and regain my confidence in a world where everyone seemed like a master chef. My first prepared dish was eggs and potatoes, then tuna fish salad. By the third day, I'd made my first pot of spaghetti; on the fourth day, I had my own concoction of "stroganoff," and so on and so forth. Between Mahmoud's shopping, my "creative" cooking, Parisa and Mahmoud's willingness to eat almost anything, and the Karimis' generous meal invitations, we weren't doing so badly where food was concerned.

So, I was torn when Nasrin suggested we consider getting domestic help. On the one hand, I had never managed domestic help, was unsure of my language skills in that regard, and probably wouldn't know what to do with a maid if I had one. Besides, we were already making progress on our own. I couldn't help feeling that having a maid was a kind of cop-out, or worse than that, just plain "uppity." Rightly or wrongly, the notion of my managing "hired help" left me uneasy as a woman of color. Would I be contributing to a world of social disparities if I hired her?

On the other hand, I wouldn't mind not having to worry about cooking and housework, especially here, where a learning curve and hefty time commitment would be involved. What had never been affordable in the States was suddenly within range, and with someone taking care of domestic duties at home, I could focus on more tempting options, even if I didn't know yet what those might be. Of course, I'd be teaching a full courseload at the Language Center come January, less than six weeks away.

Nasrin, who saw me floundering in my indecisiveness, tried to make things easier for me. "I have a friend who knows a lady looking for work," she began. "If you hired her, you'd be doing the family a favor."

Her words worked like a charm, just as she knew they would. I decided we'd give the whole thing a try, and Khanum Aghaee, who lived nearby in Khomeini Shahr, reported for work the very next week.

It wasn't an easy transition. Mrs. Aghaee was soft-spoken, mild-mannered, and, to my mind, somewhat lacking in initiative. She always seemed to need direction on what to do and how to do it, which I was neither interested in nor comfortable doing. It fed into my conflicted feelings about taking on the role of "the boss lady." Besides that, I had trouble understanding her pronunciation and pattern of speech, and no doubt she had trouble deciphering mine.

Although I did not find her cooking to be equal to the outstanding fare of Mahmoud's mother, sisters, or sisters-in-law, I knew it was an unfair standard to hold her to. And I did appreciate the breakfasts and midday meals she faithfully prepared and cleaned up afterward. But this did not keep us from having issues with each other.

She wouldn't put things in order that, to my mind, clearly needed to be put in order. I didn't appreciate that. I pointed this out to her on two or three occasions. She didn't appreciate *that*.

When Nikiar was born the summer of 1994, Ms. Aghaee had already been with us for three or four months. She surprised me one day by dressing him up in girls' clothes and tying a ribbon in his hair ("for the fun of it, because everyone loves his curls and big eyes," she said, beaming), then took him for a stroll. When I happened upon them at the corner market completely unawares, I *really* didn't appreciate it. She didn't see what the big deal was, nor did she appreciate what she saw as my glaring lack of humor. *That* was the day the collision course between us was likely set in motion.

Where did it culminate? At the foot of the staircase one day, when Parisa came down from waking up, and for the first time saw her mommy sitting on the bottom step, shedding tears.

To sum it up: Mrs. Aghaee, tired of sensing my general unhappiness with her, had had enough. In an uncharacteristically candid moment, she expressed in no uncertain terms that she wanted out (I didn't understand every word, but I definitely got the gist). I was stunned to learn she was as unhappy with me as I'd been with her. Unprepared to have her sudden absence leave a gaping hole in our daily routine, not to mention our unresolved differences, I had dissolved into tears—a tangle of confusion, raw nerves, and words hopelessly out of reach. I was due to teach at the university in thirty minutes, Mrs. Aghaee was hovering near the door, and Parisa kept asking what was wrong with Mommy.

Miraculously, Mahmoud happened to pop in from outside just then. Having kept his relationship with Mrs. Aghaee at an even keel and also being articulate in Persian, he managed to convince her to stay on with us, at least for a while longer. She reluctantly agreed. Neither she nor I liked confrontation; at the same time, neither of us liked working in an atmosphere of unresolved tension. I wondered if we would ever truly work things out.

But things *did* work out somehow. A few days after the showdown at the staircase, Mrs. Aghaee brought her mother to the house and proposed that we hire her to look after Niki exclusively. Meanwhile, she, the daughter, would continue to take care of the usual cooking and light housekeeping. Without giving it a second thought, Mahmoud agreed, and I went along.

As it turned out, my obligation to "supervise" the daughter Aghaee was almost immediately relieved by the presence of the energetic, somewhat quirky, but charismatic mother Aghaee. As the matriarch of her household, she seemed quite willing to accommodate her daughter's need to be directed while still doing a splendid job of keeping up with Niki. It made a tremendous difference in the dynamics between all of us, and Mahmoud and I held onto both of them for the rest of our stay. By the end of her nearly three years of service, when the Aghaees invited us to their household for a meal with all their family, we could see the great lengths they had gone to for us.

I am grateful for what the two "Mrs. Aghaees" (the mother and the daughter) made possible for me and for us as a family, including the priceless gift of time. Time to discover more of the kuee: its people, its social circles, its various happenings, and the lifelong friendships that would start to emerge.

***

There were other members of Mahmoud's department who would welcome us into their homes. Some had beards or "five o'clock shadows" in keeping with the ideology of the Islamic state, while others sported a clean-shaven look. Whichever the case, they showed us kindness with their food, their laughter, their family members, and by treating Parisa like one of their own. Political affiliation would not divide us.

There were additional members of the Language Center: in particular, Esfandiar Soltangheiss, the tall and lanky librarian with a smartly styled beard (more for fashion than anything else) and smiling, intelligent eyes. Recognizing me as American from the moment he first spotted me in the library, he enjoyed chatting in English with me about other Americans he'd met there and appreciated over the years. There was also Mahvash Moshiri, the center's administrative assistant. She was warm, confident, generous with her smile, and beautiful with her large and dramatic eyes. I grew instantly fond of her; she was also one of just a few university people who spoke only Persian with me. Not remembering that married women in Iran retain their surnames from birth, I didn't initially notice that she and Esfandiar were wife and husband and that they had three sweet school-age kids. I was absolutely delighted when I did learn, as it led to countless wonderful evenings and weekend outings spent between our two families.

There were also the women I came to call "the beautiful people": several wives in the kuee who, every month or so, liked to dress up, look flawlessly stunning, and gather in their different homes. There, they would eat together, dance and laugh together, and generally have a good time. One day, I was graciously invited to attend one of these "beautiful people parties" by the wife of one of Mahmoud's colleagues in the agronomy department. Since it was a party intended for ladies only, the guests were free to remove their scarves and manteaus and reveal a stunning woman beneath. Most of them were naturally beautiful to begin with — with svelte, well-exercised bodies, luxuriously healthy hair of all shades, and dramatic eyes under lavish eyebrows. On top of that, these women looked great in their sleek miniskirts, their sexy spaghetti straps (*Wherever did they find these items?* I wondered), their spiked high heels, their bangles and chokers of real gold, and their perfect makeup.

Never having pursued fashion or glamour seriously enough to have mastered them to the same degree, I felt like a fish out of water, underdressed and under-made up by comparison. The women continued to invite me to their parties just the same, always as a welcome guest. I did not sense their judgment for my not dressing or making myself up quite like them, and I'm guessing they didn't sense any judgment from me either. I could genuinely admire their ability to refine and embellish their beauty and the care and discipline it took to do so. After all, before leaving for Iran, I'd been grieving the fact that I'd have to leave the "flamenco dancer" in me behind, or at least under wraps. Ironically, here at the "beautiful people parties," I found myself challenged to rise to the occasion: to express the power, art, and full drama of my womanliness. I did respond, in the most authentic and comfortable way I knew how: by toting my guitar and, in Spanish or English, singing the prettiest ballads, spirituals, or love songs I knew. I am grateful for what I sensed and found among them. It was what I liked best about being at such gatherings: a true willingness to express, recognize, and celebrate each woman's beauty on her own terms.

There were other lovely women I met outside of the "beautiful people parties." Among them were Afagh and Shohreh, Fatimeh and Zahra (not to be confused with Mahmoud's sister Zahra), Azar, Shirin, Mashid and Soraya, dispersed throughout the four corners of the kuee. In time, after getting my bearings in my new university post, I'd find my own way to discover them.

There were yet other members of the kuee to be discovered: two gems by the names of Janet and Chris. Both were women from England who, like me, had met and married an Iranian man in their own country and relocated to Iran, where they were also raising young children. When I first arrived at the kuee, I was not aware that two other expat women were in the neighborhood. Both had been living here long enough to have an enviable command of the Persian language and enough well-earned experience to be worth seeking out. Foolishly, I shrank back from their overtures when they first reached out. Janet especially had made the effort to locate my phone number and contact me, leaving messages on our answering machine on three different occasions. At the time, I thought it might be better for me to avoid making contact with fellow westerners, in case doing so would weaken my resolve to learn, accept, and "move forward" in Iranian ways. Fortunately, one day I felt ashamed enough for not returning Janet's calls that I finally picked up the phone and dialed her number.

Almost immediately, I learned that I would find an authentic person in Janet. "If you hadn't returned this last call," she told me right then and there on the phone, "that would've been it. I was just about to give up on you."

I'm so glad I *did* call and that she hadn't given up on me. Janet, her kind and fun-loving husband Ali, and their four children folded a wonderful dimension into our lives. As for Janet herself, she proved to be as "for real" a friend as she was a communicator. Her candid humor about herself, the ups and downs of living in a new country, and her adventures and misadventures as a foreigner in Iran far from weakened my resolve to "make it." After all, if anyone had proven her willingness and ability to "step up and deliver" in a new cultural setting, it was Janet. Then in her sixth year of living in Iran, Janet could dish up a fine Persian *khoresht* (stew) and rice to match, bargain in Persian at any bazaar in Isfahan, and even follow a joke told in Persian (and laugh at all the right moments while I looked on blankly). She was witty, and "plucky," as the English say, calling situations as she saw them. But both her empathy and ability to see the humor in things made it easier for me to laugh at myself and put things in perspective. Her English dishes, with the wonderful roasted meats and vegetables that reminded me so much of Aunt Maureen's in Scotland, were just as delicious as her Persian ones. Best of all, however, was Janet's famous "pink cake," a moist confection she'd pull together from scratch, top with homemade pink frosting, and serve with tea and cream in pretty porcelain cups. It was a fancier version of tea and cake than what I recalled growing up in the States, but close enough to memories of "home" to be comforting.

My heart would always hold sacred the space of what I considered my very first "home": the communion I shared with my parents and sisters. But in these four years I'd recognize "home" in other spaces, reminiscent of that first sacred space while taking on new layers of meaning. "Home" among Mahmoud's family members. "Home" among my husband and children. The household objects in *Good Night Moon*. Tea and pink cake with my English friends.

I will always remember the kindness of the Karimis, our very first neighbors in Isfahan, and all the warm times we spent together. Their house was our "home away from home," a haven, and a second family space for Parisa. After a visit, I'd often need to coax her away before she'd agree to follow me home. Sometimes I was successful and sometimes I wasn't. One afternoon, when nothing I said could persuade her to join me, I walked toward the door, silently admitting defeat.

"Mommy!" a three-year old's voice was calling.

"Yes, Parisa?" My voice had brightened.

"Don't forget your shoes, Mommy!" Her voice had brightened, too.

"Tender moments." That's what Janet wryly used to call scenarios like this one. I slipped on the shoes I had left at the doorway. I'd be heading home by myself, evidently, Dr. Karimi's laughter thundering behind me. Tickled as a proud uncle, he'd never let me forget Parisa's advice to her mommy that day.

Chapter Nineteen

"Khanum Pahvel" And Quirky Stories About University Life

My debut as Assistant Professor of English at Isfahan University of Technology began a few weeks after we moved to the kuee. While realizing that I faced the unknown, I still faced it with excitement and anticipation.

I was grateful for the two brief years of experience I had gained from teaching English to a broad mix of international students at an Ohio college just before moving here. What made the job most fun was also what sometimes made it the most challenging: what we, as teachers, so carefully plan and present to our students is not necessarily what they end up learning or remembering. Rather, it's probably better to be prepared for the unexpected in the cross-cultural classroom. In all fairness, as I look back on my years of teaching in Iran, I suspect that my students there might also have benefited from the same advice before being introduced to their American teacher, *Khanum Pahvel* ("Ms. Powell").

I had precious little to go on when it came to teaching at an Iranian university. Before the move, there had been one admonition about teaching I'd received from an Iranian colleague whom Mahmoud and I had met as a visiting professor in the States. His advice was clear, unmovable, and surprising, coming from a person who had his own hilarious sense of humor. But he was clearly not joking when he told me solemnly and more than once, as if I in particular needed to hear it, "Remember, whatever you do, *you must never laugh, or even smile, in the classroom.*" It felt like a warning for the former Spanish instructor who had been known for her jovial and carefree style of presenting and interacting with students. Although the admonition was unsettling and I questioned whether I could really follow it, I kept the message tucked in a corner of my mind.

Up till that first day, when I finally made it to the classroom, I tried to be diligent about monitoring my expectations, careful not to envision my future classes as near blueprints of the ones I had planned in the States. Resolved to "do as the Persians do" without prejudgment or cynicism, I watched and listened for cues that would prepare me for my future role as a professor of English at a distinguished Iranian university.

So, when I dropped Parisa off at daycare one morning and noticed the children separate out to their teachers' cheerful singsong orders: *"Dokhtara ba dokhtara, pesara ba pesara!"* (*"Girls with girls [and] boys with boys!"*), I made that mental leap to the university classroom and drew some parallels. I asked myself how it would feel to teach a classroom full of *dokhtara* (young women) only: "limiting" and "repressive," or "liberating" and "empowering"? I could see the benefits of teaching an all-female group, like having to worry less about whether my hairline was visible under my hood, like maybe being able to get away with a laugh or smile in the classroom every once in a while, despite my colleague's warning. In the end, it made sense to me that with a class full of female students, I'd be much freer to "let my hair down," both literally and figuratively, to feel more comfortable in my skin.

Fitted in my simple forest green manteau with a green hood to match and armed with my well-worn *English for Engineering Students* reader in hand, I strode into the classroom with feigned confidence and ease. That is, until I heard the staccato *whoosh* of an entire roomful of people rising to their feet. I stopped, turned, and assumed my space at the front of the classroom.

Standing before me, as if at attention, was a roomful of *men*, with a sea of men's faces, some serious, some smiling, but all looking at me.

Could I possibly be in the wrong classroom? "English for Engineering Students?" I asked in English, and they all nodded. As if the "male factor" weren't disconcerting enough, the "stand-up-for-the-teacher" factor left me dumbfounded. The last time I'd experienced that kind of scenario was thirty years earlier, back in the sixties. In that era, *I* happened to be one of those students who stood in attention. And my teacher, a Catholic nun in a black and white habit, then looked comparable to how I was looking in my plain coat and hood. Stunned as I was by those first ten seconds in the classroom, there was still nothing to do but write my name on the blackboard: "Dr. Leslie Powell." I hadn't used "Powell" as a surname since before I was married, but since it was my family name at birth, it still presided as my legal name in Iranian tradition. When I turned back around to face the students, most had settled back into their seats. It was then that I could make out a sea of *women's* faces too, dotting the back end of the room. These women, like me, were shrouded in hoods or veils.

Be prepared for the unexpected …!

In my intention to be prepared, all I'd done, evidently, was to build a wrong expectation based on the faulty assumption that I'd be assigned to a classroom of women only. I didn't really mind being wrong about male and female university students being taught in separate classrooms, which was the case for students from preschool through high school. On the contrary, I somehow found comfort, a sense of normalcy, in the familiarity of a co-ed setting. Never mind that the women were sitting together at the back of the room; that was something that I, as the classroom instructor, could remedy easily enough. So, after calling the roll and carefully pronouncing each student's full name to ensure I was saying it right, I decided to set things in motion.

First, I shuffled the seating arrangement. Then I sorted the students into small groups of mixed gender to start an "icebreaking activity" in English. The questions I'd assigned were deliberately "fun" ("What color are you today, and why?"). The tone I'd set was definitely "light" ("Just be free! There are no right or wrong answers!"). The instructions I'd given were straightforward and clear ("Tell your answer to a person next to you.").

For some reason, though, what followed alternated between a conspicuous silence and almost indecipherable mumbling for the duration of the activity. I would compare the energy of those interactions to the kind I would later have with my son Nikiar as a teenager: ("So, how was your day today?" "Fine." "Well, what did you do?" "I don't know; I was at school." "I *know* you were at school, but what happened there—anything interesting?" "Not a whole lot; it was pretty much okay … "

So much for the icebreaker. However much I circulated among the clusters and encouraged them to "*Talk* to each other," the "ice" in the classroom appeared to be in no danger of breaking, thawing, or otherwise leaving the room.

Ten minutes later, I admitted defeat to myself and decided not to prolong the awkwardness of the exercise. I announced the homework for the next session and dismissed class early. Just as in the States, the classroom all but cleared within the span of ten seconds.

It was then that I met my First University Friend. One young man, no more than nineteen or twenty years old, had chosen to remain behind. Tall, with kind, brown eyes and a polished appearance, he approached me with a respectful but confident demeanor. When he introduced himself as "Behrang" and continued his rhetoric in English, I knew this was a gentleman with no ordinary command of the language. It was a pleasure to hear his mastery of English grammar, vocabulary, and diction, possibly acquired in one of the finer public academies specializing in language instruction. In fact, as he spoke, I had to wonder if he wasn't completely overqualified for the course.

"Dr. Powell, may I make a suggestion?"

"Yes, certainly—go ahead," I said, noticing myself swallow.

"Maybe in the future, you can call the ladies by just their last name and not their first. At least, not in the classroom."

"Why is that?"

"It's too personal. They don't want the male students in class to know them by their first name."

"I see," I said with composed horror, recalling how carefully and ceremoniously I'd given attention to each and every name on the roster.

"And the small groups I put together, with men and women in the same group. Was that okay, or was that also a mistake?"

He just stood there politely, looking downward and saying nothing. And it seemed he was enjoying making his point.

"Oh, okay," I responded humbly.

At any rate, I had already figured out the (singsong) answer to my question: "*Dokhtara ba dokhtara, pesara ba pesara* (Girls with girls [and] boys with boys)!" Even in the coed classroom of the university, this rule was still operative, and everyone knew it. Everyone except the new American professor on the block.

I could feel the color draining from my face as I thanked the young man, and we said goodbye. His eyes were twinkling mischievously, though not maliciously, when he left.

Concerned that my blunders would reach the ears of my direct superiors before I'd have a chance to explain, I headed straight for the central office of the *Markaze Zaban* (The Language Center) to present my case to the director, Dr. Dalili. I perceived him to be a serious man, subscribing to the "no-smile" rule of thumb with everybody. Even so, my earlier encounters with him had led me to like him and trust his fairness.

He listened attentively as I recreated the classroom scenario for him, with me as the fumbling central character. While he never cracked a smile, his eyes, like those of the young man Behrang, somehow revealed a sense of merriment.

"I see," was his initial two-word response to my humble and apologetic confession, and then, with the slightest edge of curiosity in his voice, "Anything else?"

No," I answered. But now I understand that the male and female students definitely do *not* like being put together in the same group."

His reply, delivered dryly in the form of a question, surprised me. "Oh? And how can you be sure of that?"

I studied his nearly poker face and saw that the masked merriment was still there. But he paused and held onto his serious stance before he spoke.

"But yes, even if they did like it, they're not really supposed to. So, you might want to try a different approach next time," he said calmly, leaving my dignity intact.

***

In the weeks to follow, I was to witness and ponder new things both in and out of the classroom. They continually defied my understanding of the kinds of rules and dynamics that could or could not function in coexistence. Men and women kept themselves apart at the university or at least compartmentalized. At the same time, classes were coed, and I was assigned to teach both male and female students. Women sat in the back of the classroom, but as I learned much later from a female student, this was generally by choice—and not some external mandate that relegated them to second place as I had supposed. Evidently, just as many of the female students preferred not to have their first names surveyed by their male counterparts, they also preferred to sit behind the men so as not to allow anything else of their person to be surveyed either. (Strangely, even after I heard this explanation, it didn't dawn on me until decades later that the women on the Tehran bus might *also* have preferred the back of the bus for the very same reason. I guess my experience of segregation on the Tehran bus had felt too parallel to Black history for me not to jump to conclusions.)

There were other teacher-related rules I picked up from fellow Iranian professors, including the reminder that I wasn't supposed to smile in the classroom, *ever*.

Presumably, this was because as a professor, I was to maintain clear boundaries where my authority was concerned, and because the university was, after all, a serious setting dedicated to a serious purpose. Why, then, was it so easy to detect that love for hilarity and friendship bubbling beneath the surface of even the most formal and polished of my students and colleagues? Why did I so frequently find myself in the middle of a serious conversation that could take an unexpected detour into the whimsical, mischievous, or outrageous?

There were several of these incidents, including those where I discovered that in the minds of many students, grades were open for negotiation. This forward kind of behavior—bargaining for grades—didn't make sense to me. It didn't fit with a world where students stood up for their teachers, were lavish with honorifics like *Khanum Doktor* ("Madame Doctor"), and frequently used subtle gestures of deference—the slightest bow of the head, frequent downward glances, a hand laid upon the heart—to cultivate almost a sense of intimacy while maintaining a social distance between themselves and their professors.

Somebody needed to explain that incongruence to Mohsen, another student in my English for Engineering Students class. He was quite a good-looking and amiable young man, with laughing amber eyes and a sociable nature. I remember enjoying several pleasant exchanges with him both during and after class, when he seemed genuinely curious about life in the United States and, on the flip side, my impressions of Iran and the Iranian people. With his carefree, even playful personality, he didn't quite fit my profile of the "average" university student with that aura of reserve and formality on the face of things. Yet he always maintained those small and courteous phrases and gestures meant to demonstrate his regard.

Despite his lively and charming presence, Mohsen had missed several assignments and not performed particularly well on tests. One day, close to the end of the term, he paid me a visit to my office to ask me how he had fared on the last one he took. I was delighted to tell him it looked like he was going to pass the class; he had managed to stay afloat in the course with a solid average of "10" (that is, based on a 20-point scale). One point less would have made the difference between passing and failing.

"Congratulations!" I told him sincerely.

"*Ghorbane shoma* (I'm deeply indebted)," he answered. "But I will need more points than that."

"I don't understand. What do you mean?"

"Well," he proceeded cautiously, "if you could increase my grade by a few points, my parents will be happy."

Although it was my first experience with this kind of conversation, I could see where it was heading. I now faced the choice of either ending it right there or letting it go further to satisfy my fascination and curiosity.

"How many more points do you need?" I heard myself ask.

"An '18' would be good," he said, not missing a beat.

"An '18'!" My words echoed soundly, both as a question and a declaration of disbelief. "How can you possibly ask me to raise your grade from a 10 to an *18*—I mean, just like that?"

"Look," he proposed in a matter of fact, good-natured, and slightly devious tone (as if his idea made all the sense in the world, and at the same time, not really). "You add eight points to my grade this term, see? And then next term, I'll be sure to sign up for one of your classes and you can subtract those eight points from whatever grade I get then."

Despite my shock, the proposal sounded so absurd, yet he had delivered it in such a charming way that all I could do was laugh out loud.

"Right!" I said, because I didn't know how to say in Persian, "Look, Pal, I wasn't born yesterday."

We bantered and sparred back and forth in the most amicable of ways until he finally conceded with grace and humor. His bright and talkative visits would continue in the forthcoming weeks, and we enjoyed a sweet relationship between professor and student. In a way, I felt indebted to him. If there was anyone to help prepare me for new experiences and issues to navigate at the university, Mohsen was among the best ones to do so.

But I don't think anything could have prepared me for the arrival of a certain "Mr. Farmer," as I called him, to one of my classes.

Chapter Twenty

How "Mr. Farmer" Ended Up Keeping the Farm

"Mr. Farmer," as I called him, was one of 24 university students in my English for Agricultural Students class one semester. He also happened to have been a student in one of Mahmoud's classes an earlier semester. How ironic that this mild-mannered gentleman managed to shake up my world and, without realizing it, introduce a lively dose of discord into nearly five years of marital solidarity between me and my husband.

The first time I remember him was early in the semester, when I called on him to respond to a homework item from the textbook — and in three short words of English, he said he didn't know. The second time was when he appeared on the very last day of class. The final exam had just been administered and collected, and yet there he was, weeks after not having attended or turned in a single assignment. Still avoiding my gaze, in the quietest of voices and most beautiful Persian, he politely explained that he'd come to arrange to make up the final exam he'd just missed, if I would be so kind to allow it.

I was dumbfounded by the audacity of his request, especially from a fellow who struck me as painfully shy — and had all but blown off English class till he finally remembered he would need a passing grade to graduate.

In response, I made it known that, *no*, I wasn't feeling particularly kind. And with that, I more or less sent him packing.

Wondering whether this gentleman had been trying to play me as the naïve foreigner, and torturing myself with the question, *Had I smiled too much in class?*, I hurried home, indignant and flustered. I was anxious to reconstruct the story for Mahmoud and to receive some empathy and affirmation for how I had responded. Ready or not, he received an earful when I got home. In exchange for my heartfelt story, he did have some empathy to offer, but not necessarily for the person I had in mind.

When I got to the part about how the guy wouldn't so much as look me in the eye even once, Mahmoud explained that by lowering his gaze, he was actually demonstrating respect for me—not only as a person of authority, but as a member of the opposite sex.

His comment offered a perspective I hadn't considered, deserving further exploration at least, but well, I didn't have the patience to pursue it at this point. "Never mind all that," I said. "Do you know he actually asked me if I would let him make up the final exam?"

"And?" Mahmoud asked.

"And what?" I shot back.

"And will you?" he returned, a tinge of hopefulness in his voice.

It was one of those moments when I knew intellectually that I was talking with my husband, but with great irritation, I also wondered what had happened to the "American" side of him. Then again, I recalled times in the States when I had grumbled to him about the antics of some of my ESL (English as a Second Language) students, and he had spoken on their behalf. These were times when they, from my perspective, had clearly crossed the line in their attitudes or expectations. Come to think of it, Mahmoud was once a newly-arrived ESL student himself—a fact perhaps contributing to his inclination more times than not to take *their* side.

"Of course not," I said tersely.

"Okay Babe," he answered humbly, wisely ending the subject.

Until one fine afternoon of the following week, we came upon the subject again. Only this time *Mahmoud* brought it up.

Mr. Farmer, the meek and mild, had pulled out his *first* round of arsenal by approaching my husband in his office. What did he want from my husband, the *Aqayeh Doktor Ahmadi*, his agronomy professor from two terms back? A mere favor: to approach me on his behalf with the same tired request for a makeup test.

That is, as I saw it, to pull rank on his wife.

I stood up and slapped my English for Agricultural Students textbook down on the table.

Why was I so livid over this incident as I had been about no other? It wasn't the first time I'd wrestled with questions about female status in Iran. And after living several months in this new cultural setting, I'd already visited and revisited my thoughts on the issue of female dress. I'd actually made peace with that drape of a garment; the black chador I'd secretly had nightmares about before moving here—but no longer had them. Not that I was thrilled with what appeared to be one standard of modesty expected of women and another of men, or that people were expected to conform to that mandated standard or face possible repercussions. It's not that I hadn't occasionally felt sorry for myself over having to wear an overcoat outside on those hot, hot summer days. It's not that I hadn't had to swallow back the humiliation I felt in having to rearrange or tighten up my scarf when silently signaled to do so by an official, a passerby, or even a student. Still, I'd come to sense how, for some women, the outer garment was a way to preserve their comfort or dignity or to shield themselves from the unwelcome gaze of onlookers. From that perspective, I figured it was no less dignified or valid a choice than other women's decision to accentuate their feminine form or beauty without undue concern for how others might react.

But back to the story of Mr. Farmer and the question it raises: Why was I so incensed over the role apparently expected of me as a woman in this scenario? What was the contributing factor here that made all the difference?

Up till then, any issue I'd had to confront as a woman in Iran had occurred outside of my marriage, and, for all practical purposes, outside of my husband's control. This time, my husband had been actively solicited to play a role, and by all indications, Mahmoud seemed willing to comply. But Mr. Farmer's strategy had backfired, and both men had dug their own graves on this one. On my end, the only digging I was going to do was to dig my heels in deeper, meaning *no way, no how, no make-up test.*

Stuck between wanting both to validate my feelings and to justify his role as his student's advocate, Mahmoud first tried (unsuccessfully) to appeal to my sense of humor ("Hey, do you really want to see the guy for another semester?"), and then (unsuccessfully) to my compassion ("What if he's having a bad year?"). Carefully, he built a case that in the face of Iran's struggling economy, exploding population, fierce academic competition, and alarming shortage of professional positions, the odds were stacked impossibly high against its university students—with the stakes even higher for any student facing the disgrace of failing out of school.

Mahmoud's explanation didn't cut it for me. "Then why wouldn't he be all the more careful about attending class, completing assignments, and attending the final exam on time, just like everyone else?" My emphatic tones at the end, I hoped, would signal my American-born version of justice: that no student should get special treatment and that *all students should be judged by the same rules.*

It would have been a fine time for Mahmoud to take my hands in his, exclaim, "Whatever was I thinking?" and thank me for how brilliantly I'd pointed out his oversight of basic ethics. Instead, he muttered another "Okay Babe," and something about the student now having to "take care of affairs at the farm." Although I was unsure of the details behind the statement, I picked up that my Iranian spouse was disappointed in my apparent failure to recognize that in the ups and downs of life, *everyone needs a little extra understanding every now and then.*

With neither of us moved by the other's argument and each clearly irritated with the other, we both realized we had reached a stalemate in this conversation. Fortunately, there was enough human capital invested in every other aspect of our relationship that we could avoid the land mine of this one, agree to disagree, and move on. As far as I understood, that meant that I, as Mr. Farmer's professor, would have the final say, that my preference would be honored, and that Mr. Farmer would have to deal with failing English for Agricultural Students.

Even so, realizing that my decision had not settled well with

Mahmoud and that a few days remained before final grades had to be turned in, I felt a needling pressure within me to explore the question further.

***

I took the dilemma to my colleagues at the Language Center. I also managed to insert it as a casual topic of conversation during social visits with fellow professors back at the kuee. Sorry to say, my inquiries did not help me find a clear and consistent pattern for responding to students requesting second chances. There were colleagues I liked and respected whose facial expressions, if not their words, gave away that under similar circumstances, they'd surely have given their students a make-up test. Other professors I respected just as much made it perfectly clear that if asked to do the same thing under similar circumstances, well, *they'd rather not have to*. The bottom line was that, unlike me, no one chose the categorical *No* as their response. At best, the closest response to mine was more like a categorical *it depends*. It looked like the definitive guidance I'd been hoping for was nowhere in sight.

As for Mahmoud, he had his own problems to deal with: the likes of persistent inquiries. Evidently, Mr. Farmer, the resolute and relentless, had pulled out his *second* arsenal by appearing at my husband's office door *again* one day, and the next day, and the day after that, with a new proposal. And this proposal, he carefully explained more than once, *this* proposal *Khanum Pahvel* wouldn't even have to sign off on or bother herself over!

Mahmoud recounted the request as I, *Khanum Pahvel*, took it all in: In order to graduate from the university, "Mr. F." didn't necessarily require a passing grade in English. All he needed was a way to protect his overall grade point average (GPA) from the plummeting effects of a grade gone wrong. One way to do this would be to find, somewhere, somehow, an elevated grade to fold into his GPA to counteract the effects of the English grade that threatened to cost him the farm and devastate his world.

"Wait a minute!" I protested halfway in disbelief, halfway defensively. "'Cost him the farm?' What do you mean, 'cost him the farm'? *What* farm?" It was at this point that the name "Mr. Farmer" first materialized in my mind and got stuck there. I couldn't see what this man's being granted or denied the chance for a make-up test in English possibly had to do with his keeping a farm or losing it. And even if it did, *I* surely wasn't willing to take the blame for it.

Mahmoud didn't really respond to my ranting, but instead went on with the saga of Mr. F. Anyway, he explained, in the end, Mr. F. would need the cooperation of a sympathetic professor who'd be willing to enter that elevated grade into his record. To Mr. Farmer's mind, that's where my husband could lend a hand.

"Wait a minute!" I sliced in again. "But how is it even possible for you to raise his grade when you're not his professor anymore? You haven't even had him in class for two whole terms, so then why is he coming to *you*?"

Mahmoud just looked at me straight in the eye, and I dropped the question. "So, what did you tell him?" I asked instead.

His answer surprised me. "I told him that if he had any regard or compassion for me at all, if he didn't want me to end up with a divorce on my hands, he would back off and ask his other professors for assistance on this."

Evidently, that was the only response that had made sense to Mr. Farmer. So, as Mahmoud requested, Mr. Farmer backed off in pursuit of "Plan B," leaving both Mahmoud and me relieved.

Of course, as you have probably guessed, the relief was only temporary.

Several days later, Mr. Farmer (the presumptuous and predatory) was back.

This time, however, he was not at my husband's office door but *at the doorstep of our home* at the kuee. Apparently, Mr. F had already made the rounds to all his other professors from the current term to ask for a grade hike and had come back empty-handed. "Plan B" had not panned out, and he was back to "Plan A" (that is, "A" as in "Ahmadi").

How did "Ahmadi," my husband who answered the door, respond to Mr. Farmer's arrival? While I was in the house at the time, I didn't know exactly what happened in those minutes. Totally unnerved that this student had crossed all conceivable boundaries and stood at the very threshold of our home, I'd hidden myself away in the kitchen, unable to make out what was being said. All I could hear was the deep and distant voices of the two men going back and forth in Persian at an even keel. At this point, all I wanted was for the Mr. Farmer drama to end. I can only imagine that Mahmoud, among the most patient and kind of souls, had reached that point of saturation, frustration, and weariness long before.

So, when the conversation ended, Mr. Farmer left, Mahmoud entered the kitchen, and I dared to ask him, "What happened?" all he said was, "I will take care of it." And nothing more was said of it for a long, long time.

In due time, we were able to talk about it, and I learned what had happened. Dr. Mahmoud Ahmadi, Mr. Farmer's professor from a previous class, did in fact go to the registrar to request the back records of that class and the form needed to resubmit the grade. After he had extracted an extra assignment on a suitable topic from Mr. F's hand, he turned in a higher grade. This "slight" transaction managed to raise Mr. F's overall grade point average enough to make it possible for him to graduate, and evidently, no one in the registrar's office asked any questions. It was as if the whole university somehow knew of the drama of Dr. Ahmadi, his foreign wife *Khanum Pahvel,* and Mr. Farmer—and had looked the other way mercifully. Relieved that the whole fiasco had been solved without my having to bend this time, I was only too glad to be done with it all.

We did revisit the topic, though. One vibrant evening the following term, after a completely unrelated conversation about university life, I was the one who brought it up.

"Mahmoud … I understand now why you took Mr. Farmer's side over mine. And it doesn't bother me anymore."

"Baby *Jan* (Dear Baby)!" Is that how you see the situation … that I preferred to make my student happy more than you? You think *that* was my motivation?"

"What other way is there to see it?"

"Baby! This guy came to *you* for a grade change, then he came to *me*, and more than once. And when *both* of us said "No," he showed up at our house without warning rather than backing off! Doesn't that sound a little desperate to you? I mean, if he did something like that, how do we know that the guy wouldn't do something to hurt *you*, or maybe *himself* for that matter? I didn't think it was worth the risk."

I sat silently as Mahmoud's words permeated. It wasn't the thought of Mr. Farmer as a possible threat that stunned me; it was realizing how wrong I had been about Mahmoud's thinking behind his decision.

"Okay, Mahmoud, I *was* really mad at you, but I never thought about what you just said. I guess I didn't consider the whole picture. I'm sorry."

There was a brief pause, followed by "That's okay."

"I still don't know how I feel about what happened," I said, "But *one* thing I know: When it comes to thinking about 'the other guy,' *you* are the master!"

"Yes," he said, "The Master of Disaster!"

And both of us laughed until our stomachs hurt.

***

The day finally arrived when I genuinely felt happy to learn that Mr. Farmer had safely graduated after all, presumably with his farm intact. *Mr. Farmer, should you ever read these lines, I want you to know that. It's not that I have any better grasp of your circumstances now than then. It's that I now realize I never gave myself the chance to try. In any case, I'm glad you didn't give up too easily on the farm, and I'm glad I didn't give up too easily on my husband.*

As I look back on that bizarre episode, I realize I was just as guilty, or at least just as blind as the next guy when it came to jumping to conclusions. Ironically, some of my shakiest conclusions occurred right at the points when I felt the most certain of myself. Where it came to deciding the fate of students like Mr. Farmer, I thought at the time that I was looking for answers. Had I paused to have a deeper conversation with myself, though, I might have asked if what I was really seeking was someone's *validation*: i.e., permission to give this student his "just deserts." To my mind, he had not only failed to show up for class or the final exam; he had tried to usurp my authority as a teacher by involving somebody else (who just happened to be my husband!). At the same time, I was not aware that when conflicts arise in Iranian culture, it is common to involve a third-party advocate to present an appeal, not so much a demand. That, in turn, made me realize I couldn't *really* be sure of Mr. Farmer's intentions. So, whether he had approached my husband to force my hand or simply voice an honest request, I guess I'll never know.

Following that episode with Mr. Farmer, I began noticing changes in me that I hadn't expected but became apparent when I went back to teach in America. As far as my ability to make the simplest decision on a student's work, on changing a grade, or on granting an extension, it seemed I was ruined for life. Now to my mind there was *always* another way of looking at things, and I guess I finally decided life was too short for me to try to figure those kinds of things out. Ironically, perhaps Mr. Farmer and I had more in common than I thought: Just as he had decided to check out of English class, I nearly decided to check out of university life—entirely.

Okay, I knew it might well be true that, as Abraham Lincoln has been quoted as saying, "Mercy bears richer fruit than strict justice." But even so, I thought, God forbid that "Khanum Pahvel" would have to decide between "justice" and "mercy" again in an Iranian classroom—or in any other classroom, for that matter.

Chapter Twenty-One

The Conversation Class

My first term at the Language Center had flown by, with many wonderful students and a few choice lessons for the teacher. Although each day of teaching at the university was an adventure that provided its own fulfillment, I realized after four months at the kuee that something was missing. I longed for the companionship of a more intimate community—a community of *women*. What better way to find this community, I announced one day to my husband, than to *create* one by opening our home to the women of the neighborhood for a conversation class in English? And if I could also charge a fee reasonable for participants, it would be a joyful way to supplement our income.

I was optimistic that the students would come; at least, I earnestly hoped they would. I'd been encouraged by what I perceived to be a strong "trace of English" in the air at the kuee. Even outside of the Language Center, many if not most of the faculty I'd met in the kuee had spent periods of their professional lives in English-speaking countries and had taken their spouses and children with them. What happened to them with their English is what happened to me with my Spanish after four years in Iran: the cold reality of the "use-it-or-lose-it" syndrome, plus an ardent desire to restore those hard-earned language skills. What most kuee residents had going for them, even those who'd never traveled to an English-speaking country, was a residual core of English grammar skills retained from eight or nine years of formal education in Iran, from the middle school years up through college. I recall how many a neighbor I hadn't met yet used to catch my eye in passing. She would slip me a surreptitious "*Heylo*" almost under their breath, as if to show she knew I was American and that she still remembered her English back from school days.

The fond idea of opening a class stayed with me. But how

would I locate my students, decide on a schedule, determine a fee, and fill our living room with warm, eager bodies? I wondered. Was there an office I needed to contact, an ad I needed to place, someone's permission to seek? I didn't know where to begin, which I confessed to Mahmoud one week after the idea started tugging at me.

Mahmoud knew where to begin. He pulled out a white sheet of paper from his briefcase and scripted on it in Persian:

کلاس مکالمه انگلیسی برای خانم ها در کوی استادان

دوشنبه ها و چهارشنبه ها از ساعت 3:30 تا 5:00 بعد از ظهر

کوی استادان ,پلاک ۵-۶

شماره تماس:۳۳۵۳۹۲۱

which, translated into English, read as follows:

English conversation class for ladies in the faculty residence area
Mondays and Wednesdays: 3:30 p.m. – 5 p.m.
Row 5, House #6
Call # # # – # # # #

What are you going to do with that?" I asked him.

I'm going to post copies around the kuee," he said. "So, what date do you want to begin? And how much are you planning to charge?"

Starting date? That wouldn't take long to figure out. *Planning to charge?* That would be tougher. Could I find a price low enough to be fair and welcoming, yet high enough to bring me closer to affording a visit to America every once in a while? Even with both Mahmoud and me now working full time as professors, we were earning our monthly income in *toumans*, the local denomination, within an international travel market driven by a dollar economy.

I'd lost my dad tragically to lung disease and other complications just seven months earlier. We had not been able to put enough down for my ticket home until four months after his death, and with each of us earning the rough equivalent of $100 a month, the cost of that one ticket took six months of our salaries combined. At this rate, when would I ever afford to see my family? And what of *their* hope of seeing not just me, but Mahmoud, Parisa, and any future children?

I brought my question about pricing the class to Nasrin. I really needed her help, it turns out. I was still stuck thinking in dollars while she, quite naturally, thought in terms of the touman-based salaries our neighbors were bringing home. With that in mind, she suggested a price range that would fall, she thought, within reasonable limits. Seeing that her idea of a modest price range was notably lower than mine, I thanked her for her helpful insight and went home to struggle with the question some more. In the end, I thought about my sisters back home, I thought about the families in the kuee, then I decided to opt for the higher end of Nasrin's suggested price range. I could only hope I'd done right by both sides.

Two and a half weeks later, our living room was filled with twelve women of all ages, personalities, appearances, and levels of English proficiency, eager to start class. It was September of '93, ten months since we had first moved into the kuee. By now, we had not only managed to purchase our first vehicle, a shiny blue second-hand jeep, but we had also stocked our living room with a few pieces of locally bought furniture of the *"rahati"* variety (i.e., made for comfort, not style). Although we'd already lived long enough without either purchase to be just fine without them, it felt good to offer my new students a cozy place to sit.

One of the most dramatic memories of the class for me happened in those very first minutes, when my new students and fellow neighbors began shedding their outer wraps in my presence for the first time. The one familiar member of the group was my friend Nasrin, of course, who delighted me by joining our circle, and who I also suspect had played a role in recruiting students behind the scenes. Until that moment, I'd never shared a classroom with women where we saw each other in our everyday clothes, and frankly, its novelty fascinated me. It was the first time since we'd moved into the kuee almost a year earlier that I was privileged to share an intimate space of this kind with my neighbors. And by joining this private little conversation class, they had chosen to do the same with me. Seeing the simple act of slipping off a coat, a scarf, a hood, or a chador had a strange new impact with trans-formative power. What many of them wore looked just like the pieces my girlfriends were wearing back home—a pretty turtleneck with vibrant stripes and Ann Taylor lines, a pair of designer jeans ripped at the knee and just the right shade of faded blue, a stretchy headband or large hairclip to sport a casual style. But seeing their instant transformation from "covered" to "casual" was for me more arresting than the "beautiful people" decked out in their evening wear. Even those dressed in the more familiar skirts and blouses I'd seen in Mahmoud's family had such a natural, relaxed air about them. I noted how lovely they all looked. Yet, after months of seeing them in their street attire and cloaked appearance to the outside world, seeing them this way was suddenly strange to my eyes.

Just as arresting was that everyone there was sitting in high attention, simply beaming. Setting aside our self-conscious feel-ings along with our overcoats and wraps, we promptly and unanimously agreed to the first cardinal rule of the class: to speak only English at our gatherings. Granted, a commitment of this nature required more resolve from the ladies than it did from me. But as their teacher, I felt responsible for creating a space where whatever we did, it felt worth the effort to do it in English.

We worked in pairs, swapping answers to randomly drawn questions and sharing what we learned about our partners with the others: "Tell us something you really like about yourself." "Talk about a time you were scared." "Do you think boys and girls should be treated differently?" We searched for meaning in stories from a graded reader: fantastical, philosophical, or silly tales about men waking up in locked rooms with no memory, a boy with an online "virtual fish" that granted too many wishes, a resort whose residents were secretly being controlled by drugs slipped into the water, a self-absorbed hotel manager trying to impress a celebrity guest. Moving on to a new kind of reading (Carole Jackson's popular glamour guide from the eighties, *Color Me Beautiful*), we devoted one class to ourselves and each other, deciding which fashion shades best flattered each woman's skin, hair, and eye tones. Then, there was the class devoted to my swelling, pregnant belly, when different ladies predicted, by its shape and proportions, whether I was carrying a daughter or son. That's when I figured we were getting tightknit as a group. Anyhow, when the results of my sonogram finally came in and I shared with the group that it was a daughter, one of the ladies, Parvaneh Khanum, piped up. "I don't care what any doctor says," she retorted. "Mark my words: you'll be having a son." And as it turned out, a son it was.

In class we watched movies (like *Witness* and *Awakenings*) and drew parallels to our lives. We played charades and prepared talks, debates, and made-up stories. We kept track of new terms that popped up in class and later held vocabulary competitions in teams. We focused on a "grammar feature of the week" and did spot check grammar lessons as needed. Students corrected their own errors, never those of their classmates, and many took their English beyond the classroom, circling the kuee with a buddy from class so both could practice.

How amid all the classroom agenda, the sweetness, the silliness, and the laughter we managed to share our hearts, lives, and opinions as women, wives, mothers, residents of Iran, or world citizens on things that mattered to us, I don't know, but we did. And we stuck to our pledge of "English only" while doing it.

***

It wasn't long before my daily strolls around the kuee began to take new turns, find new paths. Less anonymous than I had once been, I began hearing my name, "Leslie Khanum," or just plain "Leslie," being spoken or called from the street or one of the houses (how odd, yet wonderful, to hear my name again without embellishment once in a while!) And there would be Fatimeh, or Afagh, or Shohreh, or Zahra, or Soraya, or the lot of them together, inviting me to come along, or inside for tea, or in one of their back-yards when the cherry, apple, or mulberry trees were ripening. You never knew what news might emerge from these encounters, what unexpected gems I might discover. Like how so many of the ladies detested windy days (which I loved) but reveled in rainy ones (not my favorite) because rainy days were so rare in the region. Like how everyone had a favorite lasagna recipe to share for dinner parties. Like how, outside of class hours, one lady worked as a dentist, one as a midwife, another as an athletic director, yet another as a high school teacher who as it turned out taught English herself. Like how one of the ladies had a nephew whose name I fell in love with the instant I heard it, *Nikyar*, inspiring me to name my son "Nikiar" ("Niki") when he was born just three weeks later.

In some of the intimate, one-on-one conversations, I listened and learned of other realities, touching on the stuff of life. How one woman anguished over an unwanted pregnancy. How another had a child prodigy who was painfully bashful. After Niki was born, we'd sit in one woman's sunroom sipping tea, and she'd share beautiful insights on ways to nurture and respect our children. One out-of-town member of the class, the younger sister of a kuee member, allowed me a glimpse into her romantic affairs. She had mixed feelings about receiving yet another prospective husband into her living room while parents, siblings, and close friends looked on and offered their opinions. I ended up being part of that process one day when the suitor, a close friend of Mahmoud, arranged to come to our home to pay her "the visit." She ended up marrying another man, but through the drama of it all, our families grew close.

Chance or one-time meetings with my students at the kuee

eventually turned into routine ones, including those warm summer evenings when I'd join them and other ladies from the kuee for a nightly stroll. Chatting and laughing without a care, we'd travel the lamplit street together, a slow and steady current of mostly black shrouds and children of all ages bobbing around us. It didn't matter which kid was with who; each woman was every kid's mother, and each child belonged to everyone. Parisa later told me these evenings were among her earliest and fondest memories. As for me, I began to feel less like a curiosity in the kuee and more like a true member, a part of its fabric—even while my forest green manteau floated alongside a sea of flowing black manteaus and chadors!

We continued our lessons into the spring term, and one thing flowed into another. As I came to know the ladies of my class, I came to know their daughters too, at least enough to recognize them, to exchange genuine smiles and a greeting with them in the street or at Mr. Amin's corner store. One day in class, the ladies surprised me with a proposal that many of their teenagers had made: to open a second class, "just for girls." I had never worked with secondary school students before, and I had my insecurities. But when summer break arrived a few weeks later, I found myself with a roomful of young ladies one day, welcoming them to class.

Would the same basic teaching agenda work with this younger population? I counted myself lucky that it did. The girls had an eagerness and energy I found contagious. There was a wide range of abilities among them, depending on natural talent, exposure abroad, age, and level of confidence. Some, especially the middle schoolers, were more insecure, afraid of stumbling in front of their peers and finding themselves stumbling all the more. In moments like those I saw a kindness and solidarity among the girls that touched me. Some of the older ones would lean forward slightly, cheering the reluctant ones on with their eyes, mouthing the correct form unconsciously, ready to praise each halting effort.

The girls grew close very quickly, and in sharing their dreams, fascinations, aspirations, and spiritedness, they drew me right into their world. Feeling their vitality beneath the surface and seeing their fresh and lovely faces without scarves, I'd have loved to know something, anything of their thoughts on topics of utmost importance to budding teenage girls in the States: clothes, makeup, how to attract admirers, the latest song artists, their future dreams. But knowing that their mothers had entrusted their daughters to me, and unsure of where the boundaries for such conversations might lie, I held back, steering clear of the riskier topics and sticking to the same basic lessons I'd planned for their mothers. Even so, as I watched and listened to them—what they said, how they said it, what they *didn't* say, how they sometimes giggled or fidgeted among themselves—they reminded me so much of myself and my friends at their tender, exuberant age, and I caught myself wishing I knew more about them.

If Parisa happened to be home during class time, it would be hard to keep her and the girls away from each other. As much a giant magnet for the teenagers as they were for her, my three-year-old daughter would peek from behind a curtain with curious, admiring eyes. The girls would find her a pleasant distraction, waiting for the chance after class to scoop her up in their arms and ask permission to spoil and fuss over her at their own homes for just a little while.

What vibrant, intelligent young ladies, I told myself. *What will Parisa be like—and who will she be when she reaches their age?*

Chapter Twenty-Two

Christmas and "New Year" in the Kuee

The girls' conversation class disbanded with the end of the summer holiday and the women's class resumed. As the weeks passed, the air gradually turned from warm to tepid, to crisp. Isfahan had the sort of climate where fall slipped into winter, and December slipped into January without your noticing precisely when. Besides that, Iran's eight-month calendar year didn't line up with the twelve-month calendar I knew, and snowfall or sharp drops in temperature were rare in this part of the country. As far as I could see, there were no festive colored lights, no graceful bows, no tree-topped stars, and no elegant wreaths adorning the streets to mark the onset of the Christmas season. That being the case, I was prepared to celebrate the meaning that Christmas held for me quietly, purposefully, inconspicuously, as I had in the kuee the year before.

This year, however, would play out differently. It was perhaps ten days before Christmas Day when, as if by clockwork, several women arrived at class with bright eyes and a special greeting on their lips, the one time they spoke Persian since their solemn pledge: *Leslie Khanum, Eide shoma mobarak bashe,* meaning "Miss Leslie, may your holiday be blessed."

Their words had just begun to take hold of me when the ladies switched back to English already. "So, where's your Christmas tree?" they asked, half-curious, half-demanding. Before I could figure out what to say, or even where one *gets* a Christmas tree in Isfahan, the women began chattering among themselves. By the time class ended that day, we'd already planned to commemorate Christmas, the birthday of the beloved prophet *Isa,* at a special party in place of class the following week. I would host, and Mrs. Hamidi, my friend Janet from England, was also to come as a special guest.

They brought fancy dishes and cakes from their kitchens. They brought cards they had purchased, cards they had made, cards their children had made. One of the girls from the summer class sent a tender drawing of Joseph, Mary, and Jesus in a manger; another had created a two-foot poster of Baba Noel ("Father Christmas") meticulously finished in red and white crayon. "You can see him again on television," the ladies told me. "Baba Noel appears every year on a children's show on Christmas Day. Don't miss him," they said earnestly.

After dinner I invited them all to the living room, where they'd find what many were hoping to see: the sweet "Charlie Brown" Christmas tree that Mahmoud had cut from the roadside woods and set fittingly at the living room entrance. They cooed appreciatively at the tiny, unassuming, under-decorated tree. One of the ladies, in homage to it, dressed the glass doors beside it with a gift of decoupage: a magical scene of snowflakes and stars. It was the only "snow" I would see in Isfahan that year. We exchanged the gifts that each of us had prepared for the person whose name we'd drawn the week before. Then someone with a sharp eye grabbed my guitar from a corner and handed it to me. A round of requests immediately followed: "Leslie, please sing a Christmas song for us, your favorite." I sang three stanzas of *Silent Night* as my students—my friends—joined in with their sweet and reverent silence. They asked for another song, and I sang *The Borning Day*, a beautiful West Indian Christmas song I'd first heard sung by my earliest hero: Jamaican Black American artist Harry Belafonte.

When Baba and Mamán arrived from the village three days later, the house would still be cozy and fragrant from the leftover food, the cards and decorations, the memories of that special night the ladies from conversation class had welcomed Christmas to the kuee.

***

When class resumed in January, I was in a New Year's frame

of mind. Forgetting that Iran's New Year starts the first day of spring and not in the dead of winter, I kicked class off with an invitation for everyone to share a "New Year's resolution."

My cheery suggestion drew curious looks and blank expressions. "New Year's resolution," they repeated slowly. "What's that?"

"Well, okay," I began. "Take me, for example. Remember all those wonderful cakes and fancy dishes you brought to the Christmas party, and that, well, I ate?" I asked.

Smiling proudly, everyone nodded.

"Well, it was all *so* delicious, but I'm afraid everything has its price. So now, I suppose, it's time for me to lose the extra weight I've picked up since the party," I paused as a tiny sigh slipped out, "and also, quite frankly, since even before then."

The ladies kept listening politely, wondering whether or not they'd heard my New Year's resolution yet.

"That's all!" I continued, trying to brighten my tone and make New Year's resolutions sound fun and doable. "My resolution is to try to lose some weight and get into shape." I then quickly re-directed the question, asking the group in a perky voice, "What about the rest of you?"

Cheerfully and cooperatively, the ladies came up with their own New Year's resolutions, three months before the Iranian New Year. To be more attentive to the garden, more patient with the children, more devoted to reading, more charitable with the stray cats that came begging for handouts. Of course, "Practice more English!" came up as well. We laughed about it all and went on with the class.

But the tiny sigh that had slipped from my mouth minutes earlier had not escaped the attention of Fatimeh Dadashi, the lean, well-toned codirector of women's athletics at the university, just about my age. At the end of class, after everyone had left, she sat down to talk with me.

"You know," she said, sticking to English and looking at me earnestly, "you really can."

"Can what?"

"You really can lose your weight and get in shape. I am happy to help you, if you like."

I looked in her face and could see that she meant it. Even so, I didn't know how to respond. Besides, I'd always been kind of scared of gym teachers.

"Thank you, Fatimeh. Your offer is kind—amazing, in fact— but it's too much to ask of you—of anyone," I added. I knew what her involvement might demand from both of us.

"But it is for your New Year's resolution, right?"

"Yes," I answered, after a pause.

"It is something you need?" she pressed gently.

"Yes," I admitted to myself as much as to Fatimeh.

"We can start next week," said Fatimeh, smiling. "Two times in the week we will practice."

A feeling of exuberance suddenly came over me. I'd been offered the services of a personal trainer!

"Okay!" I answered, in spite of myself.

Fatimeh smiled again as she stood and turned to leave. I stopped her.

"We haven't talked about payment, Fatimeh. Should I pay you once a month? Twice a month? And how much should I plan for?"

Fatimeh paused, just for a moment. She hadn't been expecting the question. "It isn't for money," she answered, simply and pleasantly. "I just like to help you."

I pressed a bit harder, pointing out how much time she was offering, not to mention her expertise. I didn't want to take advantage.

When she saw I insisted, she gave me a new answer, kind of. "We can talk about it," she said pleasantly. "See you next week— and wear loose clothes!" With that, she stepped out the door with her long stride, leaving me feeling unresolved.

The next week, she came to my house. I was ready, wearing loose clothing, and she worked me in the living room. She worked me and worked me, then walked me and walked me. As pleasant as she was, it was clear that this lady meant business, that she'd taken this New Year's resolution thing seriously. At the end of our session, one hour later, I asked between breaths about payment again. "We can talk about it," she said, smiling. "See you on Thursday!"

We kept on meeting, week after week. Fatimeh's face was always bright and encouraging, and whatever she asked, she did alongside me. Eventually I gave up bringing up payment; her answer was always the same.

After a while, my huffs started to get shorter, and my stride was longer. Even between sessions, I began to notice more energy in my walking and a bounce in my step. It got easier with each meal to take less rice and reach for more fruit. My complexion began to take on a glow, and my clothes were falling in all the right places. When summer arrived and I opened class a second time for the younger set, the girls got excited with me about my "new look."

It was just around that time that Fatimeh and I both knew I was ready for independence, that I was equipped to move forward on my own. But Fatimeh had left me with more than a tremendous workout routine. Long after our sessions ended, the bounce in my step remained. Part of it came from just knowing that someone had gone to such lengths to see me realize my New Year's resolution. As for Fatimeh, her compensation lay in being that someone.

I thought back on the time I'd struggled so hard over what to charge for conversation class: how to strike the balance between earning airplane fare to see my sisters, whom I did know, and being fair to my neighbors in the kuee, most of whom I hadn't known personally before we began. As I think about it, I'm not sure I ever found that balance. All I knew at the start of class was that I wanted to offer the best to my students. In my coming to know them, they won my heart with theirs. It felt like an unfair trade in my favor: English lessons in exchange for an intimate family of women, and money on top of that. In the end, while I made every effort to give the best of my heart and teaching skills to these women, I so often felt "outgiven" by them.

Conversation class with the ladies went on for two-and-a-half years, up until the spring before we left Isfahan for our next transition. The class with the girls lasted for two wonderful summers. What became of our little group after we disbanded? One of them had a son who would grow up to interview President Obama as a correspondent for BBC, and another had a son destined to be an internationally known rap artist. One of them, a certified midwife, would play a central role in bringing my son into the world, while another (the one who helped me discover Niki's name) would leave this world prematurely while we were still living in the kuee. One of them had a daughter who married an Iranian IT engineer and resettled, of all places, in Columbus, Ohio. Another would resettle not far from Columbus, at the University of Illinois with her appointed husband. There she would develop a fondness for yoga and fitness, see her daughter (the "shy" one) flourish as an artist, teacher, and pharmacist, and dedicate herself to reading the classics of Dostoyevsky, Leo Tolstoy, and Herman Melville in English.

And three of them—Afagh, Shirin, and Nasrin—would continue to touch my life by remaining lifelong friends.

Whenever the old song "I Am Woman, Hear Me Roar" comes to mind, I think back fondly on my conversation class back at the kuee, with its powerful and diverse community of women. There's more to the story, however. After sending me their daughters for their first summer session, the ladies asked me about holding yet another class, this time for their *sons*. I was touched by their faith in my ability to engage young teenage boys on an ongoing basis, but I did not share their confidence. Besides, I'd grown far too comfortable teaching in my living room without giving thought to wearing a headscarf or coat. So, ever so gently, I passed on the chance. Having raised a teenage boy of my own (who was, after all, a "son of the kuee" himself), I wonder what I might have missed out on.

Chapter Twenty-Three

On Manners and Being Matter of Fact

From the first day I set foot into Iran, I noticed something in the demeanor and mannerisms of strangers, acquaintances, friends, and even family members that intrigued me. I could only describe it as "genteel," and if the truth be known, I found these little details in people's behavior, well, enchanting. The titles they attached to names, the hands they laid on their hearts, the heads they bowed slightly, the little expressions they voiced that made you feel practically like royalty. Expressions sprinkled here and there, like, *What would The Lady like?* (when *I*, of course, was "The Lady"), like, *It's not worthy of you* (in response to thanks for a gift or service), like, *I sacrifice myself for you* (when conveying indebtedness), and like, *May your hand never know pain* (to express gratitude for a meal or other favor that took effort). None of these expressions, of course, were meant to be taken literally. They were intended more as a kind of symbolic deference people ascribed to each other, a delicate blend of courtesy, respect, and lavish attention, all rolled into one.

The Iranians have a term for that mode of behavior: *tarof*. Of course, depending on who or what they're referring to at the time, the word *tarof* can range in meaning– from "niceties" and "courteous protocol" to "showy politeness" a little on the shallow side. As one who at least tried not to judge others' intentions, and was enamored of the evocative power of words, I was a sucker for such expressions and enjoyed my share of such gracious attention.

Then there were other times. Like when Jamshid Aqa, my eldest brother-in-law and every ounce a gentleman, made an observation among twenty-five family members gathered to see me —and did so by opening up the circle of conversation with a three-word pronouncement: "You got fat."

Turning toward my brother-in-law startled and speechless, I met his gaze in disbelief. But his eyes were so well-meaning and pleasant; he might as well have just said, "The kababs are especially juicy today." (You know, your basic conversation starter).

At moments like that and others, I gradually became aware of a strange paradox. In a land filled with the language of ritual politeness, niceties, and deference, this same language is also punctuated with comments of frankness that could shock many an unsuspecting American — and caught me off guard again and again.

My experiences at the university taught me that my students would, at one moment, stand to their feet for me, address me respectfully, and lower their gaze in silent submission — and, at another, point out some slip or gaffe I'd committed.

One day during an office visit, a student asked me, in his own way, why the simple green manteau I usually wore to work was, in effect, so "simple" and "green." (Picking up on the hint, I ended up buying a much chicer model, in sophisticated black, at a shop in Tehran with Badri's help—but I was surprised that a male student would take such liberties.) Another time, a female student with a sweet and shy voice accompanied me on my way to the Language Center. In the middle of our light conversation in Persian about dishes we liked to cook and eat, she confided that she found the way I pronounced the Persian word for "food" ("ghaza") amusing. She then broke into giggles that took some time to contain while I tried to look comfortable.

Yet again, when I was heading down the staircase after class one afternoon, a male student I didn't recognize motioned at me, with swift gestures, to pull my hood back over my partially exposed hairline, as per university regulations. There was nothing apparently hostile or disrespectful in his face, and for all I know he was trying to be helpful, but the directness of his action unsettled me.

In the case of Mahmoud's family, whom I'd always known to be generous and tenderhearted, I came to understand that what I experienced as the occasional "sling" of a frank comment was for them nothing more than a natural observation for people who are close to each other to share. And if that was the case, how could I dare approach them on those rare occasions when I thought one of their "observations" had crossed the line? Who was I to approach Jamshid Aqa, my senior by over a decade, and request that he never again make a public announcement like the one at that gathering?

It would take a few months, but at an opportune moment I finally told him in as playful tones as I could muster, "Now, Jamshid Aqa, next time we see each other, don't be saying things like '__ __ __'!" I finished the sentence by repeating the offensive three words.

"*Bashe* (Okay)," was his penitent reply, his childlike downward glance suggesting he *got* it, that he wouldn't commit the same offense twice. To his credit, he never did.

Unfortunately, I cannot claim that in the land of *tarof*, others hadn't seen *me* as lacking in the 'ABCs' of social etiquette. There were always a few details here and there that would somehow escape my attention. Like maybe it *wasn't* okay to hug or kiss a male family member at the airport, even if we *were* just arriving or saying goodbye (by the time I reached out to poor Jamshid one day, his terrified expression said it all). Or that perhaps I shouldn't have taken my guests' words at face value when they turned down my offer to bring them tea or something to eat. I shudder to think of how many other poor souls, including my faithful friends from the conversation class, left our home hungry or thirsty because I hadn't known to serve them a refreshment (fruit, a beverage, or pastry) as a matter of course. Then there was that time my husband took me to the bazaar. When the kind merchant told me I wouldn't need to pay for that beautiful ceramic dish I so admired, I missed my cue to *insist* on his naming the price. Instead, to the poor guy's dismay, I thanked him warmly for his generous gift.

Okay, I told myself when my eyes had been opened to enough of these events, *I'm going to have to do better, be more focused*. I committed to picking up and applying some of those unwritten codes of conduct—first by observation, then imitation.

Starting with the routines I'd participated in a hundred times but never initiated, I paid closer attention to how each was done. Even those common daily greetings had their own rules and rituals, not equivalent to how things worked in the States. I can still hear the sweet and classy voice of Shohreh, usually the first of the ladies to arrive at my home for conversation class every Monday and Wednesday. Although she spoke to me in English, she'd follow the Iranian protocol for greeting, practically word for word, and I did my best to follow suit:

"Hello, Leslie."

"Hello, Shohreh!"

"How are you doing?"

"Thank you; I'm very well."

"And Dr. Ahmadi, how is he?"

"Thank you; he is also fine."

"Parisa, Nikiar … are they okay?"

"Thank you very much."

"What about your father … your sisters?"

"Thank you; they are fine too. How about, uh … *your* family?"

"Thank you. They all send their hello."

"Thanks. I send my hello too."

"Thanks."

I came to understand that from an Iranian perspective, it wasn't quite enough to ask someone how *they* were; it was important to include each member of that person's family, and preferably by name, not just as part of a collective unit. At the same time, I noticed that, unlike other societies with careful rules about cross-gender relations, it was fine to ask about family members of the opposite sex. Before long, *I* was the one to start the whole line of questioning about someone's family, this time in Persian. I realized that to do this properly, I'd have to pay closer attention to the names that went with each person's family. Pleased that I'd figured out the rule that went with the ritual, I was motivated to rise to the challenge.

There *was* a shorter way of greeting and being greeted; it just took a while for me to recognize it. I mean, if one day you heard someone say to you, "Don't be tired," how would *you* take it? It took me a while to realize that all the people saying the equivalent to me in Persian (*"Khaste nabashid"*) weren't trying to suggest I was looking haggard. Rather, they were using a standard expression to wish a person refreshment and renewal after a hard day's work. The first person I recall saying it to me was one of the security guards at the kuee gate. He must have wondered why I looked at him funny instead of just responding with the standard *"Salamat bashid"* (the equivalent of "Be well"). I did catch on eventually. Who would have guessed that the day would come when I'd *also* be telling other people, "Don't be tired," in Persian?

Something else that intrigued me was the little word *"Jan"* (pronounced "Jon"). Generally used to mean "Dear" in Persian, *"Jan"* could be spoken right after someone's first name (as in *"Mahmoud Jan"* or *"Leslie Jan"*). It could also be used in isolation, generally in response to someone calling your name. I noticed, for example, that there were times when I might address Ozra, or Badri, or Mamán by name, and they'd answer me back with that tiny term of endearment (*Jan?*)—basically the equivalent of "Yes, Dear?" in Persian. What's more, I noticed Baba, and even Mahmoud's younger brother Ali, using the term with me.

Okay, I deduced with surprise and relief, *it seems it's okay to use this term across gender lines.* My observation skills were paying off.

"Leslie Khanum," Rasool Aqa addressed me at the breakfast table one morning shortly after I'd had that discussion with myself.

"Jan?" I answered, mimicking my models Ozra, Badri, Mamán, Baba, and Ali.

"Don't call me '*Jan*,'" said Rasool Aqa flatly, offering no explanation.

As I felt my cheeks flush (although I was thicker-skinned than before), I concluded then and there that *"Jan"* was one of those terms I would let others use with me but maybe pass on using myself.

***

Of course, trying to play it safe by staying within social parameters didn't always shelter me from wandering into precarious conversations. Perhaps by not expecting certain kinds of conversations in Iran, I was all the more likely to be caught off guard when they occurred. And this of course made it all the more fun for others to pull me right into them.

I remember that happening one day in the village, at a mid-afternoon stroll with a handful of female family members. One minute, we were talking about Iran's ample variety of fruits and vegetables. The next, one of the cousins, with laughing eyes, asked me to describe, in considerable detail, how I liked my "cucumbers." (Peeled or unpeeled? Shorter or longer? With or without the seeds? A little salty?) Judging from the degree of detail they solicited, the close attention they gave to my answers, and the gleeful laughter that followed each one, I gradually came to realize we had crossed over into a topic on "fruit" of a different sort. What's more, my companions had led me into the topic in a skillful way I found surprising. Crude? Hardly. Playful? Mischievous? Definitely. As they watched my eyes run the gamut of expressions—from curiosity to confusion, to realization, to astonishment, to total embarrassment—my gleeful companions became increasingly more amused with me. As to whether they considered the topic appropriate or inappropriate by their own standards, I couldn't tell. We were, after all, among ourselves—all women, all family, all married, not in mixed company. In any case, one thing led to another, and I'll admit that it made for some fun and fascinating conversation.

My favorite story came from someone who described how once, while her husband was sleeping, she snatched up a marker and sidled alongside him. Next, with some well-placed artistic strokes and a neatly knotted handkerchief, she transformed an intimate part of her husband's body into a proper little *khanum* (lady) with a proper little scarf, ready to greet the husband when he woke up. While shyness prevented me from asking her what happened next, I missed a prime opportunity to ask.

***

Now, more than thirty years since my first trip to Iran, I *still* run into conversations that catch me off guard, rules I'm not altogether sure of, and situations I don't navigate much better than I did when I first started off. Take the age-old Iranian tradition of bringing gifts for family members after coming from a long trip. Before Iran, I never had to select and buy gifts for seventy-plus family members, all while working to get myself, my husband, and my kids ready for a major trip on something of a shoestring budget. Of course, now that we've moved back to the States and have visited Iran several summers since then, you might think I've figured out the best way to plan and go about the gift-gathering process.

I *could* write an impressive list of intended recipients—names nicely written up in columns. Let's see … there were always gifts to buy for Mahmoud's eight brothers and sisters, for each of their spouses, for each of their children, and for each of their children's spouses. In addition, there were gifts to buy for Mahmoud's parents, for each of *their* siblings, for their siblings' spouses and children. I always liked lingering over writing the list, since I was pretty good at scribbling the names out. Unfortunately, it was pretty much there where my talent ended, and my questions about gift-gathering began.

I was doomed to revisit them each time we planned a trip over, because no one had given me a straight answer on the "right way" to do it: not Mahmoud, not our Iranian friends, acquaintances, or family members. The only part that ever got settled was Mahmoud's and my general agreement that he would choose for the men, and I'd focus on the women and children. Other than that, the process of selection was anyone's guess. *Should I aim to select a unique gift for each individual, I wondered, or should I stick to buying the same item for everyone? Should I spend the same amount on each person, and if so, how will doing so limit my options, squelch my creativity and gut instincts, or bar me from those special price breaks afforded by sales and package deals? Should I focus on things that are hard to find in Iran or on just any item I think folks might enjoy?*

Over the years, I managed to pick up a few gift-buying principles, mostly in the form of passing comments mumbled by well-meaning Iranian friends. Some of these tips have proven to be more useful than others. I remember picking up pantyhose, little purses, fragrant soaps, decorative pens and paper, and fashion jewelry (frequently from the clearance rack), all received with graciousness and warmth. Still, these items never generated the same enthusiasm as beauty items like makeup, face and hand creams, perfumes, scented deodorants, and for some reason, intimate apparel—generally the feminine, flowery kind. Most of these items were already available all over Iran, from the corner markets to the big city department stores. What's more, many items at comparable prices in Iran were superior in quality. Yet, time and again, the cosmetic items or other articles of adornment were by far the most popular. It's as if by giving, the giver was affirming the loveliness of the recipient, especially if the gift was beautifully packaged.

Unfortunately, distributing popular gift items among the women sometimes led to sticky situations that were hard to circumvent. For one thing, I learned it was risky to distribute gift items all at once, when everyone was gathered in one space and privy to spotting each other's parcels. Of course, everyone would thank me warmly for the lipstick, eyeliner pencil, and hand cream I'd chosen for them, politely adding, *"Daste shoma dard nakone"* ("May your hand never know pain"), and that I really shouldn't have troubled myself. There would also be one or two people who would later pull me aside and ask if maybe they could exchange their "opalescent pink" lip color for "perfect plum" instead, since the "opalescent pink" hadn't quite worked for them. I never knew what to do with those slightly used items that had been unwrapped, sampled, and returned. Then again, there was always someone happy to take them off my hands. I'd often worry whether I'd have enough gift items to go around, but things always worked out in the end. Such circumstances taught me the fun of being creative, including giving away some of my own things, things I never imagined someone might want. All it took was being a little more observant.

Like the day I noticed the young wife of one of my nephews, eyeing my new set of burgundy-colored underwear on top of my suitcase with their tags still on. I'll never know what she hoped to do with burgundy-colored lingerie several sizes too large for her. What I do know is that when she left my room that night with a burgundy bundle tucked tightly under her arm, she beamed like a new bride.

Moments like that would give me comfort. If I couldn't offer gifts of much monetary value, at least I could offer something that someone felt good about getting. The items they wanted, and sometimes asked for, would often surprise me. Something as simple as a belt, T-shirt, or blouse from my suitcase, a small stuffed toy that had seen better days, a partly used flask of perfume, or nice-smelling hair gel in a pretty bottle.

But then, days before we'd say our goodbyes and prepare to return to the States, someone would playfully clasp a bracelet of fine gold around my wrist ("We're engaged!" Badri joked on one such occasion). Someone else would stuff my suitcase with an elegant porcelain tea set or exquisitely woven cloth. And another would step forward to hang a family heirloom around my neck! How many of *these* things, I wondered, were personal items they had given up for *me*?

How could I respond to parting gifts like those? Undone by

their overwhelming generosity, I'd look at them helplessly, embarrassed about all the measly sets of hand cream, eyeliner, and pink or plum lip color I'd given out.

I never knew how to make up the difference, but that never seemed to matter to them. Evidently, what they valued was the gesture of giving more than the gift, and to their mind it was enough that I had tried my best to remember and honor each family member. As Baba had told me once or twice, the holy Qur'an teaches that it is the *intention of our hearts* more than the actual acts we perform that matters in God's eyes—that perhaps, in other words, God Himself might say, "It's the thought that counts." It also lends insight into what kind of *tarof* is okay to accept and what kind to pass on. While *tarof* obliged each of my kindhearted sisters, sisters-in-law, and other family members to insist I not wash a single dish while a guest in their home, they wouldn't have minded had I ignored their insistence and joined the kitchen crew from the heart. "You wised up on us (*Zarang shodid*), Leslie," one of the sisters quipped at me one day when I forced my way into the kitchen, plopped on the floor beside her and the others, and started scrubbing pots. However much they told me to stop, I continued, insisting on getting my fair share of *ab bazi* ("water play"). I could tell by the way they were beaming how pleased they all were that I'd figured things out.

Anyway, at the end of each summer, when the time came to say goodbye, one person after another would hug me and wet my cheek with her tears. "We'll miss you, Leslie," they'd say. "Take care of yourself and just come back soon." Touched by their tenderness, I'd kiss them back and promise I would. Then I'd turn to say goodbye to the men.

I still remember a time I reached right out, forgetting that I shouldn't be hugging them. That is, till I came to Jamshid and suddenly—in the middle of reaching—remembered. He was the same one who had gotten an unwelcome armful from me on my very first day of arriving to Iran. But when *this* time he remained there, smiling quietly and allowing me to hug him without shrinking back, I understood that what he had chosen to see at that moment was my intention only. He couldn't have left me with a better parting gift.

Upon return from the twenty-hour flight, Mahmoud would usually call to announce our safe arrival in Columbus. We'd take turns deciding whose household we'd call to alert the others, and I remember the time we called Badri's house. After Mahmoud had spoken for a minute or two, he called me and handed me the phone. A familiar voice greeted me.

"Rasool Aqa?" I asked, waiting for his confirmation.

"*Jan?*" he answered back.

Wait a minute. Hadn't Rasool Aqa once made it clear that "Jan" was off limits for our addressing each other?

His response left me speechless for just a moment, but it was a wonderful moment, nonetheless.

Chapter Twenty-Four

"It Has Come to the Attention of the University President ..."

I was on my way out of class one day when I decided to swing by the Language Center to ask a question. As always, the administrative assistant and secretary were cheerful and helpful in providing the answer. Being the only female faculty member at the Language Center for my first two years, I felt a special camaraderie with these women, and I think they felt the same toward me—which left the door open to possibilities.

As I recall, one moment they were explaining how to complete the form I had asked about, and the next we were talking about makeup—and why I never showed up to work wearing any.

"Makeup?" I echoed blankly. Their frank and unexpected question had thrown me completely. I mean, as a woman in public, wasn't I *supposed* to avoid drawing attention to myself? Evidently in the eyes of these two women, between my plain green manteau and my totally untouched face to match, I had done far too good a job of it.

"Come on, Leslie Khanum," they said confidentially now that they had my attention. "Makeup is part of your professional image, the overall 'polish' that goes with the package. All it will take is a touch here and there!"

I spent the rest of the day thinking about it. How in the world, I asked myself, could I have been teaching for more than a term already and not picked up on this question of "image"? Here I was, thinking all this time that by giving up my mascara, my lipstick, my blush and eyeliner, I'd been doing a fine job of living up to expectations. Instead, ironically, I was on the edge of being viewed as a "slacker," at least by these women and the student who'd commented on my understated manteau. Come to think of it, both ladies came to the office each day with their faces sleekly adorned. So, it wasn't as if they weren't practicing what they were preaching.

The next day after my shower, I spent extra time in front of the mirror with my cosmetics bag. The result was that I showed up in class, for the first time, with a smidgeon of black along my top lash line and coral-colored lips. I also stopped by the main office in hopes that the ladies would notice and comment.

"*Afareen* (Well done)! Now *that's* more like it!" they chirped the moment they saw me. *You* know what you're doing ... very nice! You must make up your face like this every day, okay? It makes such a difference."

I was happy to see them so excited. As for me, I was happy to have a reason to get up a little earlier in the morning, apply a little "sunshine" to my face, and feel, I admit, a little brighter about myself.

A week went by before a university staff member, a man with a kind and soft-spoken demeanor, stopped into my classroom after I had dismissed the class and politely asked to sit at an empty desk across from me.

"It has come to the attention of the university president," he said, in English, looking off to the side and choosing his words carefully, "that you've been coming to class looking 'different' these days. He respectfully suggests it would probably be better if you toned down a bit. That's all," he added, rising from the desk and not wishing to prolong the agony for either of us. Still avoiding my gaze and feeling my silence, he laid his hand on his heart before exiting quickly.

Wow. I had never met the university president; I didn't even know what he looked like. How was it that he knew I had touched up my face a bit? Why did it matter that much that I had? Most of all, how did it square with what my well-meaning, well-made-up colleagues in the office had told me? On the long walk home, I pondered and pondered as my heart was stinging. Nothing like this had happened since my encounter with the "moral police" in Hamadan three months earlier.

When I told Mahmoud about the day's encounter, plus the chain of events leading up to this outcome, he shook his head slightly as if trying to clear it. But I will always appreciate his kindness for not overreacting. He did give me food for thought, however.

"I suppose," he began thoughtfully, between sips of hot tea, "that if on the first day you had shown up in the classroom with makeup, it wouldn't have been a big deal. But if after weeks of coming to class with no makeup at all, you suddenly show up with lipstick and liner, some could wonder what the heck was going on. I mean, what would your Spanish students in Ohio think if suddenly, one day, you showed up in class wearing a miniskirt and spiked high heels? They wouldn't know what to think either. And here, even if it didn't matter to most of your students, I'm guessing one or two felt they had to report you."

Okay, I wondered, but *now* what was I supposed to do? What did it mean for me to "tone down a bit"? Should I return to the classroom plain faced and back to square one? That would also feel a little humiliating.

After putting our heads together, Mahmoud and I came up with a "best guess" approach, which I'd put to the test the very next day. I'd show up in class with a "modified" look: the eyeliner would stay; the lipstick would go.

Three weeks went by with that plan in effect, and I'm happy to say we heard no more reports. Eventually, I introduced a touch of lip gloss, which was a little less bright and considerably sheerer. As the days went by without a word from the president, I felt satisfied that I had found the right balance. Either that or someone had decided to cut me some slack. It hadn't been the first time, I was guessing, and it wouldn't be the last.

I still remember that warm autumn day in the season of Ramadan (*Ramazan* in Persian), the holy month on the lunar calendar when between the hours of dawn and dusk, all Muslims are called to a period of dedicated fasting in consecration to God. The point and benefit of the exercise are to remind those who fast that the true source of their sustenance, whether physical or spiritual, comes from God alone. It is also to remind partakers of the fast to be genuinely and actively compassionate toward one another, especially to those who go without physical food or drink because they don't have the means to acquire them. Because Iran is an Islamic republic, it is assumed that nearly all its residents will observe this significant Islamic holiday, and that if they do not, they should at least be discreet about it.

It was late morning of the second or third day of this holy season when I walked into the university classroom to conduct business as usual with my English for engineering students. For whatever reason, the air in the building felt palpably arid that morning. Its stark dryness had scoured my tongue and throat, leaving me with that "cotton mouth" feeling. So, without giving it a second thought, I asked one of my students in the front row if he'd be so kind as to fetch me a glass of water from the kitchenette down the hall.

Without a word and being the gentleman he was, the student gave a slight nod, rose dutifully from his seat, and made his way into the hallway. When he returned minutes later, supporting the long, wet glass on a saucer, I barely noticed the marked hush that fell upon the students as I gratefully took the glass from his hand and nearly emptied it in one, long, refreshing draught.

While I was still drinking, a student with a boyish face who was sitting near the back of the room punctured the silence:

"But Teacher ... aren't you *fasting*?"

I looked into his eyes, uncommonly blue and wide with surprise, and the silence in the room all at once became apparent. Every student was looking at me, waiting for an answer. The fact was I *wasn't* fasting. Even so, I'd never have made such a public display of drinking water had I known it was off-limits to every onlooker, and on such a brutally arid day at that. What was I to do in a moment like this one?

"Not even water?" I heard myself say.

They all tossed their heads in a solemn "No."

Placing the glass back on its saucer, I laid the two items gently on the lectern, then drew my incriminating arms away.

"I'm so sorry," was all I knew to say.

It was then—through my students—that perhaps I experienced what Baba had once referred to as the "true spirit of Ramadan."

"That's okay, Teacher. You didn't know!" a compassionate voice piped up from the back of the room. It was the same student with bright blue eyes and a boyish face.

Although no one else breathed a word of response, this young man's words were just enough. He had transformed the awkwardness into a moment of grace. Immediately after his words tumbled out, I could feel myself and the students relax. Some nodded ever so slightly, some smiled shyly, and others looked plain relieved. I'm sure they could see how grateful I was to be understood and allowed to simply proceed with class. I never did hear from the president (although something tells me he probably got wind of it).

As for the young man who retrieved the water in the first place, I wish he could have collected five toumans for every astonished look he drew in the corridor with that gleaming, forbidden water glass and saucer in hand. He probably couldn't wait to get back to the classroom and hand over the damning evidence. If that was the case, he never once flinched or let on in my presence. I give him a lot of credit for that.

***

Students would not always be so stoic or contained. Just like their teacher, they couldn't always be prepared for the unexpected. In an ordinary lesson, anything could happen at a given moment, even during something as mundane as an English lesson on the "present continuous" form of the verb.

"What are they doing?" I asked one day. We were looking at a picture in my students' grammar book. The book had been written and printed in England, which explained the drawing of a young man and woman blissfully dancing together in their Western party clothes. Considering the place and the times, I probably should have moved on to the next picture—or at least called on a student who knew his grammar. That way he could simply have answered with, "They are dancing," it would have been right, and we'd have been done with it. Instead, I called on some poor student who, shifting uncomfortably in his seat, took an unsuccessful stab at my question.

"They are doing …" he began haltingly.

How can I guide him to the right answer?, I asked myself. *Maybe if I put his words into Persian, he'd see the parallel error in logic and try again.*

"'*Darand mikonand* …'?" I said in a questioning tone.

It was the literal translation of, "They are doing," but evidently, in Persian, the phrase had an entirely different connotation (as in, "They are doing *it*.")

After a moment of absolute silence, the class broke into uproarious laughter while I stood helplessly looking on. The students appeared to be just as helpless. It took several minutes and a few valiant efforts before they were able to stifle themselves. I'll grant they had *tried* to spare my feelings, but it simply had been too perfect a moment, one of absolute blundering, where I the teacher had stepped right into it.

There were times when I, too, had to grapple with how to respond to my students' unexpected behavior, particularly in areas that ruffled my feathers. My biggest emotional challenge came on test days, at moments when I sensed more was going on between some students than what met the eye. This suspected behavior, which I generally called "cheating," pushed all kinds of buttons in me, both in Iran and back in the States. I tended to take such acts personally as a breach of trust. Over time, I came to realize that what I called "student cheating," a moral infraction and a disrespect to academic authorities, many students simply viewed as what they had to do to "get everyone through" a challenging educational system. A distinctly "all for one, and one for all" kind of attitude.

That's what made rooting out such behavior so much tougher

in Iran. In America, where competition is openly touted, there were generally enough students opposed to someone copying their work that they'd set up their own defenses against those who would try. In Iran, it seemed that even some of the best and brightest students didn't mind sharing their answers with the less prepared. Passing answers hand-to-hand underneath chadors, sitting in strategic configurations around the exam hall, and sending signals in such subtle or sophisticated ways that they were barely detectable, some students had their system down to a science. The fact that there was no formal policy on cheating in most, if any, universities didn't help. Sometimes when I'd point out my suspicions to fellow faculty members, proctoring with me in the same exam hall, they'd simply chuckle and nod their heads, half-amused by the students' covert collaborations. It might have been nice to have another American teacher to talk things through with, to serve as a sympathetic sounding board, but my lovely colleague from Kentucky, Carolyn, would not arrive at the kuee or Language Center for another year.

One exceptionally bright student, noting my sense of powerlessness one day, tried to relieve my distress with some well-meaning advice. "Really," he said, "maybe you should just forget about it. No matter what you do or how hard you try, there's nothing you can do to stop them. In the end, the students will always find a way around you." I can't say I found his comments too comforting.

But just as had been true in the States, for every student whose actions distressed me, there were so many others who impressed me daily with their talents and knowledge, thoughts and dreams, humor, curiosity, and personalities. For a place like Isfahan University of Technology, which claimed its share of the country's top minds in science, agriculture, and engineering, it also revealed a population with a whole other range of giftedness.

I remember the strapping and self-assured engineering student who appeared in my office one day. He had come to borrow a handbook of mine on how to prepare for standardized testing in

English. At some point after I handed it over, he asked to see a photo of my children. Although his request surprised me (he didn't strike me as "the sentimental type"), I pulled out a recent photo of Niki, who at the time was all of three months old. The student studied it closely for nearly a minute, returned the photo, thanked me, and left. Two days later he returned, presenting me with a tender portrait of Niki—a stunning likeness in watercolor, accented in exquisite shades of blue. It found a special place on our bedroom wall. But I didn't see my handbook after that!

***

Another surprising display of student talent would come after two of Mahmoud's agricultural engineering students asked for the chance to entertain us with a small recital of Persian classical music. They had wanted to thank him, they explained, for "always being there for the students." I thought back to the day of a recent protest on campus when students had blocked entry to parts of the university due to some unresolved grievances tied to food service limitations and other issues. That same day, some of the students approached Mahmoud, asking if he'd take their concerns to administration. Mahmoud agreed—and did so in a way that all parties felt respected. Now, several weeks later at the end of the term, this small recital in our home would allow for an intimate way to say *thank you* to both Mahmoud the professor and Mahmoud the man. We invited a small circle of students and colleagues, and I even cooked dinner myself. Excited and nervous, I looked forward to meeting the students who had chosen to honor my husband in this way.

Imagine my surprise when, upon opening the door, I saw two familiar figures standing at the entrance. These young men happened to be former students of *mine* as well, having completed "English for Agricultural Students" in the past semester! They greeted me brightly with smiling eyes, cradling classical instruments of Iran in their arms.

After a casual period of food, conversation, and laughter, the students pulled out their instruments and assumed silent, reflective poses. One was gently embracing the *setar*, a handheld lute with a mystical voice. The other balanced the hollow *tombak*, a drum-like instrument, between his legs. Taking our cues from these young musicians, the rest of us quietly chose our places, forming a circle on the carpet around the room. In those moments before the first notes were struck, the air throbbed with anticipation, awaiting the sound of an ancient past.

It made its entrance in graceful tremors, against a soft and resonant pulse. The tremors arose from the strings of the setar, the hypnotic dark pulse from the tones of the tombak. Sometimes, their voices merged and blended, and sometimes they played against each other. The alternate sounds of swelling and silence lured us in steadily like a tidal wave, then suddenly carried us off to who knows where. And although the sounds were far from Western, something about them pulled at my heartstrings, like a familiar voice that I couldn't quite place.

My heart was still full when our guests said goodbye. Forgetting myself, I reached out to our student musicians, to take their hands in mine. As soon as I did, they both shrank back with startled eyes. In my moment of abandon, I had forgotten how reaching across genders could lead to confusion, precisely as it just had.

What could I do to recover the moment? Deeply embarrassed and as startled as they were, I reached out a second time, hoping they'd reconsider taking my hand. But no, the conviction of their faith and their respect for my husband simply did not allow them.

I took a breath and steadied myself. Then, looking from one young man to the other, I laid a hand on my heart for each of them. In an instant, bright smiles lit their faces again, and they bowed their heads and responded in kind. Grateful to see their comfort restored, I stood at the doorway beside my husband as we bid them good night, a night that closed as warmly as it had begun.

But I would have loved to overhear their conversation about me, this quizzical American teacher of theirs, once they slipped into their car, shut the door, and drove off!

Chapter Twenty-Five

Reflections on Women and Feminine Beauty

For some time before my first trip to Iran, including that time with those haunting dreams, it had not escaped my attention that affronts like "Death to America" and references to America as "The Great Satan" were circulating in Iran. I also realized that back in America, things were being said about Iran (like "terrorist," "fanatical," or "axis of evil") that were equally outrageous. Even so, I couldn't help but wonder how I would fare as one of a few scattered American citizens in the country (as compared to the 41,000 or so Americans living in Iran right before the revolution) once people discovered my country of origin. I decided it wouldn't be a bad idea for me to keep a low profile with my appearance—not only to honor my understanding of Islamic standards of modesty, but also to avoid standing out as an American in Iran. I soon learned from both my Iranian family and others who had my best interests at heart that making myself as inconspicuous as possible would not always result in my going unnoticed. In fact, it often ended up having the opposite effect. How was it that in the very country where I thought I'd have to give up the "flamenco dancer" in me, there would be plenty of people to remind me not to neglect her drama, her vitality, her flair and sense of style?

My two female colleagues from their Language Center were not the only ones who saw me as a candidate for their beauty tips and interventions. There had also been Fatimeh Dadashi, the physical education director from my conversation class, who'd walked and whittled me back into physical shape. Of course, there was my Iranian family too. In the spirit of helpfulness, one day my mother-in-law took it upon herself to mix a concoction of natural henna root powder and water and apply its magic to my hair.

It was a long and laborious process, mostly for Mamán—and yes, it turned my hair a deep orange. There was also Ali's wife Ashraf, the skilled beautician and natural beauty who frequently focused her attention on me. Up till then, I hadn't understood how some Iranian women take the familiar notion of suffering for the sake of beauty to new heights. The popular Persian phrase, *"Mano bekosh, vali khoshgelam kon."* ("Kill me, but make me beautiful.") summed it up well.

I still remember my first experience of a "deluxe facial," Persian style, compliments of Ashraf. I could have said "no," and I *wanted* to say "no," but I didn't know how to without risking offending her. So, armed with a pair of tweezers, a tiny pair of scissors and a strand of thread (or *band*) held tautly in her hands, my stunning young sister-in-law bent over me, gently asking me to lie still with my head on a pillow. Then, for several minutes of dogged determination, painstaking patience, and precision, she sculpted my historically sparse and scattered eyebrows into a perfect shape never before realized on my face.

Unfortunately, the pain was also exquisite, making my eyes steep with tears, but Ashraf's work with me had just begun. All the while coaxing me on with sweet tones ("Leslie … Leslie Jan … just lie still for a little longer … okay? *Afareen!*"), she proceeded to apply the relentless rolling pressure of the taut thread across the entire surface of my face, stripping and mowing away any trace of surface skin cells or microscopic hairs. The other female members of my family, who of course had the eyes to recognize the process, told me how beautifully my face "glowed" after undergoing the "band." From the way I was feeling inside my skin at the time, I didn't doubt it.

Evidently, the issue of attaining and maintaining beauty was serious business among women in Iran; it had been for thousands of years. One look at classical illustrations of Persians from centuries past confirms a longstanding penchant for pleasing form, line, and color in both their garments and the adornment of the face. How, then, had I overlooked all those cues that might have changed the way I presented myself to the Iranian public eye? It's not as if I'd never seen those finely made-up faces on my first flight to Iran or at the Language Center, the fashion flair of the "beautiful people" in my neighborhood, the meticulously sculpted hands and nails of family, neighbors, and friends, the intricate gold ornaments that hung from the necks, earlobes, and wrists of women everywhere. There was no denying that some of the most exquisite and feminine jewelry and clothing I owned came from the generous hands of Iranian women. So, what was it that kept it all from registering, that kept me locked in some understated, under-glamorized mode of appearance? What kept me from recognizing this thriving presence of feminine glamour all around, inviting me to come out of the mothballs and maybe cultivate some for myself?

I don't know whether it was just me or my Western eyes, but for my first months in Iran, the presence of a chador or manteau and scarf on a woman kept me from noticing much of anything else about her physically. To my understanding, these outer garments were meant to function as a kind of shroud, serving to mask a woman's beauty. With this notion so firmly entrenched, these garments struck me as a kind of uniform, where I perceived one garment as basically the same as the next and one woman's image fairly indistinguishable from another's. As long as this picture shaped my thinking, I unconsciously strove to maintain the same nondescript image of myself.

It wasn't until I gave in to trading my familiar green coat for a new one in Tehran that I began to see all the variations that factored into the design of a manteau. The day I went to the shop with Badri, she carefully thumbed her way through several racks, thinking "chic," "sharp," and "professional" on behalf of her American sister-in-law, the university professor. After thirty minutes or so, I left the store wearing the model Badri had recommended: a black manteau in a crisp and lightweight finished cotton. It gently hugged my waist and flared gracefully at the hem around my ankles, and the lining of its generously cut collar and cuffs sported a smart black-on-gray plaid design. When I modeled my coat to the other sisters, they chirped and fussed over me, praising Badri's selection and spending several fascinating minutes gently showing me the difference between merely *putting on* a scarf and artfully *draping* it into something stylish.

As we tinkered with our collars and buttons, making the most of the outer package, I realized I'd come to a subtle shift in my relationship with the manteau or hijab in general. It's not that I felt better about having to wear it or that I wouldn't have welcomed the chance to opt out. But it had far less to do with my sense of womanhood or overall happiness than I'd figured initially.

I'd observed so many Iranian women around me—my family, neighbors, students, friends—each one, no doubt, with her own thoughts on hijab. Every day I would see them going about their business, expressing their feminine style and vitality. And from time to time, I'd tell myself that wearing the manteau was a small price to pay for the privilege of living among them. Perhaps one day I'd find the courage to ask some of them to share their perspectives on hijab with me. But I'd need to hold off till my own fears and struggles with hijab weren't so easy to see through, I thought.

Even so, from the day I put on my new manteau, my eyes began to discern the details and distinguishing traits of all manner of fashion—just as my eyes had started noticing the subtle spectrum of color in a mountain range that had once seemed only brown or gray. As I started noticing clothing designs, I saw just how attentively women would "dress" their faces to match, from the flowing lines adorning their lids to their perfectly cut and fashioned eyebrows. Secretly proud to now carry a pair of my own (compliments of Ashraf), I thought back fondly on a favorite Persian love poem Mahmoud had often wooed me with in our courtship days, an homage to the arresting power of a single brow:

The executioner's blade
is sharply curved.
So is the eyebrow of my beloved.
Both cut till you bleed—
But oh! The difference in how
this one cuts
and that one cuts!

[Translated version, Poet Unknown]

Ashraf did more than reform my eyebrows and scale my face. With the wielding power of her pencils and powders, lipsticks and liners, hairbrush, and ornaments, she'd treat me to the best of her masterful arts. Some of the looks I liked more than others, but under her hand, there were magical moments when I felt my most beautiful.

I remember lying in my bed one night, sorting through my reflections on the nature of beauty in Iran. For me, the fascination lay in the point that, just as in the States, "modesty" was not necessarily equated with the absence of beauty. Rather, beauty could be showcased as art while still presented within a modest frame.

Of course, there were varying opinions on this point in Iran. In our own huge family on any given day, you could spot quite a range of "preferred presentations" among the women—from the platinum blonde cousin with the heavy black eyeliner to the scarf-clad aunt with the faded lipstick. But my friend Behrang (the first university student I met) once told me that according to the teachings of the holy Qur'an, modesty wasn't so much a focus on prescribed rules of presentation as on the kindness of the inner person. It was a concept I'd also heard from the Bible, emphasizing the "hidden beauty of the heart" over outer adornment.

This concept also corresponded with my earliest memories of lessons on beauty, as spoken by Mom to her three young daughters when she was in her early thirties. At four years old, I didn't much notice my mom's natural beauty—she was just "Mom." But she had a way with words to get her points across about beauty to her little ones:

"You never want to wear a dress," she said, "that's so loud and fancy that people will say 'Hello, Dress! Where are you going with that girl?' Instead, you want to wear a dress—or choose makeup—where people will see *you* and say 'Hello, Girl! Aren't you just lovely!'" Down the road, she would also remind me what my namesake, Black American entertainer of the sixties Leslie Uggams, had mentioned in the *Leslie Uggams Beauty Book*: "Just because one dab of perfume is alluring, it doesn't mean five dabs of perfume are five times more alluring!"

Mom practiced what she preached. I vaguely remember how, back in the day, she liked to wear clothing with solid colors, classic cuts, and a special flair here and there. And as for makeup, I can't remember a time she displayed much more than a well-sculpted brow or a pretty shade of red on her beautifully curved lips. It wasn't until I was a young woman myself and Mom was in her fifties that I recognized how stunning she was.

I believe her perspective on beauty influenced all three of her daughters. Pat, with her stylish fashions, light strokes of makeup, and softly swept hairstyles, was the queen of elegance. And when she traded some elegance for edginess with her afros, dashikis, and earrings during the Black power era of the seventies, she looked just as great. And Sylvia, a fresh-faced beauty with her flowing skirts, embroidered blouses, and no makeup at all, attracted people and suitors with her vibrancy and kindness.

As for me, while fashion in clothing rarely captured my interest, I was the one among the three of us who pushed the boundaries most when it came to experimenting with cosmetics and different looks. I'm grateful that during my teenage years Mom was tolerant of my makeup choices: the off-white eyeliner that went gummy by the end of day, the pastel shades of blue and green I smudged a little too generously onto my lids with my finger, the overly-orange blush on my cheeks. Then again, whenever I asked her opinion, she would always tell it to me straight.

Eventually I stopped asking and decided to recalibrate on my own. However, I was always fascinated enough with the transformative power of makeup to be open to others' interventions—from the beauty consultant at Macy's cosmetic counter to Ashraf, who felt confident in her expertise.

On Identity and Being Black American in Iran

Other notions and practices I discovered in Iran around beauty were less settling and harder to reckon with. When handing out makeup items for family members while visiting from abroad, I noticed that, despite the wide range of complexion tones among the women in our family, nearly everyone seemed to prefer the paler foundation shades to the deeper-toned ones. One day, when one of Mahmoud's sisters selected a foundation that I thought was several shades too light for her, I asked her about it.

"Parvin, have you ever considered choosing a shade that matches your own natural skin tone—you know, something that might blend in better, and maybe enhance your own pretty color?"

"Oh no," she explained without hesitating. "For fancy occasions, we generally like to use 'pancake' on our faces. It helps show off the eye and lip color more dramatically."

"Pancake?" I paused, thinking back on times I had seen Parvin and other family members just before leaving for a wedding or some other festivity. Suddenly I remembered the look she was referring to: faces "set" in a combination of milk-white pressed powder, dark eyeliner and bright lip tones that made for a porcelain doll effect.

"Don't you all do the same in America?" Parvin asked.

"Not really," I answered. "At least not that I've noticed. Generally, women try to find a color that matches their own skin tone. That means a light foundation for women with light-toned complexions and a darker foundation for women with dark-toned complexions. And for Black women like me, there are now special lines of foundations."

Parvin looked at me contemplatively.

"So, then, you would describe yourself as 'black'?"

"Well, of course I would," I answered tightly, trying to hold on to my wits and see where the conversation was going.

"Because looking at you, many might describe you as what we call *sabze*—maybe more 'olive-skinned' than 'black.'"

I was not prepared for the moment; I had not really expected to have a conversation with my Iranian family about race. Following the revolution, Americans were so few and far between in Iran that my nationality alone grabbed people's attention, with skin color perhaps a secondary factor. Besides that, the topic of race was not something I heard people talk about. Not because it was a social taboo, but rather because race as a concept was not fully developed—at least not compared to the States. Yet here we were, talking about skin color. It was the first time I remembered having had such a conversation, although, yes, I was the one who had brought up the topic.

But as I studied Parvin's face, I began to realize we were talking on two entirely different planes, and on two different levels of emotional energy. Parvin was talking about the use of language to describe *color at face value,* in terms of shade alone. I, in contrast, had taken her reference to my skin tone as a gauge of not only my racial heritage, but also of my racial identity and pride. I'd experienced conversations of that nature back in the States, both in and outside of the Black community, and could still feel the battle scars of times I or others had been designated "in" or "out" by someone else's criteria. I never understood why we as Black people did such things to each other, consciously or unconsciously. I did remember how Mom used to reference Jesus' words on the futility of "a kingdom divided against itself."

"That may be so, Parvin," I said carefully, "but I still prefer to call myself 'Black.'"

Parvin considered me quietly again, and then said, "I see." But *did* she see in precisely the same way as I did, with the same measure of passion, history, and social significance attached to concepts and conversations around race? I wasn't so sure, but even if she didn't, her face now registered a dawning awareness that I had just said something important, something perhaps worth talking about sometime soon. As for me, I wondered if I had the language skills to navigate such a complex conversation on what it meant for me and so many to be Black in America. Over time, I would learn, and my efforts were rewarded by listening ears.

At any rate, I noticed she didn't refer to me as "sabze" after that. Nor do I recall a future dress-up occasion when she or any of the other sisters dressed their faces with white pancake powder, or again achieved a similar effect. Deliberate? Coincidental? As attentive as Parvin and the sisters were, I like to think it was.

It wasn't the last time I'd have conversations with people that touched on issues of color. When Nikiar was born, his complexion looked more like his father's, while Parisa's complexion looked more like her mother's. When the topic came up in conversation one day, Baba, with a relaxed smile, explained the contrast between Niki's and Parisa's skin tones as likely an act of "divine justice," where God might have seen it as only "fair" that one child would take after the mother and the other after the father in this respect. We laughed appreciatively at Baba's witty analysis, and nothing more was said about it. At least not then.

But when the older of the two "Mrs. Aghaees" was tending to Niki one day, she casually suggested to me, intending to be helpful for all I know, that if Parisa and I ate more apples, our skin "might get lighter, like Niki's." I bristled, telling her it wasn't my goal for either me or my daughter to turn lighter. So, she simply shrugged and went back to business with Niki and housework. But with Parisa there, listening quietly in the room, the damaging seed had already been planted.

I do not remember exactly when four-year-old Parisa told me, "Mommy, I want to be white," or whether it happened before or after that moment with Mrs. Aghaee. Whenever it was, her words sliced through my heart like a razor. How much had she heard or experienced *here*, of all places, to come to that painful conclusion? Had I been so naïve as to think that in Iran my children would be safely removed from the burden of being assessed by skin color, from absorbing a world where (just as in America) lighter was somehow better? A world where Parisa, her brother, and her mother would likely be in spaces where they'd be "the only ones" (i.e., the only Blacks among non-Black people)?

Evidently, my telling Parisa how pretty she was, singing her special love songs at night ("*I Like You as You Are*," or "*Parisa … I just met a girl named Parisa …*,") and tucking her in nightly with her pretty Black dolls hadn't reached far enough to take root in her heart, to counteract her discomfort with what she wasn't. Her sweet, rounded nose, plump lips, nut-brown complexion, thick black spirals—none of which closely matched her cousins' features—needed to be celebrated. Every day. And Niki's features needed to be celebrated too. Not that the sweeping lashes of Parisa's eyes or Niki's wavy brown hair from their *father's* side weren't equally worthy of being celebrated. But if I could have turned the clock back to redo *just one thing* when making the move, I'd have scoured the bookstores for more picture books besides just *The Snowy Day* (Ezra Jack Keats) and *Molly the Brave and Me* (Jane O'Connor): the kind of books with kids in the story who looked like Parisa and Niki. Kids whose presence on the pages confirmed to the children that they counted too. Unfortunately, those books I was thinking of were out of reach, away in America. Not much help to us here.

It was my feeling embraced in a new community, the range of rich skin tones in the people around me, Mahmoud's affinity with the Black kids in Newark neighborhoods (where he used to sell Italian ices in the summer), and his longstanding attention to race issues in America even while he was living in Iran—that had led me to view Iranians as fellow "people of color." But it was too simplistic of me to presume that Iranians necessarily identified as people of color.

First, the term Iranian traces back to the root word *Aryan*—historically linked to a Caucasian, Indo-European genealogy—so other lines of Iranian ancestry are simply not reflected in the term.

Second, the concepts of race and racial identity were not a developed part of Iran's national consciousness or discussion, nor was the notion of "minority pride" acknowledged in Iran the same way as in America. Finally, the fact that Iran had once had its own Black, White, and Indigenous slave trade from 1500-1900—and that consequently, a separate community of Afro-Iranians in southern Iran represented roughly ten percent of the total population—was neither widely known of nor commonly discussed (I didn't know myself), even in Iran. And at the time, there were no known initiatives for Black Iranians to be affirmed as part of the Iranian demographic. Perhaps my blanket view of Iranians as fellow "people of color" was a product of my own wishful thinking.

Even so, there were *also* Iranians, in both Iran and America, who empathized with the struggles of Black people in the USA. Some did identify as people of color, supporting a common cause of freedom from prejudice and political or psychological suppression.

I remember when one of Mahmoud's older nephews, then in his mid-twenties, asked me to share my memories of the civil rights movement in the United States, particularly during the sixties. As soon as I began talking, it was clear he already knew many of the key details, events, and people involved—from Rosa Parks to Malcolm X, to Stokely Carmichael, to Dr. Martin Luther King Jr., to world boxing champion converted to Islam, Muhammad Ali. What I didn't bring up, what I couldn't find words for, was my black-and-white TV memories as a nine-year-old of the hosing, the clubbing, the lunging police dogs tearing at peacefully protesting Black folk at the civil rights marches—while my parents, sisters, and I watched together in shock. To my nine-year-old memory, the lunging dogs were the worst images of all. To talk about them would be like pulling a scab off a crusted wound.

My nephew interrupted that private replay in my mind when he asked if I realized that during the Iranian hostage crisis, the Black hostages were among the first ones released, that the gesture had been made to acknowledge the struggle Blacks faced in

America. I nodded in silence, not ready to say more. While I appreciated that expression of support toward Black Americans, I would not have wished for a longer sentence of captivity on any of my fellow Americans, Black or otherwise.

Years later, in the summer of 2008 when we were visiting Iran from the States, I could also feel a general furor and enthusiasm not only in my Iranian family, but in the whole country about this young, eloquent, and idealistic presidential candidate named Barack Obama, and the fact that he was also Black American. Mamán, in particular, was taken by the energy and warmth she saw in him, and also by his "radiant smile." For some, it didn't hurt that his name "Barack" came from a Semitic root they recognized as meaning "blessing." Then again, not every Iranian was on the same page regarding Mr. Obama. I had already come to discover starkly contrasting political leanings among members of my Iranian family on American politics. At the same time, given the well-known occurrence of Black oppression in American history, all the Iranians who spoke to me about Obama seemed to give points to America for ultimately voting in a Black American president. Did my being Black play a role in their remarks to me about Obama, or was there a heartfelt affinity there? I can only guess.

***

But what about me and my own Black identity? How could I stay connected with this integral part of me? What would I need to do to keep it alive in the total absence of a Black community?

I soon realized that regardless of whatever fear I felt of losing touch with this part of me, being Black was inseparable from who I was, how I saw myself, and the experiences and people who had shaped me. Not that I was consciously thinking of myself in terms of my race, no more than I did of my age or my gender identity. But while I wasn't keeping a pulse on my Blackness, the imprint of my lifetime as a Black American did its own thing in *me*—bubbling to the surface, nudging, or swelling with emotion, usually when something external awakened or triggered it:

Like when I looked in the mirror and saw my sisters' features reflected in mine.

Like when I ran out of my Black hair care products from the States and could find no local products to make my hair bouncy, hydrated, and happy. (I finally figured it out, though, when my nephew Mohammed offered me some of his coconut oil!)

Like when Mahmoud would introduce me to guests and be asked at some point, "Is she biracial? (*"Do-rag-ast?"*), as if I weren't present to speak for myself.

Like the day I learned that blackface performances were an antiquated but ongoing tradition in some Iranian festivities.

Like when one day after class, an atypically older student in army clothes asked me flatly in English, his eyes confronting mine, "So, are you one of those 'high-yellow' (light-skinned) Blacks?" While he did get a rise out of me (which I tried my best to conceal), he also struck me as troubled and angry—with me, with the world, with who knew what—so I let it go. "*But, where on earth did he pick up that term?*" I wondered, "*Certainly not in Iran.*" I had not heard that label in twenty years; the first and last time I had heard it was from Mom, when I was a teenager. It was a particularly offensive term for her, Mom had confided; in high school she'd been taunted with that label and others, by members of both White and Black races, for the exceptionally light complexion she had no choice in being born with.

Like when Mahmoud recounted a scene at the flea market—the time when an unfamiliar woman approached him surreptitiously and asked him the question (referring to me), "Why did you choose *her* when you could have married a blonde?" His answer: "I chose her because she was the one I wanted." End of discussion.

Like when a friend or family member would align their arm with mine and point out how our skin colors were nearly a match, leaving me with mixed feelings. In the States, I used to feel uneasy and awkward when a White friend would try to "equate" us by doing the same, as if skin color were the only factor for resolving racial inequities in America. In Iran, I felt even less sure of what comparing our skin tones meant to the person making the comparison.

Like when I got no acknowledging glance of a shared racial heritage in response to mine from Farideh Khanum, the Black Iranian teacher at the kuee's daycare center.

And especially when I saw the impact of a careless word or action directed toward my children due to their complexion or features, and I didn't know how to fix it for them.

I had experienced moments like these in one form or another as a familiar component of being Black in America. It was something I'd learned to accept and manage there, to prevent it from derailing me from my self-esteem or long-term goals. But when I relocated to Iran, I was somehow unprepared to deal with similar moments in a different setting, where I wasn't as sure of the cultural context or the nuance of words. Besides, I wanted to believe that a population like Iranians, commonly subject to other peoples' prejudice and misconceptions, would not fall into discriminating attitudes themselves. How quickly I had forgotten that even I as a person of color had secretly battled my own fears and notions about Iran. But in the end, it was my consciousness as a Black American that would catch me in the act and hold me accountable whenever I started making assumptions about Iranians or any other group of people.

In any case, I realized that if not racial prejudice per se, *colorism* would be an issue I'd face in Iran—I, my children, and my darker-skinned Iranian relatives. It wouldn't prevent me from appreciating my life there or the special people who had mostly been kind to me, but it wouldn't shield me or the children from its presence or impact as part of life there, even as it was in America and other parts of the world.

Nevertheless, there were things in Iran reminiscent of my

girlhood days with extended family in Cleveland, Ohio, especially on social occasions. The free-flowing laughter over practically anything. The gestures that came with a good, raucous story. The jubilant spirit of Black folk dancing. And the endless stream of aunts, uncles, cousins, and other relatives whenever we all got together. While Cleveland's tempting smells were of grits, biscuits, eggs, and bacon, and Iran's were of sizzling kababs and rice, it was all about being part of a big, vivacious family that created a space for "home" in both worlds.

There were other times my heart would also fill up in Iran—like when I'd sing and play my guitar to the tune of spirituals, gospel pieces, or other traditional songs by Black composers. I could be alone, or it could be a precious moment when I was invited to *Share a song from your culture, Leslie Khanum*—as I was by family members, as I was by the ladies in my conversation class, as I was by "the beautiful people" in the kuee. If God has given me any gift, it is the ability to be transported and connected spiritually through song. So, when I played certain numbers, they would often take me back to my college years at Twelfth Baptist Church, a historic Black church in Roxbury, Massachusetts, under the impassioned leadership of Reverend Doctor Michael E. Haynes. There was also Bette Jo, her sister Nora, and their parents, Deacon and Mrs. Tony—my doting city family away from home. There was Gene, my first official sweetheart, and Oscar, one of Gene's best friends who was as close as a brother to me. In song, I could instantly reconnect with them and all the church body, unrestricted by barriers of time and space. I could almost smell the cornbread and the seasoned collards simmering, awaiting us from the basement after Sunday worship. Or I could hear chicken frying in the Tonys' kitchen on afternoons when I hung out with them.

When I finished singing and opened my eyes, I was back in Iran—my heart revived and my spirit fed—with my Iranian friends and family, applauding, nodding, smiling, and welcoming me back. One or two people would even have tears in their eyes.

Of course, reconnecting with my Black church community in Boston by closing my eyes and imagining could never be a substitute for enjoying a current, ongoing, face-to-face fellowship with people who looked like me and shared common experiences. So, as much as I loved my Iranian family and took joy in their affection—and I did—the absence of Black relationships was still a loss I was living with. And, well, "forever" would be a long time to do without.

Chapter Twenty-Seven

Other Observations as "an American in General"

There was more to take in of this fascinating county than through my eyes as a Black American alone. For one thing, I had *other* discussions and observations about color in Iran that had nothing to do with race. While not as "deep" as those that touched on racial issues, they were just as interesting in their own way to my "American in general" self, who had been born and raised in the USA.

I was continually intrigued by the number of women who, despite having to cover their hair in public, changed their hair color as frequently as they might buy a new pair of shoes to match an outfit. I remember Esmat's fun-loving sister Effat, whom we would see at family gatherings every few months in Tehran or the village. It seemed that every time I saw her, she was sporting a different hair color—sometimes brown, sometimes black, sometimes strawberry blonde. In the back of my mind, I wondered when she'd finally decide on the shade that suited her best, and one day, out of curiosity, I just asked her.

"Why do I have to make up my mind?" she asked me, surprised, in a good-natured voice, "Why can't I just be dark-haired in winter, blonde in the spring … and maybe something else in between? The operative word is 'variety (*tanavo*),' Leslie! That's what makes life, and fashion, fun!"

I suppose that in my American-leaning way of thinking ("American-leaning" at least at that time), I carried a notion that there was probably a "perfect hair shade" (maybe two at the most) to go with each person's coloring—and that the "beauty challenge" for those who were interested was to go out and find it. I had never thought of hair color as a kind of fashion accessory that could change with the season, match your wardrobe, or just be different for the sheer fun of it. The funny thing was that, after seeing Effat's "switches" from shade to shade a few times, I couldn't decide which "look" suited her, either. She was starting to look good in all of them! And as I started noticing how many hair shades were circulating among Iranian women, and how many of them probably came from a bottle, I discovered that just about any hair color on a woman was game for fashion—that is, any color except for gray. Over time, however, as I reached my salt-and-pepper years, I learned a way to redirect a conversation with a well-meaning sister-in-law who suggested I cover my gray. All I had to do was point to my husband's glorious natural silver-gray highlights and declare triumphantly, "But we're a set!" They'd laugh at my mock self-righteousness and admit they had to agree. Maybe it would just be a matter of time before gray also counted as "*tanavo*"?

***

Finally, as a U.S. American, I was fascinated by how a former thriving U.S. presence had left its ghosts and footprints behind, despite the near zero visibility of American nationals in Iran during the early to mid 90s. Signs and displays printed in English populated the streets and shops of every urban area, from major cities like Tehran and Isfahan to the smaller neighboring towns. If it hadn't been for all the chipped paint and faded signs, you might have thought the Americans and Europeans had never left. What's more, on the shelves of some of those shops were products whose names, save a missing letter or two, bore a striking resemblance to popular brands in the States: a fragrance called "*Charle*," a facial cream in a dark-blue jar marked "*Nozema*," mascara in a familiar-looking pink and green tube labeled "*Mabeline*." Other unexpected "ghosts" in other forms and voices could also show up anywhere, like the day I heard a wordless version of the passionate Tom Jones' hit of the sixties, "Delilah," blasting from the airwaves of a Tehrani radio station.

At first, I couldn't make sense of it. If sometimes I felt Iran was a space for Americans to creep through cautiously and unnoticed, at least when in public, then why these surprises at every turn? What was it that led people to reach out so frequently to me? There were always the acknowledging nods from folks in the street, the gracious assistance at shops or the airport, the steady invitations to people's homes, the good-natured questions on American popular culture. Judging from all the teens in our family, with their well-kept collections of posters and music by Michael Jackson, José Feliciano, Jim Morrison, and The Doors (unearthed from who knows where), it appeared that my young nephews and nieces knew far more of the works, the lyrics, and the lives of these artists than I did.

When it came to the university, I could walk through the campus on the anniversary of the revolution and be greeted warmly by students, with their hands on their hearts, on their way to a "Death to America" rally.

Throughout the four years I lived in Iran, it seemed that the Iranians I knew had little problem distinguishing between the politics and the people of the USA. I have always been deeply grateful for their ability to do so. What accounted for their generosity of spirit toward me or other Americans, I could only guess. Was it an interest in and curiosity about American people, who were way out of reach most of the time? Was it because they noticed how hard I was trying to "do as the Persians do"? Was it because they'd taken to heart the Qur'an's teaching to always show kindness to foreigners? Or were they simply doing what came to them naturally, in light of a legacy of Persian hospitality?

Whatever it was in that spirit of generosity, it managed to reach me, melting my fears and slowly transforming my way of seeing things. It struck me one day in a single moment when a sister of Mahmoud stepped out to greet me. Once I had cringed at the sight of a dark flowing garment, but that phase was gone, a thing of my past. Now, among my most beautiful and heartwarming sights was Badri's unmade-up face in her black chador, smiling her kind and radiant smile.

Chapter Twenty-Eight

"Something in the Air"

It was the day from hell and from heaven.

For sure, it was inexcusably hot and no day to be in a car (*And, I grumbled to myself, having to wear a manteau on top of it all doesn't help*). Unfortunately, that was the only way we were going to get to the "perfect picnic spot" that Dr. Ali had promised to find us "somewhere outside of Isfahan."

Without the benefit of the slightest breeze, we (a dated car and our newly acquired jeep, each carrying an assorted mix of two families), rambled along what seemed to be an endless stretch of dusty road. One family consisted of Ali Hamidi (or "Dr. Ali"), Mahmoud's colleague from the university; Janet, Ali's wife from England and my spunky confidante from the kuee; and the couple's two sons and two daughters, ages thirteen, eleven, eight, and five. The other family was ours: Mahmoud, Parisa, who was only three at the time, and I, who at five months pregnant, was both showing and feeling it. Imprisoned in our deluxe car-shaped ovens, we were practically melding together in our own juices like a fine Persian stew of meat and bitter lemons.

On either side of the road lay endless stretches of parched ground dotted with tufts of stubborn grass poking through the cracks—not exactly your scenic view. The unchanging scenery, mile after mile, added to our misery, leaving us with the illusion that we were making no headway toward reaching the promised land. But no matter; there was nothing to do at that point but to bump along for what felt like hours and hours.

Finally, we arrived at "the spot"—an oasis of four knotted trees that squared off a small plot of shady and slightly greener land just down the roadside.

The vehicle doors swung wide open, and out we piled in various stages of disarray. Even the still, hot air was a welcome relief from the intense heat of the crowded car chambers. With renewed energy and eyes on our destination, we trudged down the shoulder of the road loaded with blankets, pails of food, and picnic equipment. Not ten minutes later, we were seated on blankets under the shade on a small patch of paradise, chatting while enjoying a delicious sandwich lunch and each other's company.

We were blissfully unaware of the signs that nature offered us, stealthily accumulating around and above our heads in the form of fidgety, sporadic air currents and a strange yellow cast filling the sky.

As if she knew something the rest of us didn't, three-year-old Parisa broke away from our circle, jubilantly running up a nearby hill and laughing fiendishly as she went. As we watched her clamber up on chubby legs, our eyes suddenly met with the sky, now fully swollen with an eerie, yellow-brown light. Something Big and Lofty was coming from a distance; I just didn't know what.

Moments later It was upon us: the full-blown fury of a sandstorm. Wind, sand, and dust unleashed their stinging rage on our arms and legs, then into our eyes, mouths, and nostrils. At the same time, a grainy blur of deep brown blinded the earth and sky with a jolting and terrifying force. I lost all sense of time and space and could see no one. I could only hear the startled, stifled voices of my companions. Among them was Mahmoud's, bellowing his daughter's and wife's names.

But, fighting to keep my balance, my bearings, and my wits, I shielded my face with my arms and began bulldozing my way up the hill to find Parisa. I could almost hear my own heart pounding until I suddenly heard myself screaming, "PAR-EEEEEEEE …!"

Grit instantly invaded my tongue. Was it filling up Parisa's lungs too? Was she a little heap thrown on the ground somewhere, unable even to whimper for help? What if the wind had knocked her over and slammed her head against a rock? How could nature be so cruel? My panic swelled wilder than any sandstorm.

But terror gave way to indescribable joy and relief when I

caught a glimpse of Parisa's tiny figure, fairly flying down the hill toward me. In a paradoxical moment of generosity, the sandstorm had been kind, propelling Parisa toward her mom, straight into my open arms. I clasped her against my pregnant belly and released a wordless groan of thanks from a deep place inside me.

Seconds later I felt a firm hand curl around my waist, pulling me against a body covered in grit. It was Mahmoud, who seemed to have come out of nowhere to reclaim and shelter his daughter and me. *How was it that, once again, he appeared at such a right moment?* Things like that often happened with Mahmoud, somehow.

***

Apparently satisfied with the work it had done, the sandstorm then disappeared as quickly and mysteriously as it had come. The sky returned to its natural blue luster, and the sun was suddenly back again, pointing us out to each other in all our disheveled glory. A comb would have been nice at this point, and everyone and everything were dusted with a thin layer of sand and grit. But thank God, we were safe.

It took several minutes to clean up the mess the storm had left behind. Not surprisingly, several of the china plates and glass cups that Janet had brought were shattered, and all of them were filled or coated with sand. The ever-resourceful Janet, who always knew what to say and do, filled a basin with one of the water jugs she had brought and set us all to work. Soon, every jagged fragment had been collected, every dirty cup and plate washed, every blanket shaken out and tidily laid back in place. Once again, we were seated upon them, holding the steaming warmth of brimming hot teacups in our hands for some badly needed comfort.

Seeking to recover equilibrium each in our own way, some of us chattered endlessly, comparing facts and feelings about the sandstorm. Others, I included, just sat quietly, sucking on sugar cubes and nursing our tea. In any event, we were soon to discover we weren't the only ones who had been affected by the strange, surreal act of nature.

While sitting quietly on the ground, I noticed something unusual. It was all happening so fast, or perhaps my mind was still in the fog of the sandstorm frenzy. But just a few feet away, something was rapidly making its way toward me—something silent, something black, something sinuous and undulating ...

In Iran, many report that much, if not most of its snake population is venomous. Furthermore, they say, the venom of snakes that dwell in the sandy regions, where water is short, tends to be all the more potent. I had already heard strange stories from Mahmoud's family about snakes. Baba had shared firsthand reports of snakes that had made their way into jeeps, as if to seek vengeance after being glanced by rocks. Of snakes, posed and ready to strike in the shadows of caves where family members were wandering.

But back on my patch of paradise, I suddenly recognized two things: (1) chances were it was a venomous snake, and (2) I was sitting directly in its path. Whether it was denial, disorientation, paralysis from fear, resignation, or the plain lethargy of a woman five months pregnant that kept me firmly planted on the ground, I cannot say. As if I had been posing for the most suspenseful, most bizarre moment of a horror film, I sat immobilized, quietly observing the creature head straight toward me. Seconds later it slithered under the hem of my green cotton manteau (which I happened to be wearing at the time) and disappeared out of sight.

In a remote part of my brain, I could hear my companions begging me at the top of their lungs to jump to my feet. Their screaming, however, was of no assistance and to absolutely no avail. After all, presumably *they* didn't have a snake slithering somewhere on *their* body, much less with an unborn baby nearby.

I was utterly alone in this moment of decision: i.e., whether to stand to my feet and risk agitating the snake to attack, or to stay seated and risk giving the snake more time to think about it. The weight of my decision was heightened all the more by my awareness that an innocent life was growing inside of me.

It wouldn't be exactly accurate for me to say that, after what seemed an eternity of considering my two options, I finally jumped to my feet. It was more like I rocked and shimmied and wig-wagged my way up (If you've never been pregnant, you just can't understand.)

As if the invisible director of my fantasy film had planned to heighten the suspense, the snake cooperated by *not* falling right out as expected. It took its own sweet time, a good seven or eight seconds if not more. I'll never know what it was doing there or how it managed to escape the pull of gravity for so long before finally dropping from my person to the ground. In any case, I owe it a world of thanks for deciding to keep its mouth shut during its visit.

Perhaps that's why I experienced such a powerful surge of un-expected emotions—a bizarre blend of relief and guilt—when seconds later my hero of a husband stepped forward and lashed it with a large stick, crushing its head and killing it.

In contrast, three-year-old Parisa experienced no conflict of feeling whatsoever. She sobbed inconsolably as she demanded to know why Daddy had killed the "poor worm." As I glanced at the dark, limp creature, all three feet long and already looking shriv-eled, part of me had to agree with her. It *was* a poor worm indeed, probably just as much a disoriented victim of the sandstorm as we had been—and just trying to find its way back to where it had been before being involuntarily cast into the horror flick.

Not coincidentally, some ten minutes later we discovered another snake, quite possibly the mate, zigzagging in the vicinity. Sorry to say, it met with the same unjust fate as the worm.

It remains a day I'll always remember with both terror and awe. Like that blinding night of the blizzard in Boston, when my yellow Toyota snagged a patch of ice and spun out of control across the highway, or that sparkling day in the waters of Mazatlán, Mexico, when I barely broke loose from the suck of the undertow. What might have ended in terrible tragedy turned to unbelievable moments of grace—that, and the raw and humbling reminder that we're not as much in control as we think.

Years later, Mahmoud and I still feel both gratitude toward and remorse about the snake. Perhaps our best moment of vindication came from Nikiar's succinct version of the event, which he offered three years after his birth when asked (by his Great Aunt Annise in the States) if he knew the Story of the Snake. "Yes. Daddy killed the snake and I comed out." End of story.

Chapter Twenty-Nine

On Having and Rearing Babies

When Nikiar ("Niki") Firouz Ahmadi "comed out" on September 1, 1994, it had been two years since we had moved to Iran, one week before the projected due date of September 8, and four months after the day of the snake. His first name, which I discovered and fell in love with just three weeks before his birth, is Persian for "companion to goodness," or just "good friend," depending on who is doing the translation. The second name, "Firouz" (meaning "victor" in Persian), was after his Iranian grandfather. I wouldn't have wanted it any other way, and I was so glad his daddy went along with me in choosing our son's name. Of course, I had never really expected to use the name at all, since based on the sonogram, the doctor had predicted with 95 percent certainty that the baby would be a girl. When he announced otherwise at the moment of delivery, my mind flashed back to Parvaneh Khanum, the lady in my conversation class who just weeks earlier had insisted that I'd give birth to a son. I marveled to myself that she'd been right all along.

I'd gone to see the doctor that morning simply for a routine check. After examining me, he announced that since his schedule was open and the due date was "close enough," I should plan on meeting him in the delivery room in a couple of hours. "In other words," he said, matter-of-factly, "Congratulations! You're going to be a mother again today!"

I was almost too stunned to process the doctor's words, let alone process my feelings about the decision. From that moment on, I allowed myself to slip into a kind of passive mode where, like the day of the visiting snake, I "went along" without much resistance. I couldn't blame my reaction on language confusion, as the doctor had been educated in the United States and spoke

English, both well and comfortably, the entire time. Looking back, I think it would have been better for me to *ask*, at least, about the option of waiting until natural labor chose to kick in. For all I knew, he might have had no issue with sending me home that day to do just that.

Why didn't I just ask, then? For better or worse, back home in the States I had grown up in circles, and perhaps in a general era where a doctor's word (including my father's) was generally not subject to question, negotiation, or discussion. On top of that, I was still operating on my mostly unconscious resolve to "do as the Persians do" while in Iran. Of course, by not asking, I had no way of knowing whether inducing labor on or near the expected date actually *was* common practice in Iran, or just something that varied from doctor to doctor. All to say that perhaps things would have gone differently that day had I been more willing to speak up.

Since I *didn't* speak up and things proceeded as they did, I can only be too grateful for the able and reassuring presence of Zahra—not Zahra my sister-in-law, but the professional midwife in the kuee whom I had met in the conversation class. Since men, including husbands, were not allowed in hospital delivery wards out of respect for the privacy of the female patients, it was Zahra, not Mahmoud, who accompanied me to the doctor's that day. She never left my side—from the time she took me home to collect my things to the time they wheeled me into the Isfahan Hospital delivery room, to everything else that came after that.

I was *not* looking forward to being induced. I'd been down that road once before in the States three years earlier, when my pregnancy-induced hypertension came to a head and Parisa, not due for another three weeks, had entered into fetal distress. I remembered how they'd hooked me up to the IV-unit, dispensing Pitocin into my veins and forcing my uterus into contracting. Once the contractions started rolling, the brute churning force was relentless, leaving me moaning between each breath. The nurses had given me something "to take the edge off," and I remembered asking myself: *If this is how it feels "with the edge off," who could possibly bear what it's like when it's not off?* It was an intense window of accelerated wrenching, but mercifully, it was also a brief one: not three hours later and next to no pushing, Parisa came safely through, a healthy little girl.

In Nikiar's case, I'd meant to have a conversation with Zahra about pain management, but we never did. Each time I brought up the topic, all she would say was "We can talk about it." Too bad I'd forgotten what my fitness trainer Fatemeh meant by that phrase whenever I asked how much to pay her for coaching. In the days leading up to Niki's birth, I'd relearn the hard way what the phrase "We can talk about it" had *really* meant all along whenever I asked about managing pain.

On the day of the event, when the contractions started rolling fast and furious and the intensity shot up a notch or two higher, I politely asked Zahra when we would get around to talking about managing my pain. This time, Zahra broke the news with her gentlest voice and a note of apology:

"Leslie Jan, it's better that you feel it when your baby is coming; that way, you can help her come into the world. It is the natural way … so maybe ask God for a little *sabr* (patience). I'll be here with you the whole time, okay?" Her reassuring smile was like an angel's.

Breathless, I answered by nodding my head. But my heart had already plunged to the pit of my stomach while the pangs obliged me to writhe on the bed. I concluded that pain meds in childbirth *weren't* standard procedure, and at this point at least, not really an option. So, I closed my eyes as my body and flailing limbs took over and Zahra steadied me with the calming touch of her hand.

What was the silver lining? With all its intensity, my labor was even shorter than it had been with Parisa (not quite two hours this time around). And with the doctor and Zahra present, I gave birth to a lovely and healthy baby *boy*. From the way Zahra ladled him so tenderly into my arms, it looked as if a part of her had given birth too. Her beautiful face was flooded with joy for me, for herself, and for the life she had helped me bring into the world.

But it was a moment my heart ached for Mahmoud to share

with me. And I wondered if my heart felt like his did the day of our wedding, when no one from his immediate family could be there to laugh and cry with him.

***

Between periods of nursing and a visit that evening from my dear friend and neighbor Nasrin Karimi, I slept eighteen hours in the recovery ward. When Mahmoud proudly brought his wife and new son home the next morning, we were greeted by our excited three-year-old daughter, who couldn't wait to see her brother. But Parisa wasn't the only one; her *Ammeh* (Aunt) Badri was excitedly waiting there too. In keeping with Iranian family tradition, she had arranged to come from Tehran to spend the next few weeks with us and help in any way she could. She might have stayed even longer if she hadn't had four children of her own.

Judging from Badri's constant attending, you might have thought *I* was the newborn in need of care. Never once letting me lift a finger, she cooked me delicious puddings and soups, pureeing them to extract the maximum value from every ingredient and urging me to finish every drop. Not only would they renew my strength, she said, but they would also ensure the best diet for my nursing son. She also urged me to nap whenever I could, and if Niki wasn't napping near me, he'd be under her tender and watchful eye.

I was never more grateful for that watchful eye than the day she walked in on Parisa, Niki, and me in the living room. I imagine what she saw was a classic scene in many families' lives, involving a protective mother, her innocent newborn child, and a disgruntled older sibling who at least *looked* like she was about to do something horrible. Just before my impulses took over, when I was about to unleash my tongue on Parisa and make her feel ten times more dejected than she did already, Badri joined us, announcing her presence with a cajoling voice.

"Par-Par!" she chirped, addressing her unhappy niece by a pet name. "Par-Par, *look* … can you see? Niki Jan is looking right up at you. He's looking up at his big sister!"

She encircled Parisa in the crook of her arm and gently pulled her close to her brother. Then, looking at me with coaxing eyes, she asked in a single glance for me to trust Parisa with her brother.

The look in her eyes instantly reached me in the same way her voice had reached Parisa. The next thing I knew, I was placing Niki right smack into Parisa's little girl arms while Badri supported them from underneath.

With Badri's reassuring presence among us, I watched Parisa's eyes connect with her brother's for the first time. When four-week-old Niki considered Parisa with his large, liquid eyes, and then broke into a delighted smile, it looked like he had never seen anything so beautiful. In that instant, everything changed. It was as if the children were meeting each other for the very first time—and for brother and sister, it was love at first sight. It's been pretty much that way ever since. Their encounter in that moment helped set the foundation for a sweet and strong bond between them—one that has flourished into their adulthood.

Badri had shown yet another example of what I came to think of as a "no fault" approach with children: gentle correction without pointing the finger. I had seen Mahmoud's family apply it time and again, when the cousins were locked in a standoff, or a child had made off with somebody's toy, or someone had spouted off something horrendous. The adult response was generally the same: a gentle appeal where no child was singled out. I can still hear the basic script in my head, halfway between spoken and sung, and almost delivered like a nursery rhyme.

"Good Children of Mine, Good Children of Mine! Be nice to each other and try to be kind. Okay? Be good to each other, as I know you are. There, that's better!" (paraphrased).

Truth be told, things *weren't* always better at the point of pronouncement. It might actually have been a disastrous moment, the absolutely worst point of a conflict or squabble. Even if it was, the adults would generally repeat their message just the same and wait for the passion to subside. It always did. In the meantime, the children would have heard a measure of faith expressed in them that they'd have a chance to live up to. It reminded me of what Mamán had said the day she prepared French fries for a fussy Parisa: "The first lesson a child needs to learn in life is that she is loved. Once she learns that, everything else will fall into place over time." And from what I'd already seen and heard, kind words spoken with a gentle spirit went a long way toward impacting a heart.

Even so, I wasn't convinced that a soft approach was all there was to raising a child. A side of me, influenced by memories of how my mom and dad raised me, remained concerned that too much "softness" could lead to "spoiling." Mom sometimes referred to that kind of parenting as "killing with kindness"—or leaving children subject to future dangers if they didn't learn to manage their own behavior. Consequently, in my own childhood, a switch, a paddle, or the palm of a hand was sometimes applied when we misbehaved. And while I never felt comfortable spanking my own children, I had surmised that a stern voice, or look, of reprimand was still called for.

Not coincidentally, the parenting guides from the states I'd chosen had suggested that a little "firmness" was sometimes needed to help instill the desired behaviors. So back in the day, when Parisa was a newborn in Columbus and cried several times a night, my handbook advised parents to wait three or four minutes before entering the room to offer comfort. In the process, the handbook explained, I would allow my crying baby the chance to learn some "self-comforting skills." Chances were that she'd settle back to sleep on her own, and take a baby step closer, I supposed, toward that prized American ideal of *self-reliance*.

My strategy was met with mixed reviews, particularly from Parisa, who, despite my best efforts, enjoyed her share of being walked up and down the halls at night by her sleep-deprived parents—mostly her soft-hearted father. Who knows? Perhaps the "Iranian side" of her would have nothing to do with the "firm" approach, especially where a lesson in self-reliance threatened to replace the comforting feel of a warm adult.

Her Iranian family members didn't buy the notion of "independence over comfort" either. We never had a conversation about it; we didn't have to for me to get the message. I remember those one or two nights when, within a minute or two of Niki's starting to cry, Badri slipped softly into our bedroom and gently delivered him to our bed, right where I was positioned to nurse him.

For someone as tenderhearted as Badri, it must have been tough enough to see her nephew sleeping in a separate room when, to her way of thinking, he clearly belonged in the same room as his parents. But for her to overhear him crying, even for two minutes, was probably too hard for her to bear. I'm guessing it also would have been too hard for us ever to talk about a topic as touchy as "good mothering," so she never spoke a word about it. I, in turn, didn't return Niki to his room after she brought him to me to nurse him.

In the end, I spent two full nights with my infant son nestled beside me the whole time. Those were the two nights when we both slept through till morning. Yet … how can I put it? One side of me was sound asleep, and another, sensing this tender breathing parcel, stayed fully vigilant. It's a memory of a strong and wordless communion when neither of us stirred.

Years later, when we were back in the States, and by a curious turn of events I found myself teaching Spanish to child welfare professionals, I overheard three caseworkers talking one day. Turns out they were expressing their angst over mothers who slept beside their infant children. *How could adults be so irresponsible,* they marveled, *by leaving their children at such physical risk?* Keeping my memories to myself, I stood by silently, savoring the irony. *If only they knew my secret,* I thought. And how could it be that what one culture saw as "responsible parenting," another saw, plainly and simply as "child neglect," or even worse?

What made it all so interesting was that each side could make its claim with equally staunch levels of conviction. I'd see my Iranian family members let their little ones stay up at night till they practically dropped (because no one had told them to go to bed). Then again, sometimes they'd see *me* park my little ones in a big, lonely bedroom to sleep on their own. At other times, I'd see Niki's aunts empty warm, sugar-loaded tea down my son's eager throat before I could figure out how to ask them politely to stop. But had they ever seen me in Columbus, spooning that bland stuff I sometimes gave Parisa from a baby food jar, they just might have wondered when I'd buckle down and cook for my kid.

Of course, things didn't always stop at "interesting." I remember how terribly flustered I got one afternoon when we were staying at Ozra's house, and Ozra tried to help me with bathing Parisa. So then, I asked myself, was taking Parisa out of my arms, then giving me an on-the-spot demonstration, Ozra's way of telling me I didn't know how to bathe my own daughter? It didn't help that I was buck naked in the shower when she first walked in. Simultaneously embarrassed and seething, I felt stripped of personal boundaries on two major counts and had no idea of how to address it—or even if I should. Ozra, after all, was the eldest sister who had played a role in raising most of her siblings.

I had other struggles around boundaries. From the early days of Parisa's arrival, Jamshid's wife Mahmonir took a special liking to her, calling her *"Dokhtaram"* ("My Daughter") whenever she spent time with her. I didn't let it bother me much, as long as I didn't dwell on it. I will admit, it got harder and harder once she started referring to Parisa as "my daughter" to everyone, including me, her "real mom." Although I never voiced a word of protest except to my husband, I felt myself bristle whenever she used that term of endearment. It certainly would have helped had I known that *"Dokhtaram"* can also be translated simply as "My Girl." As things stood, however, I concluded that Mahmonir had gone too far. Was she trying to suggest something about my mothering skills, I wondered, by claiming Parisa as her own? Once, when Parisa was two, Mahmonir even asked to "borrow" her for a weekend. She and Parisa had spent plenty of time playing together, so Parisa didn't mind a bit, and Mahmonir had given no reason for me to distrust her. I didn't want to be viewed as petty and overprotective. So, in a split-second decision, I told her, "Yes." Both Parisa and Mahmonir were elated, and off they went.

When Mahmonir brought her back, she proudly announced that she had "potty-trained" Parisa in those two days. Just held her a few times, for a few minutes, over the pot each day until Parisa caught on to how it worked—just as it had worked long ago with her own young children. Mahmonir was elated and expected I'd be too, but I'll admit I was secretly less than thrilled—okay, I was furious. *She might have just asked me*, I thought to myself. *After all*, I kept stewing, *Parisa is **my** child*.

***

So where did *Mahmoud* figure into the mix of such moments, when perspectives could get muddled, and tempers could flare? At once husband, brother, in-law, and son, was he there to step in when my heart was reeling, or burning, or craving an advocate?

To be honest, not really. And yet that was the wonder of it: his very ability *not* to step into it. Not that you couldn't take him aside or count on him to feel the weight of your burden. But it was his nature to *listen*, not to take sides or offer solutions, and that was both the maddening and beautiful side of him. His gentle silence kept you from feeling self-satisfied, as if yours were the only side to consider. In short, he would listen just enough, but not *too* much. And when he did choose to say something, it was usually the same message, words that he has lived by (and have served me as his wife for more than three decades).

"Just let the fever pass," he'd say, "before you say or do anything." For Mahmoud, fanning the flames was never an option.

In the end, as much as a part of me wished Mahmoud would talk someone else into seeing *my* side of things sometimes, it wasn't so much that he "wasn't there" for me as that he was present for *all* of us. And when I look back, it was the far better solution.

***

Things got easier, and I got wiser and happier as a mom, once I loosened my grip on a need for "boundaries" and the notion that Parisa and Niki "belonged" to their parents alone. It happened little by little, starting in Isfahan, where I learned to see Parisa and Niki not so much as Mahmoud's and my children as everyone's children, just like the rest did. The world around me became my teacher: friends and visitors who came to call, neighbors from around the kuee, the ladies and girls from conversation class. I marveled at how freely they'd enter a space and start wooing our kids with a single glance. There was no holding back, no asking permission—just a playful courtship with a look or a smile, then scooping them up like a favorite rag doll.

"How are you doing, *Amoo* ('Uncle')?" the men would croon, signaling that the children should call them likewise.

"Hello, *Khaleh Jan* ('Dear Auntie)!'" the ladies would coo, with the same intention.

"Ay … *Shaytoon*!" someone would say every once in a while. (I was okay with it once I finally realized that the word didn't mean "Satan," as it sounded to me, but "little devil" or "little rascal" instead!)

I wondered when the children might shrink from such over-tures, but there was never a time they didn't love it. The moments were so real and genuinely affectionate, and they could feel it.

During visits with family, it was all that and more. Between the grandparents, aunts and uncles, great aunts and great uncles, and two dozen cousins or so, someone was always lavishing their at-tention on the children. The older cousins, ranging from nine years old and up, would take it upon themselves to entertain Parisa, Niki, or both, sometimes for hours at a time. Depending on where we were visiting, they might cart them about the farm to visit the animals, or to the neighborhood streets to try a new kind of ice cream. At the end of the day, when to my mind it was time for us to "take them back," someone would ask to keep them still longer, like overnight at their house if we weren't there already.

There was even a time when Ghazaleh, Parvin's sweet eleven-year-old daughter, was so taken with Niki that she begged us to let him stay at their home in the village ("Just for a week," she said), so that she and her mother Parvin could care for him while we were in Isfahan. I knew I could trust our son with Parvin, and I knew Ghazaleh's intentions were good, but I still felt deeply conflicted about leaving our eight-month-old in someone else's care for a whole week, even if that "someone else" was family. But because it was family, and because Parvin was so assuring, and because Mahmoud was comfortable with it, and because I couldn't bear hurting my young niece's heart, I acquiesced in the end, still questioning my better judgment.

At the end of one of the longest weeks of my life, we returned to the village to pick up Niki. I was overjoyed to see his face, and yes, he was happy to see us too. But my greatest comfort came from what I saw *before* Niki saw us: the bright eyes of a child laughing gleefully with his cousins—not just with Ghazaleh, but with Jaber and Ghazal too. Although he'd been away from his parents for a week, apparently he hadn't felt away from the circle of people he counted as *home*.

It didn't happen overnight, but it was all finally starting to sink in. I began to grasp the meaning behind the saying, "It takes a village to raise a child." Once I did, Mahmonir's pet names for Parisa were no longer an issue, and Ozra could share tips to her heart's content. Now that I didn't feel as threatened (and was also much better about locking the shower room), I might even have been willing to learn a thing or two from their wisdom.

***

With the passing of the weeks and months, I saw the imprint of many loving hands on the budding lives of Parisa and Niki. I knew that *I* hadn't taught them to suck on fresh lemons, to quip and quibble in Persian with their cousins, to dance with their arms stretched high. I knew that *I* hadn't told Parisa, as her uncle Rasool had, that if she didn't behave and finish her breakfast, "Lu Lu" (the Iranian equivalent of "the boogeyman") might snatch her up and carry her off. And I could never spin the tale of "The Three Little Goats," "The Golden Rooster," or "The Fox and the Bee" with the spellbinding power on the kids that Mahmonir could. Nor could I, like their uncle Ali, hold my own on a cantering stallion while keeping them safe in the crook of my arm.

Like many other American girls, Parisa loved playing "dress-up" in her mother's fanciest dresses and heels. But from the ethereal look you saw in her eyes, you could also tell she felt just as beautiful wrapped in Mahmonir's blue-floral chador, robed in her cousin Minoo's Indian dresses, or with her *Mamán Bozorg's* ("grandmother's") scarf adorning her head. She'd seen the beauty in these women who loved her, and she "dressed up" in the essence she saw in each one. Although now she's her own woman in her jeans and natural curls, I still see that passion for life and beauty she learned from them.

Chapter Thirty

The Mark of Two "Villages"

It wasn't only the women in the family who left their impression on Parisa.

One evening at the village, I spotted her standing in the shadows, watching her *Baba Bozorg* (grandfather) in prayer. No more aware of my presence than Baba was of hers, Parisa remained transfixed while I observed quietly. She watched him start from a standing position, then slowly crouch forward toward the ground. As he leaned on his hands from a kneeling position and touched his head once, then again, to the floor, Parisa started copying her grandfather's gestures. She was no more than three years old at the time, yet as she mirrored Baba in those private moments, her face reflected a sense of the holy. Parisa, who had learned "The Lord's Prayer" from her mother (just as I had from mine), had always touched me with her child's tendency to see with her soul.

As powerful a memory as it was for me, Baba never knew of his little granddaughter's presence, nor of how his example might have touched her that night.

And what about Niki, his little grandson? He was under two (and Parisa under five) when we left Iran for America. Since *everyone* had lavished their attention on Niki, how could we know the particular role Firooz Aqa (the grandparent he'd been named after) had played in shaping Niki's life?

It wasn't a question of his trying to shape *anyone*. What Baba and Mamán aspired to do was to *love* their family, from the eldest son to the smallest grandchild—not try to change them. Not that they were perfect or always successful, and not that they could always see their way clearly. But from what I could observe, *they really tried* to do right by their children and children's children. As

Mamán had always believed (namely, *that the most important thing for them to learn is that they are loved*), perhaps the impact of that belief in some way would reach all of us.

The awareness of that influence would surface when I least expected it: the day Mahmoud and I went to the American Interests Section of the Swiss Embassy in Tehran when Niki was one year old. We had gone there to arrange for Niki's American passport, since as the child of an American national, he was entitled to one. The official conducting the interview was polite and formal, with something of a no-nonsense manner, and was perhaps in her fifties. She spoke English well in her Iranian accent, and sitting behind her typewriter, she directed most of her questions to me.

"Your son's name, please?"

"Nikiar Firouz Ahmadi," I answered.

She paused before asking the next question.

"And does he not have … an American part to his name?"

"His full name is 'Nikiar Firouz Ahmadi,'" I repeated.

She paused again, peering briefly over her glasses at Mahmoud, then looked back at me.

"Do you mean they didn't let you name your own son … not even his middle name?"

Now *I* looked at Mahmoud, sitting quietly to the side. I admired him for holding his tongue.

"Actually," I said politely, "*I'm* the one who chose his name…I mean, all of it."

First, she looked bewildered, then intrigued. She started talking about her history at the embassy, about all the American spouses she had interviewed there. When she got to the stunning part—that her interviewees had included Betty Mahmoody, the same American woman from *Not Without My Daughter*—I was the one to change expression. Betty Mahmoody's name and story still continued to cross my path! The Iranians often explained such things as "fate," or "destiny," or *ghesmat*, as they called it in Persian—the same force that brought Mahmoud and me together, as Pastor Bob from Old South Church had conjectured. Were these recurrences nothing more than that? *Ghesmat* or no *ghesmat,* it was wonderful to recognize that Ms. Mahmoody's story no longer had the same threatening hold on me. It was nice to feel for her, but without the angst. Her story was hers and mine was mine.

The woman went on to explain that I was the first American woman she'd met who had claimed a fully Iranian name for her child. Hoping for an explanation, she looked at me and paused.

I didn't need to think about it. "I wanted our son to be named after his Iranian grandfather, whose name is 'Firooz,'" I told her. "If Niki—I mean Nikiar—can grow up to have any of his grandfather's qualities, I will be grateful."

The official took timely care of the paperwork needed for Nikiar's passport. And Mahmoud and I left the embassy in a happier state than when we had come. I took one last glance behind me before we exited the building and noticed that the same official was still watching us as we left.

***

Two decades went by and Nikiar grew up, just as his sister did. No longer that dewy-eyed cherub from Isfahan, he evolved into a beautiful character in his own right. I also saw how the coexistence of two distinctive "villages," his families from both Iran and America, left its mark on him. (This included a mysterious and unmistakable mark from his Grandfather Powell, "Doc," although the two of them never met: His deep and resonant voice, the noisy way he yawns or says "Yello?" when answering the telephone, his well-formed legs and towering stature, the impossible, quirky, and often profound questions he still likes to ask.)

But *how,* and *through what prisms* did Nikiar and his sister develop and see themselves in the midst and clamor of multiple heritages—cultural, racial, and also religious? How did they manage to negotiate and reconcile the different parts of themselves along the way? The most honest answer I can offer is *gradually*…with *discovery, trepidation, growing pains, integrity, and rediscovery* (each of those words containing a book in itself). And at different stages, settings, reflections, cross-roads, and decisions along the way. They drew what they could from both sets of families—both *because* of us and *in spite of* us. And over time, they figured things out for themselves—with the love and help of each other perhaps most of all.

In the end, I'm deeply proud of the people they've become—and are still becoming. And so is their father.

But let's not stop here. How can I talk about raising children, especially when the children are Nikiar and Parisa, and fail to talk about Mahmoud in his role as their dad? In their infancy or young adulthood, their peaceful or stressful seasons, their being in Iran or America, he's remained their steadfast hero, and mine as well. What's made it so much fun is the kind of man he is: a perfect blend of wise and humble, transparent and unpredictable. The children have described it better than anyone:

"He's the kind of dad," they'd say, "whose sweet smell you still remember from the times he walked and sang you to sleep."

"He can stop a quarrel before it starts by making you laugh at what you were mad about. At those rare times when he does get mad, he gets over it fast and won't bring it up later."

"But he might come by with a plate full of grapes and say, only halfway joking, 'Help me finish these up; they're starting to go bad.'"

"At dinner he'll 'fight' you for that last piece of kabab, when you both know he'll let you have it in the end."

"In the evening, he'll call you from whatever you're doing to admire a sunset or a moonlit sky."

"You can share your secrets or tell him your troubles, and you know he won't judge you for any of them. But sometime later, if your ears are tuned, he might tell a story that was just what you needed."

Basically, they fell in love with him for the same reasons I did, and they absolutely adore him.

Over decades Mahmoud has managed to embody the best his family has passed on to him, mingle it with his own magic, and keep it alive with his wife and children. I can only hope that after all these years some of that essence has rubbed off on me. In any case, he has been the father they've needed.

I had never imagined how soon after our move to Iran, I would lose mine.

Chapter Thirty-One

"God Rest Their Souls": Reflections on Death

It was February of 1993 when I received the most unwelcome call of my life, when my sister Patricia reluctantly announced that my father had died far sooner than any of us had expected.

I was in Isfahan when it happened and had been living there for less than a year. And Dad, along with my two sisters, was in the States at the time. The painful details surrounding my father's death at age sixty-nine, and the fact that I'd be thousands of miles away when he died, remain buried in another story for another time.

I was devastated by Dad's passing, but Mahmoud was too. Still, he did his best to comfort me. When the reality of it finally hit me, two nights after he died, I sank headlong into his chest, sobbing, shaking, wetting his neck. As he locked his warm arms around me, he began singing a sweet song to me in Persian—a faraway melody, soft and low. I didn't catch what the words were saying, but I had never heard his singing voice so serious, so beautiful. I hung onto every note, every lilt and tremor in his voice, till I fell asleep.

Feeling alone in this world that my dad had just exited, I grieved like a wounded creature in the wild. What I desperately longed for was time alone: time to retreat, to grieve, to plan the belated trip home, to sort it all out in my head and heart. I was not yet aware of the Islamic tradition calling for forty days to mourn the death of a loved one. Nor had I heard of the family tradition of gathering at times throughout that forty-day period, to remember the loved one and comfort each other.

That is, not until the day Mahmoud gently mentioned, as if in passing, that seventeen family members from the three family checkpoints of Saveh, Tehran, and the village had rented a minibus and were coming to Isfahan, both to pay their respects and to keep our company for seven days.

I don't know what Mahmoud was hoping for in terms of a reaction, but I'm sure my wide-eyed response disappointed him. *Coming to Isfahan? For seven days?* How could this be? I hardly had the know-how to host a houseful of Iranian guests competently even when I *wasn't* in a state of total grief. I understood the family's intentions, and I loved and appreciated them for their tender hearts, but panic has its own sordid way of sabotaging gratitude in no time flat. I asked myself how I could possibly present a welcoming face when all I felt was a need to hide away and nurse my own battered heart?

"And how will we manage to cook, shop, do laundry for, and otherwise take adequate care of seventeen people for seven days?" I asked Mahmoud, my voice starting to crumble.

Mahmoud smoothed back a lock of my hair with his fingers. "Don't worry. You won't have to."

Now totally overcome, I said nothing. Was my sweet husband in total denial?

I was about to find out. The minibus had been rented, and they were already heading our way, Mahmoud added, not meeting my gaze.

I wince at how I must have appeared to the seventeen weary passengers of the minibus, who after five to eight hours on the road piled out and greeted me with heartfelt affection. I could feel myself shift from frenzied, to stilted, to flakey, to spacey, then back to frenzied all over again. Shortly after receiving them, I recalled that important Iranian custom of serving tea. I wandered aimlessly about the kitchen like a fool, looking for that good kind of aromatic loose tea one serves to guests. I knew, of course, that even if I managed to find it, I would have no idea how to prepare, let alone serve it properly to seventeen road-weary relatives.

I think Nadereh, always observant and quick to assess, felt sorry for me. She happened to enter the kitchen when she saw me standing there, opening and closing drawers in a daze. "What are you doing, Leslie?" she asked gently, but with a hint of playfulness in her voice.

"I want to make tea," I said, feeling my eyes dampen. The operative term here was *want to*, a far cry from *can*, but Nadereh had already figured that out. She proceeded discreetly.

"Come on," she said cheerfully. "I have a better idea. Why don't *I* make the tea?"

"But you're our guests," I said in a small, uncertain voice, terrified she would be able to see right through me and read the subtext: *And I have no idea whatsoever what I'm doing.*

"Leslie," she answered warmly but firmly, "thank you so much, but you're not even to *come* to the kitchen so long as we're here, understand? We're here for *you*, to take care of *you*. That's why we came."

Even as my inner voice of pride began to condemn and nag at me, protesting that it was still my home and my responsibility to run it, Nadereh led me gently back to the sitting room and sat me down beside a circle of people. I looked up at her, not knowing what to say.

"I'll be right back," she said.

I remember sitting there compliantly, right where Nadereh had seated me, until she returned with not one cup, not two, but a whole tray of steaming hot tea for everyone. It was fragrant, comforting, and delicious. So was dinner, served as if by magic hands, the kind I'd read about in fairy tales as a child. So was the next day's breakfast and lunch, and every meal to come after that. So was every conversation I had with every person, who one way or the other asked, or said, or did the right thing, for seven days. Seven days that passed like a dream.

At different times throughout those days, I vaguely remember being surrounded by chatter and laughter, even music with dancing. I somewhat recall walks in the fresh air with one, or two, or ten people beside me. There were hot showers and partial nights of sleep in between. Although I wasn't totally ready for it, life was going on and taking me along gently, as part of the healing. Thank God, the magic hands of my family were there to guide me. I love them.

Amid the hazy dreaminess, one memory shines brightly. In the sitting room where Nadereh had served that first tray of tea, I was surrounded by people who were keeping me company. At some point, after the tea had thawed my numbness and eased my pain, Rasool Aqa—known not to mince words when he felt he needed to—silenced our pockets of conversation by clearing his throat:

"As we all know, we have come to Isfahan to stand with Leslie Khanum and her family in America and to remember her father, *Aqayeh Doctor Pahvel*, God rest his soul, who gave his blessing to Leslie Khanum's joining our family in Iran. May I suggest we now join in a period of silence, dedicated to his memory."

As the room grew silent, our collective presence ignited like a flame. It filled the whole room and every chamber of my soul, quieting my questions and transporting me to the Transcendent. And it lingers in my soul's memory to this day.

***

That kind of presence—the kind that finds a special voice in shared silence—cannot be confined to a single time, space, or continent. It spills beyond a single memory and merges with other memories and commemorations. Like my memory of walking to the muffled sound of the wind ... of walking silently in the company of relatives and friends. To where? To the graveside of Mahmoud's young cousin Mohammad, who died way before his time ... to the gravesides of our beloved university colleagues Dr. Karimi, Dr. Dalili, and Dr. Gharemani in Isfahan. To the graveside of my mother, Margaret Minerva Dunn Powell in Connecticut. And much later, after we'd returned from Iran to the States, to the adjoining graveside of my father, Charles Porter Powell, MD.

Khoda biamorze. God rest their souls.

Chapter Thirty-Two

The Road Between Hearts: Leaving Home to Return Home

After nearly four years of living in Iran, Mahmoud and I had the conversation that took us to the road leading back to America.

Were we working in sync with a "master plan," a mapped-out trajectory of our lives to guide our decision? How about, *Let's start a new life in Iran and see how it goes*—that was about it. There were really no time frames, no deadlines, no schedules, no checklists to go by. It just happened to be January 1996 when the conversation happened.

And it was much, much harder than I thought it would be.

I'm not talking about the conversation itself. I'm talking about neither of us wanting to have the conversation to begin with. We each knew that once we broached the subject, it could lead to a change in our lives that at least one of us might not be ready for. The question of where we'd ultimately call "home" was too big for both of us—fraught with the risk of terrible loss, a dream shattered. Perhaps especially for Mahmoud.

Yet from the beginning he had promised we would return to America if I felt I could not spend the rest of my life in Iran. Another person might have seen no reason to raise the question unless *I* brought it up, but not Mahmoud. My guess is he knew I'd have reasons of my own to *avoid* the topic, however wise it might be to discuss it. Who, after all, would want to feel responsible for casting a shadow on someone else's dream—especially if that someone was her own spouse?

And so, Mahmoud took it upon himself to raise the question so I wouldn't have to. I will always love him for that selfless decision, and it will also always haunt me a little.

I came home from teaching class one day to find Mahmoud alone in the dining room, scrutinizing some papers he was clutching.

He seemed unaware of my arrival, but his words spilled out the moment I spoke his name.

"It's coming," he said, looking like someone had slapped him.

"What do you mean, 'It's coming'?" I asked. "Is something wrong?"

"The extension the US gave me as a permanent resident living outside of America is about to run out. If I don't go back in the next six months, I can lose my permanent residency for good."

The space filled up with our stark silence. Beyond the shock, I didn't know how to process what I'd heard or what would be appropriate to say. So, I stayed quiet until Mahmoud was ready to speak again.

"I guess we can't postpone a decision any longer," he finally said, shattering the silence.

What? Had four years already gone by that quickly? A season flowing with family, community, and tightknit friendships? Apart from enjoying work, hadn't we finally found time to enjoy things *besides* work? Was it possible that we now had *two* children: a five-year-old speaking fluent Persian and a toddler mouthing his first words in Persian too? As for me, hadn't I managed to feed my hunger for *learning* language, for *teaching* language, for discovering something new each day, for being a source of others' discoveries as well? Had I not found a place to walk with God, learn of God, and see God's face in the face of others?

And rather than lose all contact with the "flamenco dancer" within me, hadn't I actually become *reacquainted* with her—not on my own, but with the help and examples of others? Like Zahra, my whirling, exuberant sister-in-law. Like the other sisters-in-law, who would grab my wrists and teach me to dance with my arms and hands. Like my female colleagues from the Language Center, who had urged me to make my face pretty every day. Like the women from the "beautiful people" parties, who had asked me to sing my heart on the guitar for them!

Everything I had feared I'd miss out on in life—the color and glamour, the music and laughter, the lush and flowing landscapes, a space to acknowledge my ethnic and spiritual heritage, the hands of friendship and spirit of fellowship—I had found it all with my family and the people in Iran. When faced with the choice to exclude or enfold me, to show distrust or suspend their doubt, to try to change me or simply accept me, in most cases people had chosen the latter.

For all these reasons, I felt just as relieved as Mahmoud to hold off on the decision. But now, time had run out—and like it or not, we were squarely faced with having to choose.

We started off making empty comments about US immigration laws—all the hoops to jump through, all the red tape attached. We asked meaningless questions: why reentry permits for green card holders were called "white passports" anyway, why they were renewed every two years and not four. Neither of us cared about the answers, of course. Our need was to fill up the silence with chatter, to avoid being the first to say something wrong—too terribly honest, too close to the heart—about how to feel, about what to do.

I mean, how could I say even something as simple as *My father is gone; I need my sisters and my sisters need me*, without risking his hearing it as something else … like *My feelings and sisters matter more than yours*. How could I air the emotions I had managed to bury for far too long? I knew once I opened my mouth and got started, I couldn't be sure of what would spill out.

Ms. Aghaee (the younger one) walked in from the kitchen, seeking direction.

"Pardon. Would you like lunch now, before I pick up Parisa from daycare? Or do I fetch her first and serve lunch when we return?"

It was a nice, straightforward question—and a welcome interruption. Mahmoud decided to extend the interruption even further:

"*Ghorbanat* ('Much obliged'); *I'll* pick up Parisa from daycare. We can all eat lunch when I bring her back."

And with that, Mahmoud stood up, gathered the papers, stuffed them into a drawer, and out the door he went.

From Mahmoud's perspective, we could pick up the matter later, tomorrow, next week … not now in any case. But there was no getting around it; it was time to decide, and neither Mahmoud nor I could have it both ways. There was simply no path to easy answers.

Of course, some considerations were clearer than others—where all it took was "doing the math." It would take both our salaries for six full months to purchase four airline tickets for a visit with my family in the States. If we stayed in Iran, we'd have to forego those visits on any regular basis. That kind of factor was cut and dried—a plain and logical reason to leave.

But there were other questions—deeper and more baffling.

"Are we being fair?" I asked Mahmoud late one night as I lay in bed beside him, my eyes pinned to the ceiling.

"Fair to *who*, Baby Jan??" murmured Mahmoud, who had nearly drifted off to sleep.

"To our children: Parisa and Niki. Is it really fair to pluck them out of this world and transplant them into another—just like that?"

There was a pause, an indecipherable silence. Perhaps Mahmoud was now asleep? I listened for the telltale shift in his breathing rhythm. But no, I heard no change; he was wide awake.

"What do you *mean* 'Is it fair?', Baby? Isn't this plan the plan you wanted: for the children to have connection with their family and culture and identity in America? Isn't that exactly the kind of "fair" we are trying to do?" His voice sounded weary, but not from sleepiness.

"I know, I know … but I've been thinking. We know my family in America will know how to see them, but what about everyone else? What will our children's culture be, and how will they manage when everyone else tries to define them? When some see them as "Black," others as "Brown," still others as "Iranian," or maybe just "immigrant"—depending on who is looking —do we want them to go through the pain of all that?

"They *will* go through it, whether they stay here or go back," said Mahmoud, "but they will also become stronger, find the best of themselves from Iran and America, and hopefully we walk through it with them."

"We will. But taking the kids there means taking them away from *here*. Away from flesh and blood they *know*, from family *who already know and adore them*. And how can we take them from Mamán and Baba—especially since their grandparents in America are already gone? Is *that* fair?" I could feel my throat knotting up, my guilt welling.

The room filled up with silence again, until Mahmoud gently broke it:

"… But their *Aunt Pat and Aunt Sylvia* aren't already gone."

Voiceless, I snuggled close to my husband as my eyes filled up. I couldn't deny it: I longed for my children to be close to my sisters—their two aunts in America. And to their one Black American cousin, Emily, too. And it wasn't just that. I longed for my homeland, my culture as an American and Black American, my friends, a church home. For the pleasure of walking without a headscarf or coat, of enjoying a movie I could truly relate to, of going to the library and finding a book I could actually read. And of picture books with people who looked like our children.

I longed for *all* of it; I just couldn't say it to Mahmoud. But Mahmoud knew. He spoke gently into my ear while my tears trickled down:

"Listen to me, Baby Jan: it's okay. We are going back—really! The kids will have more choices in the US—what they can study, what they can wear, and where they can worship. Let's just sleep now and be happy about *that*. The rest of it … we will have to take it day by day. Okay?"

I wiped my tears.

"Okay," I agreed, "Enough talk for one day! Let's go to sleep!" and I closed my eyes. Mahmoud did too. This time, the darkness and silence were comforting. For half a minute, anyway. I opened my eyes again. "Mahmoud?" I said. I wasn't "off" yet.

He turned his head toward me, his eyes met mine, and then he started laughing at me! But it was a kind laugh; that was all I needed. And the sheet began quivering with our mingled laughter!

"Yes?" said Mahmoud.

"Goodnight, Mahmoud Jan!"

"Goodnight, Baby."

***

I was unaware at the time that the pain of our dilemma wasn't limited to just Mahmoud and me. As I learned later from Mahmoud, he had already talked privately with his parents about the inevitable decision we faced. Yet, as agonizing as it was for them, they gave him the gift of only their unconditional love and support.

"You must go while you still have time to reestablish your-selves. You must think of what's best for your wife and children," Baba had told Mahmoud in an almost steady voice, his heart prob-ably breaking as he spoke, of course, of his *own* grandchildren, son, and daughter-in-law. It wasn't the first time Baba had had a conversation of this nature with a family member. No doubt, he could still feel the sting of the talk he'd had years earlier with his baby brother Said, when Said confirmed his and Maureen's decision to move to Scotland. Yet even with that memory haunting them, he and Mamán were resolved not to hinder us.

But by committing to send us back with their blessings, Baba and Mamán had won my heart's loyalty forever. Knowing they would be waiting for us on the other side of the world, we'd seek to return to them again and again.

***

In the end, and for our own sake (perhaps mainly for mine), Mahmoud came up with a true but surface explanation for those who asked why it was "best" for us to return to the States at that time. A "proper" rationale that sounded good and made sense. One we could deliver and that others could hear. Namely, just as Baba had said, we needed to leave the door open for reestablishing ourselves in America professionally while there was still time, before we were rendered "too old" or "irrelevant." It was enough of an explanation to avoid having to reveal the more deeply personal needs.

And after returning home, what then? The only plan we had, if one could call it that, was for the four of us to stay with my older sister Pat and her husband Jim in Massachusetts while we figured out the next steps. The prospects were at once exciting, promising, and anxiety-producing. *What kind of future awaits us*, I wondered, *and realistically, what are the possibilities?* I'd already grown fond of the thought of resettling in Boston—a return to my roots, to the general region of my growing-up years, to the homes of my sisters and two of Mahmoud's cousins, and, thankfully, Mahmoud was game for it. Not that we wouldn't miss life in Columbus, the beautiful and beloved city where we met, the university town that had been so good to us. But back in Iran, I had found such joy in the regular visits we'd made with Mahmoud's family members, I yearned for that same joy with my sisters in Massachusetts. Not only that, but my closest friends (Evelyn from junior high school and Debbie from college) still lived in New England. And if Mahmoud and I could start over in Boston, I could reconnect with my former church family at Twelfth Baptist Church—where my ties to the members, the precious memories, and the jubilant sounds of gospel worship still ran deep. I knew that none of these plans were promised, but they were my dreams, nonetheless.

***

But then, what about *Mahmoud*—beloved son, nephew, cousin, brother, uncle, professor, and husband—whose intimate place in my world is what opened this whole other new world to me to begin with? What would he do with this dream retracted? Where was the compass to reset his path? How could I make *his* feelings count too, and reach what was hiding behind those eyes?

"How are you doing with this … change of plans?" I asked him one evening on the patio when I dared to try.

He switched his gaze from where he was staring and turned it toward me, his eyes reflecting the moonlit skies. "You are pretty, aren't you?" he said, smiling faintly while crickets sang brightly in the background.

In that moment, I understood that words wouldn't do it for Mahmoud, nor would it help him to "talk things out." Plainly and simply, he would anchor his peace by doing right by his family. And if the stunning, unsettling truth was that "family" mostly meant *me* and the children in this case, how could I do anything less than honor him—to make it easier in any way I could? In those final days, I sensed, it would be by living life fully with him and his loved ones, by laughing instead of crying with them, by showing a heart of gratitude to them, and by leaving him a space for his most private feelings.

On the day of our early morning departure, we were jammed together with Ahmadi kin in Baba and Mamán's village home. There we said our goodbyes to each other, some with words and others with tears: silent, constrained, yet softly streaming and un-ashamed. And I thought back on the saying Mamán shared when her grandchild Parisa first saw her and ran straight to her arms: *A road can always be found between two hearts.*

So, yes, our greatest treasure in Iran was our connections with *people*, heart to heart, beginning with our Iranian family. And the foundation was Baba and Mamán.

***

Beyond the space in our hearts they had filled, they wanted to stock our suitcases with the material riches of their store: Mamán's neat packets of harvested walnuts, rose petals, and dried herbs, plus mint and rock candy for pain below the gut. And, of course, the embroidered pillowcases, the bright knitted socks, the tea sets and chess sets, the gold earrings, pendants, and bracelets, the customized drapes, the thick and downy blankets …

"But how will we *ever* fit these colossal blankets into our suitcases?" I groaned to Mahmoud in a rare private moment. "It's just impossible! We have to tell Mamán and Baba we're leaving them behind."

Mahmoud squeezed his bright eyes at me with his double-barreled blink.

"Don't worry about it, Baby Jan; everything works out! Just wait and be a little bit patient, okay? At the right time, we can play with ear."

"I believe the term you mean is 'Play it *by* ear,'" I answered back, then started giggling like a middle-schooler with a serious crush. "It *really* is time to visit the US again—you're forgetting your English!" I teased.

"Okay, okay: have it your way. It's 'Play *by* ear,' then!" He answered with such a fun-loving nature that I had to kiss him right there on the spot!

These were some of the moments I loved him most.

It would likely cost us another two hundred dollars to cover the excess baggage charges, but there was no use refusing any of it. Somehow, we made room for all of it, even those things we could find in the States; Mamán's fresh walnuts would always taste better anyhow. The stuff we'd first brought when we moved to Iran would be kept here in storage or, better yet, put to use till our later return.

In keeping with the Islamic tradition associated with departures, Mamán had a copy of the Qur'an in hand, her mouth gently pronouncing the words of blessing she always spoke while lifting the heavy, gold-leafed volume above and around our heads: "May God keep and protect you; may God stand behind you and be your strong support…" We had to duck to accommodate ourselves to her petite stature. As I rose to straighten myself, I noticed her bright, silent tears. We hugged, leaving so much unsaid in hopes of a future day.

I wish I had done the same with Baba—leaving things unsaid, I mean. Instead, awkwardly knitting my words together, I tried to leave him with a funny little sentiment. Expressing a big one risked being too much for either side to handle.

"Baba Jan ... I'm going to remember how you used to direct me to my place at the table during mealtimes, the place for the daughter-in-law ..."

Actually, it was the closest I'd come to admitting to either of us that I had noticed—and sometimes struggled with—being told where to sit at the table, wondering where my gender figured into it all. But none of that mattered to me anymore.

Baba paused for a moment, his damp eyes pondering my statement. Slowly, his face brightened, taking on a mischievous expression, and he surprised me with his spunky retort.

"'Place for the daughter-in-law,' you said? 'Place for the *daughter-in-law*'? Leslie Khanum, those were the times I was asking you to sit at the *place of honor*."

So much for my astute cultural observations. Four years ... *four entire years* of having sat at the table with Baba and Mamán, and only now, right before leaving, had I realized the message behind Baba's seating directions all along. Apparently in Iran, the farther up a table they placed you, the more honored a guest you were. Baba's generous-hearted efforts had been wasted on me, evidently. I felt like a total idiot, yet it was worth that stunning revelation.

Clearing my throat once or twice, I looked back at Baba apologetically, only to be met by his radiant smile and bright eyes, and we enjoyed one more laugh together.

"Okay," I said.

Longing to go back home to America, yet realizing I was also leaving home, I couldn't wait till our next return.

Chapter Thirty-Three

Flipping the Switch

The transition to the States from Iran was hard at first, but somehow we managed to "flip the switch" and settle back into life in America. I realize we were privileged to have the choice and blessed to have managed to pull it off. Still, I can't believe that when I first shed my manteau, my arms felt cold in seventy-degree weather!

Goosebumps in summer weren't the only challenge I had to adjust to. I had to stop jumping out of my skin each time I heard the *click* of a car door unlocking from the remote-control button on somebody's keychain (*Who invented that thing while we were away?*) I had to learn to drive a car again—without forgetting that a red light really *did* mean "STOP." And how many times did I hear the words *"Friends"* and *"Seinfeld"* before realizing they didn't refer to real people but to two hit comedy shows everyone seemed to know about except *me*? Oh, and there was this new little thing called "email" that Mahmoud and I had to sit down and learn to use.

As for five-year-old Parisa and two-year-old Nikiar, for all practical purposes they were diving into America and "the American experience" for the very first time. Sometimes it was amusing to watch their reactions as the immigrant children they were at the time. The McDonald's "Happy Meals" got them all worked up about the toys they would find inside the boxes … but they were not enamored by the food that came with them. ("What's this?" I remember Niki saying with a perplexed expression as he held up a cheeseburger with only one bite in it.)

Talk about feeling "behind the times." But I believed we'd find our way soon enough. Not surprisingly, the children were the first to start catching on; it wasn't long before they loved French fries and chicken McNuggets like most other American kids.

But after four years of scant communication between my sisters and me, and with me feeling like the guiltiest party, what about the three of *us*? Would *we* be able to find our way to each other again?

***

From the moment we arrived at the Boston airport, my big sister Pat and brother-in-law Jim gathered us up—Mahmoud, Parisa, Nikiar, and me—and sheltered the four of us under their wings in a townhouse accustomed to housing two. In the four months of our stay there, they fed us, clothed us to some extent, and shoved money into our pockets whenever we needed a bundle. They caught Mahmoud and me up on national, international, and local affairs and gave us email and internet lessons. Evidently, this was the year Hotmail premiered, and the first flip mobile phone went on sale. It was also the year Osama bin Laden declared war on America, and Nelson Mandela announced he would not stand for reelection as president of South Africa in 1999. And tragically, somewhere between twenty and thirty Black churches in Mississippi had been set fire to and burned to the ground.

I grieved I'd been out of the loop for so long.

In Nikiar's and Parisa's eyes, Pat and Jim instantly became a True Aunt and True Uncle, being clearly talented in popcorn popping, daily outings, lots of laughter, and nightly snuggling with bedtime stories—complete with picture books in English, of course. Perhaps not coincidentally, the children's favorite storybook was Aliki's *Nice New Neighbors*, memorably narrated by their Aunt Pat, the best storyteller ever!

As for setting a deadline for finding jobs and our own living space, Jim or Pat never stated or even implied a time frame. And whenever Mahmoud asked, Jim always answered, and his answer was always the same: "You're welcome to stay with us for as long as it takes."

"That is really good of you; thank you, Jim!" Mahmoud said

from his heart the first time Jim said it. "Okay, we will play with ear, then."

"Pardon me?" Jim said.

Sylvia and Don, my younger sister and brother-in-law who lived twenty-five minutes away, came by once a week or so to visit with a dish or two to share. And when Sylvia, beloved music teacher of second graders, first bounced in—crooning a silly welcome song in her zany but sweetly delicate voice—I recognized the same affectionate and fun-loving sister I had always known. I enjoyed watching the children and their eyes grow wide as their Aunt Sylvia won them over in fifteen seconds flat.

As for me, my heart skipped as I reached out to six-year-old Emily, my one and only Black American niece. When we had left America four years earlier, Don and Sylvia's daughter was barely two. How much she had grown since then! How beautiful she was! When I gave my best hug and she hugged me back politely, I felt a mix of elation, affection, longing, and guilt. *Dear God*, I prayed silently, *help us find each other again!*

But somehow, I knew that we, the three Powell sisters, *had* found our way back to each other. Between the special meals, the late-night sharing, the laughter ignited by old time "Powell humor," the entrusting of secrets, the affirming words, the swapping of stories and sometimes tears, it felt clear to me that being reconnected was what we *all* wanted—with no guilt trips, no blaming, no questions asked, no strings attached. In the end, my sisters reached out with their own distinct styles, but with the same substance as Baba and Maman's, the same spirit as in a "road between hearts." It made me think back to our mother; how, in her final year of life, she'd written to each of us, expressing her wish and prayer that we, as sisters, would always stay close.

I will always love Pat and Sylvia—and Jim and Don—for being there for us, ready and willing, when we needed them most.

Even so, just because we had reconnected didn't mean we all agreed on *how long, how often,* and *how planned* our visits together should be. Having just arrived from Iran after four years of separation and a lifestyle where siblings could drop in on each other at any time, I was sold on the bonding value of that "open-door policy," domestic style. As it was, I was still determined that Mahmoud and I would resettle in the Boston area, so that my sisters and other family members would be relatively close by. These included two of Mahmoud's first cousins and their respective families, who, remarkably, happened to live in neighboring towns. So, like an earnest convert turned preacher, I proposed to Pat and Sylvia that we practice this open-door policy with each other ("for a visit, for a meal, for a sleepover … whatever!")—not noticing how silent the room had become …

But when Sylvia finally chirped, "We should talk about this!" in a voice a little too cheery and with a pause a little too long, I picked up the *real* message: *"I'm not ready for this conversation. If it's all the same to you, let's change the subject (!)"*

I was disappointed by the ambivalent response, but I also realized I had overwhelmed my poor sisters. After all, *I* was the one needing recalibration after being away from my own family culture, as influenced mostly by my father's side. A culture whose members tended to visit in moderation and schedule events *ahead* of time. In any case, once I realized my *own* need to readjust, it became easier to find my way back to life in America. To be in charge of my own agenda. To get around on my own again. To do my own shopping, cooking, and cleaning. To plan ahead for get-togethers with my sisters and be moderate about passing the time when we did. In short, to do almost everything that had been second nature to me before leaving for Iran.

***

What were the hardest things to readjust to? A big one was having to rely more on strangers than family whenever childcare was called for (both Pat and Sylvia and my brothers-in-law worked full-time). Another was learning to live again without the refreshment of a daily nap. The quirkiest challenge was getting through saying a sentence in Spanish without Persian words spilling out instead. I really had to work hard on that one.

Still, I managed to find part-time work teaching Spanish again at my alma mater, Gordon College, and English as a Second Language at Boston College. Mahmoud was able to work for one of his cousins, who actually owned a Persian rug shop not far from Don and Sylvia's place! But with our growing family and the pressing need to reintegrate with full-time professional work again, we knew that, practically speaking, our best bet would be to return to Columbus, where a familiar community, a much lower cost of living, and former professional contacts already awaited us. Thank God, within three months of our return, Ohio State rehired me as a full-time Spanish instructor and Mahmoud in a postdoctoral position in agronomy research.

And so, again with mixed feelings, we packed up our paltry belongings and headed back to Columbus to reestablish our lives. But it also added to the painful trail of beloved family members left behind.

Chapter Thirty-Four
Change

It's 2011, fifteen years since we first left Iran for the States. I'm guessing it will take me another fifteen years to process what it has meant to leave Iran, to come back to America, to sort out the gains and losses—for myself, at least. With a few exceptions, Mahmoud and I still speak carefully around that topic, in case one or the other might step on an unresolved issue or reopen a scar of grief or loss. Parisa, an anthropology major in her first year of college and blessed with the hand of an artist and writer, has penned some reflective gems in her journal about her ties to the land of her earliest memories:

There's something so romantic
about billowing wheat.
It's a golden color;
nostalgic, like an old
sepia-toned photograph.

(from Parisa's journal, 2011)

And even Nikiar, who was less than two when we took him from Iran to America, has his own layered thoughts at the age of sixteen:

"Every time we visit Iran for a few weeks in the summer, I wonder how my life would be different if we had stayed. Life in the village with my cousins and grandparents feels simpler and more carefree somehow, although I'm sure it isn't really. People have problems everywhere—internal problems, external problems. There are great things, too, in both Iran and America—but while the countries struggle with getting along, it makes it harder to hold onto both places the way I want."

Still, up till now our family has managed to make it back to Iran every two years since '96, even if just for two or three weeks. There was the summer of '98, of 2000, of 2002 ... all the way up through 2008. But now it's been three full years since I've roamed through Baba's wheat fields, felt Duzaj's radiant nights, and seen her stars. That lingering interim, when faltering finances led to an extra year between visits, ended up making the wait too long. How could thirty-six months, just nine months longer than the usual interim, so change the Iran I remembered from last time?

It wasn't the extra months themselves; it was Mamán. During that period, before we could reach her on time, she slipped away into a coma following a kidney infection. It happened both softly and impactfully, just as she had lived her life keeping the family together. She died at age 85 on Valentine's Day, February 14, 2011, leaving Baba, her sweetheart of more than seventy years, devastated. Over one thousand mourners attended her funeral in Duzaj, home of 1300 residents, beloved village of wheat fields and tiny red poppies.

I wish I had known her better, asked her about her life, and explored life in general with her, as I had with Baba. But Mamán was not one who connected through conversations; conversations simply were not her thing. She connected by simply being there, by being among us—usually just sitting relaxed and contented beside Baba.

Without Mamán, life will not be the same for any of us.

***

Spring has now arrived in the village, and we've finally made it over here. I sit quietly in Parvin's newly built, comfortable, and "updated" home, observing what's happening around and inside me. Settled in an armchair across from Baba, I keep him company as he lies sleeping on the sofa. The others, a mix of family and drop-in neighbors, are gathered a few feet away at a dining room table. They chatter and help themselves to Parvin's delicious fried fish, yogurt with cucumbers, herbed rice, and pickled vegetables from a large lazy Susan. The long, bordered tablecloth, which had once decked the floor like a rolled-out carpet for fifteen to twenty guests, is nowhere in sight. Since when has Parvin's house been so full of furniture?

I feel odd sitting off from the rest, but there's no space at the table to seat us all anyhow. The young folk in their teens and twenties are nestled in various rooms throughout the house with their plates of food, cell phones, PCs, and each other's company. Even at the dinner table people are doing their own thing. Which conversation do I tune in to? It's useless to try; the clandestine satellite television is on full blast with no one fully attending, but no one is fully ignoring it either. *Befarmaeed Sham* ("Dinner is Served"), the reality TV show of cooking one-upmanship among everyday Iranians, has taken the whole nation captive. Young folk and old, male and female, seem intrigued by its focus on food innovations, exquisite flavors, and supreme presentation with a competitive edge. It was filmed in England, but all its contestants are originally from Iran.

Other new satellite shows have gained popularity alongside the swirling MTV images and smooth sounds of Beyoncé, Shakira, and other stars from the 21st century. Among them are the Persian equivalent of *So You Think You Can Dance* and a slew of rap artists, Persian and non-Persian. There are new soap operas too: glitzy imports from Korea, India, Latin America, and Los Angeles too, with its mega Iranian presence. The locally filmed Iranian serials have also been updated. Make no mistake; what their characters forfeit in glitz and glamour, they more than make up for in spunk and melodrama. Seems everyone here knows the deeds of the villainous housewife determined to do in her husband's brother. Yes, planting drugs in his truck might set things in motion to usurp his inheritance. Will she manage to pull off her dirty scheme, or will her inept behaviors give her away? Her no-frills manteau and hood do not distract from the shady gleam in her mascara-laced eyes. How many times and in how many households have I seen her onscreen, vying for our attention and shamelessly threatening to rob us of each other's company?

I glance over at Baba, still lying quietly. He's sleeping an awful lot these days. I still wince at remembering how he struggled to his feet to receive me when we first arrived to greet him.

My thoughts take me further than I had intended, and my grieving soul revisits the question:

What's happening to the Iran I once knew? With the passing of Mamán and all she stood for—simplicity, devotion, an intangible wholesomeness—what other things may be slipping away? What is the fate of this generation? How will Mamán's grandchildren (and the rest of us) fare without her?

A two-week visit in May is not long enough to evaluate, especially when I have only my eyes, my ears, my own needs, and my sad and nostalgic heart to judge with. I want to be reasonable, but there are some things I just want the way I remember them.

I still want the charm of the trickling water ducts, like the one that used to trickle alongside the street beside Badri's house. Just why did the city have to plug them with concrete, transforming my "streamlets" into crusted scars? ("I dunno, *Zan Daee*, I'm guessing they've got a better drainage system now," Amin tells me plainly and simply one day, puzzled by my indignation.)

I still want the intimacy of gathering at mealtimes where we're seated around the tablecloth, down on the carpet.

I still want that daily standard set before me, one in which materialism and glitz don't matter as much as family and neighbors and people's feelings, where spending time together doesn't compete with the seductiveness of media or the worries of getting ahead. A world that doesn't have the "same-old/same-old" trappings, temptations, and bills of goods I face each day in America. And I want Baba to feel well again.

As Mahmoud and I move from household to household, making our visits, I unconsciously look for familiar signs of yesterday. But the greater my angst, the more changes I notice. The most striking reminder that time is passing is in the transformation of nieces and nephews. They were mostly children when I first knew them, but now they are young adults in their teens and twenties. Some are in the university, and some seek admission, here or abroad. A lucky few are on a career track (Badri's son is in social services, Parvin's daughter in family counseling), while several are jobless in the glutted work world. Most are unmarried and living with their parents.

I must say, though, our nieces look exceptionally beautiful these days. I don't know if it's their fashion finesse or simply that they've grown so gracefully into womanhood.

Why do I see it now as I hadn't before? Whatever the case, their eyes are more sparkly, their hair more luxurious, their complexions dewier, their makeup softer and lovelier. I tell them admiringly I like their look, and to my surprise, they say they like *mine*. They touch my silver hair and say *these* days people are paying top dollar for the drama of silver highlights, that natural is "in" — "enhanced natural," of course! They speak with more confidence, laugh with more ease, showcase their skills in the household and kitchen. I watch one of them don a sleek beige manteau that hugs halfway between her hips and knees. Her manicured feet in sandals are flawless. She grabs a long, flowing scarf of black chiffon that smells of Chanel, and she uses it to loosely frame her face and shoulders (all with a mere toss or two of her hand). She pops on a pair of shades, and her vintage "glam" look is now complete.

"Where are you going?" I ask her, intrigued. "Out," she says vaguely, not meaning to be flippant. "I have a few things to do. I won't be long." I later learn that "out" can mean going shopping, doing an errand, or heading for a walk along the river or park. It could mean hanging with friends of one or both genders, or up on the roof, taking a smoke or getting "bronzed" in the sun. (Evidently, I note, the white powder "pancake" look is no longer in!) It could mean taking a day trip, or even spending the night, to go somewhere sightseeing all by oneself. And by the way, public transportation looks different these days. When traveling on a bus or train, ladies either form their own clusters or find their space in a group of mixed genders.

There are also the nephews who have grown up on me. Strapping young men who still have sweet smiles and call me *Zan Daee* ("Uncle's Wife"). They take me to the bazaar, trim my hair fashionably, help me decide which glasses frames look best on me, and offer their hand when we trudge up a hill for family picnics. On the way up, someone might pick me a handful of wildflowers or perhaps offer me a drag from the gurgling hookah (*ghelyoon*) when we get to the top. When I recoil, no one holds it against me, and if I slightly reprove them on the health risks of tobacco, they listen dutifully. (Just like their cousins Parisa and Nikiar, over the years they sometimes had to put up with my strait-laced, protective talk and hopes for them.)

Sensing my maternal sentiment and restlessness, one of the nephews mentions they miss Parisa and Nikiar, who couldn't join us for this last-minute trip. I can feel they really mean it, and I'm happy we share this common affection.

Best of all, nephews and nieces tell me their stories—the dreams and frustrations that fuel their lives. A couple of them amaze me by talking in *English* with me for the very first time, yet another surprise. One or two have taken a wife; another has just suffered a bitter divorce at age thirty. He's determined to pick up the shattered pieces and keep moving forward for the sake of his seven-year-old son. If he can get a visa one way or another, he'll take them both to America and get his PhD in sports psychology. "Help me navigate the system," he implores me. "I want the opportunity, like my Uncle Mahmoud had." I see both determination and desperation in his eyes. I suddenly think of the nephew who resettled in Norway, another who has recently left for Spain, the niece who has made it to Canada against all odds. And what are the rest of them thinking and hoping, I wonder? Each mind is like a gold nugget waiting to be discovered.

Before it's too late, thank God, I finally figure out I can simply *ask* if they'll share with me. It happens one warm afternoon in Nadereh's house when most of the older adults are napping. "I want to know what you're thinking," I say to a handful of nieces and nephews, "how life and events have impacted you in recent weeks, months, perhaps even years." I'm touched by how receptive they are.

We gather in one of the back rooms where the *cooler* is blowing. We form a circle down on the carpet (hmm … I notice sitting like this used to be easier), and I start asking questions.

"Tell me, how do you think your lives are different from those of your parents—I mean when they were your age?"

There's a pause and not everyone answers - some are in reflective mode like me. But I do get a few takers.

"People were happier then."

"Life is harder now."

"And too expensive to get married—which leads to other issues."

"You can't trust people as much."

"…or count on a lasting relationship."

"So, people take what they can get."

Although I've heard it among American youth too, I didn't expect such a somber review from the younger members of my Iranian family. With the recent passing of their Mamán Bozorg, are they also feeling a wave of nostalgia?

Pointing out how most of their parents were already married at around their age, they blame their plight on soaring prices, not enough jobs, too much free time, and satellite television—whose subliminal messages focus on sex and not on commitment, they say.

On top of that, they add, young people are freer to come and go as they like, without having to give an account to their elders.

I'm not sure how to take their comments. "So, you're saying that maybe these new freedoms are a bad thing?"

Not a bad thing," they clarify. "It's good to have freedoms … but we may not always know the best way to use them."

I'm intrigued—and impressed—by the self-critiquing, by the distinctions they draw. In case they have even more thoughts to share, I sit and wait quietly, hoping they'll continue.

"It's a matter of balance," someone starts up again. "In the past, parents decided too much for their children; they imposed too many rules and controls. Nowadays parents are starting to let up, allowing their children, both men and women, to make their own choices. Choices about who they marry, choices about the friends they make, even choices about what they *do* with their friends—including the most intimate, private decisions. So, these days our generation is starting to be more open with parents."

"And *that's* a good thing?" I ask, wanting to know if I'm getting the point.

"It can be, of course," someone else chimes in, "as long as we also remember to listen. It's not that we don't still need our parents' guidance, you know."

Yes, I do know, I think to myself, but I don't share it out loud. Instead, I decide to seize the moment and ask what still lies at the core of my heart.

"So then, what exactly *have* you learned from your parents? Have the things they taught you made a difference? And what about Baba Bozorg and Mamán Bozorg? Now that your Mamán Bozorg is gone and your Baba Bozorg is … how he is, do they still have a place in this generation?"

I'm surprised by the emotion I hear in my voice, and I think to myself, "Man, where did *that* come from?" I just hope my wording didn't come off too heavy.

"Oh, wow. Baba Bozorg and Mamán Bozorg," a nephew says softly, as if he doesn't know how to begin to respond. "Well, there was nothing like Mamán Bozorg's kindness—we could always count on that, and on her patience. And I've learned from watching Baba Bozorg that in the end, money is not all that important. But being forgiving is."

The room falls silent for a moment or two, and I see something registering on all their faces. Memories of when one or both grandparents had overlooked some offense they'd committed, noticing some little triumph or virtue instead. Revisiting some of my own such moments, I join the circle of their gratitude.

The topic evolves into reflections on parents. How one mother is trustworthy; she never betrays her children's secrets. How another is forthright; you know where you stand with her, so when she tells you she's proud of you, you can totally trust that. How one dad makes a point of seeing things fairly, judging young folk and old by the exact same standard. How someone else's dad "shows what it takes to be a husband and father: by both loving his family and being willing to pay the price."

How *all* the parents, in fact, have paid a high price one way or another, and have done so gladly for the sake of their children. How they voice such pride in their kids' education. Looking up to their kids, a few have been inspired to go back for more schooling themselves.

I listen to these young people whom I've so come to value. Their words are lovely, but *they* are lovelier. Their eyes are bright; their faces are earnest, and they haven't shrunk back from my angst or intensity. I can also hear the pride in *their* voices. And that's when I get the answer to my questions. That's when I grasp what they've absorbed and embraced from their parents and grandparents.

I remember when most of these young folk were small—all those genuine moments when their Baba Bozorg would cradle this one or that one in a tender squeeze, just because. You could hear his contented, deep-throated "Mmmmmm …!" slipping out as he savored the moment. Now, fifteen years later, I see his grown grandchildren—my nephews and nieces—bending over him tenderly, helping him stand, adjusting his pillow, kissing him softly, and saying they love him. And my question gets answered all over again.

"*Zan Daee*," someone says gently, calling me back to the conversation I've managed to drift away from. "Zan Daee," he says again, beaming, "and *then*, of course, there's my Uncle Mahmoud (*Mahmoud Daee*)!"

My ear perks up as he brings up his uncle whose home is America. I am touched that Jaber is including my husband in this intimate tribute to parents and grandparents. After all, Mahmoud is neither a parent nor a grandparent to anyone present. But for fifteen years I've seen him struggle, trying earnestly to do right by his family on *two* sides of the world. I find it at once eerie and amazing that a nephew who lives continents apart from us is so appreciatively attuned to his uncle's struggle.

"Uncle Mahmoud," he starts explaining, "Uncle Mahmoud tries so hard. He doesn't want to hurt anyone. After all these years, he's never forgotten us, and he hasn't forgotten his homeland. Like him, I want to get the highest degree and make a difference with my fellow Iranians." He's in his third year of college, studying agronomy, just like Mahmoud did.

He is still beaming, and I want to hug him, but I don't. Instead, I beam a smile right back at him and tell him just what I'm thinking. "That's *exactly* what I see you doing, Jaber Jan. Be successful! (*Mo'afagh bashid!*)" Judging from the look on his face, I can tell I found the right words.

Having just mentioned their Uncle Mahmoud, the young folk then decide it's time to remember their "Uncle's Wife."

"Zan Daee Leslie," says one of them kindly, "there's a phrase we have here; it's called "Seeing the glass half-full instead of half-empty." Are you familiar with that expression?"

So, it's not just an American phrase? I muse to myself and tell her, "I think so."

"Well, that phrase describes *you*," she says. "I like how you always choose to speak to the positive side of things, how you choose to see the glass half full. It's a helpful thing, and I want to follow your example."

At first, I just smile, touch her hand, and say nothing. Truth be told, if ever I saw my world, and even *myself*, as a half-empty glass, it's now, with my heart still grieving and a world I love, changing. Yet somehow, my niece can still see me with generous eyes. In that moment *she* becomes the example. In the same loving spirit I've seen in her grandparents, she inspires me to be what *she* sees in me, to rise to the challenge of her faith in me.

"Thank you," I now say with gratitude to her and to all of them—and it gets me thinking.

It's one of those sweet (and sometimes annoying) ironies of life: that you can start out seeking the answer to *one* thing and wind up finding the answer to another. In talking with the young folk in our family, I was seeking reassurance that the Ahmadi legacy would stay valued and that what Baba and Mamán had taught us wouldn't be lost. What I needed to know was another insight: *how one honors a legacy without standing in the way of change.* How to move forward wisely without hanging on too hard.

My nieces and nephews have actually set the example. They do it each time I see them with Baba. They don't expect him to conform to the towering image of the Baba Bozorg they knew in the past. They don't pressure their grandfather to "hurry up and get over Mamán" any more than they ask me to cover my gray. No, they love on their grandfather, they go with my gray, they're awed by the photos of Parisa in her natural curls, and they show themselves gracious in the face of change. Isn't that exactly what Baba and Mamán did when they first welcomed a Black American Christian bride into their lives?

Not that change is always good. With change comes the risk of loss, of failure, of making wrong choices. But change is also inevitable, and with it lies potential for new opportunities. It's as true in Iran as it is in America. Can I do any less than my Iranian family by not being open to it?

Like my nieces and nephews and family before them, I will try to be gracious in the face of change.

***

It's June 26, one day after our twenty-third wedding anniversary. It's been nearly a month since our return from Iran. From the kitchen, I can hear Mahmoud on the telephone with his sister Parvin; he's been keeping close tabs on what's happening back home. At first it sounds like he's laughing … but then I realize he's crying.

"*Pas, rahat shod digeh! Khoda biamorze* (Well, he's comfortable finally! God rest his soul)," he's trying to say in a steady voice. Of course, he's speaking of Baba. I drop what I'm doing and rush to join him at the telephone.

We should have been prepared, but neither of us is. My heart is sinking, my thoughts racing. Losing Baba and Mamán in the same year represents the biggest change for all of us. But Baba had been telling us all along. He had tried to tell us in Saveh, in the village, at moments on the couch or in his bed. He had started to mention how "tired" he was, bring up little questions about his finances, share things he'd "always wanted to tell" us, wave a weak hand in protest when we'd coax him to take just one more bite. Even smiling seemed to use up his energy. And there was something in the way we all said "goodbye" the day Mahmoud and I had to leave for the airport—something fragile, painful, tender, and lingering.

Now, one month later, we're on the phone with Parvin. Right now, it's a time mostly for crying, for reaching out to family members. It feels too big to do anything else. We'll do our best to help each other through it. But we know each must face their pain separately too.

Over the coming days and weeks, we go back and forth over the phone, offering comfort, accepting comfort. With Mahmoud and me trapped back in Columbus, I wonder which sensation is worse: the raw pain of being there with family, where everything is happening, or the emptiness of being one step removed. In any case, we reach across continents in our fragmented, marathon phone conversations, piecing our feelings together.

***

The day of Baba's funeral, they said, was a massive outpouring of love and grief. Flooding the weathered mosque of the village were the mingled tears of fifteen hundred. People had gathered from neighboring regions, from every faith, age, and station of life. People whose property and grandparents' property had been quietly protected under Baba's hand.

The hundreds who'd eaten inside his home, laughed at his stories, sought his wisdom, or asked for his help would never forget the heart of this man. Like me, they were grieving the loss of a second father.

***

As for Baba in his final weeks, for some time now, he'd been ready to go—to put his affairs from this earth aside. After the loss of his lifetime companion, he waited two months for his brother from Scotland. Then he waited three months for Mahmoud and me. He hoped and hoped we could make ourselves ready, but he couldn't and wouldn't wait forever. Most of his children had made peace with that, and Parvin was with him when Baba was ready. Taking one last spoonful of food for her sake, Baba relaxed in her arms when he died.

"But moments before it happened," she added, "his eyes were fixed on a point on the wall … then his whole face lit up in a beautiful smile. I didn't dare interrupt to ask him why."

***

Even at the end of his life, Baba does something unexpected. A smile? The kind that lit up his face? I think I know that smile; I like to think I've seen it before. Could it have been similar to the smile he was beaming the day he whispered, "And trust in God; trust only in God"? Was it the same light in his eyes as on the day he shared his heart, saying, "Leslie Khanum, when you give yourself over to God's care, there's no safer place to be, no better thing to do"?

***

As each day goes by back here in Columbus, I sit with my thoughts, remembering my resolve to be "gracious with change."

But a moment comes when I'm suddenly mindful of all the things that *have stayed the same*.

I review the events of our recent visit—and conclude that despite the extra buzz, gadgets, and other contemporary distractions even in the village, we somehow made time to find each other—laughing and crying and swapping details. That we ate like kings, scaled mountainsides, made time for naps in the afternoon …

… That the brothers and sisters still saw me as one of them, sharing tender details of Mamán's last days. Nadereh had brought fresh flowers for her daily, singing to her in the hospital room as she lay in her coma. Zahra had "tried to beg and bargain with God … until I felt His peace to let go and accept." I'm grateful we could all still huddle, surrounded by pillows and emptied tea glasses, discovering common experiences, and sharing our hearts. We were even laughing out loud at points. Evidently, before Mamán got as sick as she did, she had tricked Baba at the hospital in a game of memory and wits called *jenagh* and got the upper hand. *Man*, we said, marveling, *they were such a pair!*

The nephews and nieces still made time for me, too, even if it meant cutting classes sometimes. And although they are mostly all grown up now, I will still always be their "Zan Daee."

And now that Mahmoud and I are back in Columbus (I am writing and teaching, and Mahmoud is running a landscaping business while teaching part-time), we find comfort in the phone call and video exchanges from across the miles. The cheer flows freely to and from our voices, and everyone's calling each other "Jan."

Epilogue

"I have spent so many years returning to this place,
seeing the slow changes
in the stretching apricot and walnut trees
mirror the changing portrait of my family:
births, marriages, and the empty spaces of those who have died
or left for new lives abroad."

—Parisa, from her journal, 2013

Can it really be the 2020s? Since Baba and Maman's passing in 2011, it's been harder to make regular visits back to Iran. Ticket prices started climbing dramatically and have stayed aloft ever since. Before the price hike, we had managed to return as a foursome every two to three years, mostly summers during the school break, with Mahmoud and me covering all the expenses. We'd spend most of our days at Baba and Maman's old farm in the village—the family's sacred watering hole for reconnecting, reminiscing, laughing, dancing, eating fabulously, or simply hanging out and about.

When traveling every two years became unaffordable, and Parisa and Niki reached college age and beyond, our nuclear foursome had no choice but to dig deeper, each one of us, into our pockets, space out our visits to every *five* years, and show up in dwindling parties of three, two, or one at a time.

What still draws us? Each of us has their own story to tell. For Mahmoud, who night after night, year after year, *still* has dreams that take place in Iran, his heart remains in his homeland, and I suspect it always will. From what I have tasted of his intimate world, whether in Duzaj the village, Tehran, or Saveh, I cannot blame him.

What draws me is a yearning to rekindle in me the spirit of Heidi, still dwelling among the people there who love and claim me as family. And while still holding sacred the life, family, and people of my homeland, I'm drawn to stay mindful of what I learned in that other beloved universe, that altered existence, that other Space and Time that have deepened me in the here and now.

What draws Nikiar and Parisa has been their memories of a magical childhood in their earliest years—of being absolutely doted on and loved. Loved by grandparents, aunts and uncles, and cousins so much older than they were—even when their Persian wasn't fully developed, or when Parisa got into squabbles with her same-age cousins, or when Niki accidentally set a hayloft on fire!

And although Parisa and Nikiar are no longer children, now living their lives in the USA, the imprint from their memories of Iran remains. It's a primal feeling that comes alive in them when they are there - or even when they're simply *thinking* of there. Parisa's journals are filled with phrases and sketches that expose her nostalgia and ignite her yearnings for things of the past: *rosewater and pistachio ice cream, the sweet orange ripeness of a full moon, bridges descending into the night-lit water, saying 'goodnight' to the home of my first memories.* And Nikiar, inspired by *his* memories of the village and his grandfather, was motivated to complete his MBA to enable projects of local communities to thrive.

As time passes, the number of people who gather at the village watering hole is steadily shrinking. Some have been lost to old age and illness; others are in search of new freedoms and opportunities. So many of Parisa and Niki's cousins, especially, have already been scattered to the wind, transplanted to different parts of the globe. Some of them, just like my husband, have taken a non-Iranian spouse. So far, all of them have been amazingly resourceful, successfully rebuilding their lives one by one: this one in Germany, this one in Turkey, this one in Spain (or Italy, or Norway, or Canada, or England). Others are setting their sights on the USA—applying for school or casting their lot to win a visa by lottery. All are hoping for a chance to chart their own course. As for those who remain in Iran, their success lies in their resoluteness, resilience, and independent constitution in the face of challenges too sensitive to articulate. Their parents, Mahmoud's brothers and sisters, are proud and stand humbly in awe of them. As do I.

With the expansion of social media and other communication technologies, my nieces, nephews, and I now stay in touch as we couldn't in the past, keeping up with each other from all over the globe. And while technology doesn't always cooperate in all circumstances, in some ways we're communicating and hearing each other much better than ever before. A shared experience of cultural displacement and the gains and losses that come with it build new roads of understanding and affection between us. Not only that—but these nieces and nephews, who spoke only in Persian as toddlers and teenagers, are now sharing their thoughts with me in fluent English! I can hardly grasp that they are the same age or older than I was when I first stepped into their world called Iran.

***

I decide there's a purpose and place for my memories, alive in my head all these thirty-some years. They bring me richness and wisdom, and incredible comfort, and something to draw from as I face the future.

So, I'll keep myself open to what comes with change and entrust my cherished memories to you.

Thank you for walking this "road between hearts" with me.

Acknowledgments

There are too many to name, but some stand out. I thank the following beautiful people:

To Mahmoud, my love and my hero, a quiet strength. You are too unassuming to accept how central you are to this whole story. But that's your humility and one of the reasons I love you so much.

To our children Parisa and Nikiar ("Niki"): Your heartfelt ways of cheering me on and practical ways of giving support have always had a powerful impact on me.

To my Iranian family members, both inside and outside of Iran: You've embodied in your daily lives—both then and now—what I consider the highest and kindest ideals of Iranian culture. And from the very beginning you have accepted me, just as I am.

To my sisters Patricia and Sylvia: Your fervor to learn the missing parts of my story from thirty-plus years ago deepens our bond even more. I love you.

To Emily, the one niece I have who was born and raised in the USA: Your creative talents and caring heart have been constant and precious gifts.

To Evelyn: You have given me nothing less than your all—your time, your honest input, your needed encouragement, and most of all, your unconditional love and belief in this project.

To Zari: Your trusting me to tell my story as a non-Iranian in Iran, plus the multiple times you read through and proofread the manuscript, spoke volumes and touched me more deeply than you probably knew.

To Melody: As extraordinarily gifted as I see you as an author, speaker, activist, and advocate who is also Iranian American, what touches me even more is your heartfelt humanity.

To Nan and the project team at Muse Literary Publishing: Your spirit of enthusiasm, creativity, and collaboration made our work together rewarding.

To my primary editors Faith and Gail (the latter from "The Savvy Red Pen"): While always expressing belief in my voice, you each inspired and guided me to stretch as a writer.

To the members of my writing community who walked this journey with me—in particular, Eddye and the :55 sprint writers' group, Merle and the memoir writers' group, and the original "pod sisters" memoir writers' group (Kathryn, Lisa, Marilynn, Toby, Wendy), along with Alexa, Elizabeth, Linda, Nicole, and both literal and figurative "good neighbor" Andrew.

To Joyce: Your quiet discipline, clear and genteel way with words, and striving for excellence while remembering to live life fully, all continue to inspire me.

To Rachel ("State of Sparkle"): Your dedicated coaching skills, knowledge of the publishing industry, and loving spirit kept me informed and on task.

To Mary L.: Your immeasurable generosity of time and technological support simply cannot be overstated.

To Mary S.: With your amazing abilities, you kept me organized. And with your kind and beautiful smile, you kept me buoyed.

To Kathy: who expressed belief in this project and faith that it would surely come to fruition, you kept hope alive in my heart for these many years.

And to the members of the Persian Student Association (PSA) at The Ohio State University: Your absolute welcoming of me into your community, your interest in what I had to say about my life in Iran, and your sincere wish to see my book make its way into the world are what often fed my soul and propelled me forward.

A Note from the Author

Dear Reader,

Thank you so much for reading and traveling *The Road Between Hearts* with me! Writing and sharing this memoir with you has allowed me to revisit one of the most eye-opening periods of my life. I'm honored you chose to spend time with my story, and I hope it moved you, opened your heart or mind in new ways, or simply transported you for a while. I warmly invite you to continue the journey by visiting my website and signing up for my monthly newsletter.

From my heart to yours,
Leslie Powell Ahmadi

VISIT:
https://www.lesliepowellahmadi.com/welcomereader.html.

About the Author

 **Leslie Powell Ahmadi is a** cross-cultural educator, language coach, and former university professor whose lifelong fascination with global cultures began in childhood. Raised in Connecticut, she imagined foreign lands before ever setting foot in one—and later turned that early curiosity into a career. Fluent in Spanish and conversant in Persian (*Farsi*), Leslie has taught Spanish and English as a Second Language, lived and worked in Iran, and earned a Ph.D. in Foreign Language and Culture Education from The Ohio State University. Her personal and professional journeys have taken her across continents, deepening her commitment to fostering understanding across cultures.

Her debut book, *The Road Between Two Hearts: A Memoir of A Black American Woman Discovering Iran*, is a deeply personal account of her journey as a Black American Christian woman navigating fear, identity, and transformation in her husband's homeland of Iran. Spanning the years 1992 to 2011 and beyond, the book offers a rare and intimate portrait of the lives of everyday Iranian people.

Leslie lives in Columbus, Ohio, with her husband Mahmoud, and continues to consult, train, and speak on cultural diversity, language, and global understanding.

www.ingramcontent.com/pod-product-compliance
Lightning Source LLC
Chambersburg PA
CBHW020903060726
47591CB00004B/1064